Astrological Psychology, Western Esotericism, and the Transpersonal

Sue Lewis

HopeWell

Knutsford, England

First published in the UK in 2015 by HopeWell

HopeWell
130 Grove Park, Knutsford
Cheshire WA16 8QD, UK

Editor: Barry Hopewell

Cover art: *Elemental Mandala for Sue Lewis*
by Cathy Wallace
Cover design: Barry Hopewell

Astrological charts reproduced using Cathar software,
www.catharsoftware.com

ISBN: 978-0-9558339-8-4

Dedication

In memory of Nicholas Goodrick-Clarke, without whose inspirational two-year MA in Western Esotericism and tremendous intellectual encouragement, all this would not have come together.

Acknowledgements and Disclaimer

Thank you to Barry for editing and publishing this book, to Joyce for encouraging me to become a Huber astrologer, and to the many scholars, colleagues, and friends whose works are cited in this volume. Thanks also to my partner Terry for his tolerance and support throughout the book's conception and production.

I take full responsibility for the opinions expressed, and for any errors and omissions.

Contents

Foreword

In the 1990s, when I first became aware of the work of Bruno & Louise Huber, I was increasingly impressed by the way in which their practical approach of 'astrological psychology' integrated the then apparently disparate fields of growth psychology, spirituality and astrology. I was sufficiently enthused to pursue the Diploma Course of the English Huber School and experience its power for myself.

Over time, I was lucky enough to be able to meet and study with the Hubers themselves, and discover their depths of knowledge and wisdom, which were shared with serious intent and gentle humour. Sue Lewis was a fellow student during this period, and as it happens we received our Diplomas at the same time.

Since then we have both remained active within the 'Huber family' of those involved in this work, through our various services to the Astrological Psychology Association and disseminating the teachings.

The Hubers' work began as a practice borne of experience and extensive research, and has subsequently been documented in the series of books first published in German by their Institute in Switzerland and subsequently as part of an expanded range in English by HopeWell.

But what of taking a step back, with a more objective look at the Hubers' approach, where it came from, its main influences and its place in the contemporary scene? It is into this ground that Sue Lewis steps, supported by the richness of her astrological and astrological psychology background plus the fruit of her Masters degree in Western Esotericism.

The result you will find in this book is a *tour de force*, teasing out the key developments in the various fields that led to the development of astrological psychology by the Hubers, initially working at Roberto Assagioli's *Istituto Psicosintesi* in Florence. The Hubers' approach is seen as a natural development in the spirit of the times, building on the work of predecessors including Ptolemy, Marsilio Ficino, Helena Blavatsky, Alan Leo, Alice Bailey, Roberto Assagioli and Dane Rudhyar. This is supported with full academic rigour by comprehensive quotes, notes, bibliography and indexes.

But this is not just an academic work. The Huber approach is essentially practical and, in helping the reader to understand the process, Sue exposes her own birth charts, together with personal experiences that they have helped her to understand and move beyond. She is to be congratulated for showing the courage to expose her hidden depths.

Finally, Sue takes a look at contemporary trends in science, philosophy, psychology, astrology - including key thinkers such as Iain McGilchrist, Ken Wilber, Stan Grof, Richard Tarnas, Irvin László, Jorge Ferrer, Bernadette Brady - and draws a picture that is very much aligned with the direction taken by the Hubers from the 1950s, truly on the leading edge of their times.

Sue has performed a great service to us all, in putting in all the hours and detailed effort needed to produce a work such as this, while at the same time retaining a broad historical overview of the context. I hope that you will find it as rewarding to read as I have.

Barry Hopewell
Trustee of the Astrological Psychology Association
Managing Editor, HopeWell

Introduction

Synopsis of the Study

This study considers the historical, philosophical, and spiritual background that encouraged the development of astrological psychology in the mid-twentieth century, and its relationship to the discipline and methodology of Western esotericism. Astrological psychology directly translates the German title Astrologisch-Psychologisches given by Bruno and Louise Huber to the institute they founded in Zürich, in 1964, and their method, its origins, objectives, and scope are central to this work. This method is non-predictive and rejects swathes of astrological material on judgements and horary, and keyword cribs, deviating sufficiently from this standard fare for many historians of astrology to neglect mention of it. Yet it does belong to a tradition epitomized by the *Castle of Knowledge* (1556), which illustrates a book on astronomy by the Welsh mathematician and physician, Robert Recorde. He contrasts the 'wheele of Fortune, whose ruler is Ignoraunce' with the 'Sphere of Destinye, whose governour is Knowledge', advising readers to check sources carefully and beware of being deceived by authority.[1] The Hubers heeded this advice and listened to stories of clients, adopting fluid methods of interpretation to consider the whole person from inner motivation to environmental pressure. Their path to self-knowledge and self-integration, guided by the intimate relationship between humanity, earth, and the cosmos in turn opens the way to a reciprocal engagement with the wellbeing of our planet. It shares common ground with esoteric currents from time immemorial and transpersonal philosophy of recent decades.

1. John S. Mebane, *Renaissance Magic and the Return of the Golden Age: The Occult Tradition of Marlowe, Jonson, and Shakespeare* (Lincoln and London: University of Nebraska Press, 1992), pp. 75-77, and op. 110; <en.wikipedia.org/wiki/Robert_Recorde> [accessed 30 September 1014].

The book has five chapters with sub-sections. Chapter 1 covers the early lives of the Hubers leading to the founding of their Swiss school and its expansion overseas, the seminal influences of Alice Bailey, Roberto Assagioli, the spiritual in art, and how and why Huber astrology took a different course from the psychological astrology of Liz Greene. Chapter 2 explores the academic discipline of Western esotericism, ways in which astrological psychology conforms to its characteristics, and controversies within the discipline. The central chapter takes a historical perspective, selecting philosophers and movements that prefigure astrological psychology. Bruno Huber attributes his assertion that astrology is 'the foremost expression of esoteric thinking' to the interface between man and the cosmos documented by early observers and diviners in ancient Mesopotamia.[2] Which of the Alexandrian wisdom streams are most pertinent to Huber astrology, and how important were Ptolemy's *Tetrabiblos*, Alfonso el Sabio's *Tablas*, and the *Corpus Hermeticum* transmitted from Asia Minor to fifteenth-century Florence for translation by Marsilio Ficino? Alan Leo and Dane Rudhyar were salient figures in twentieth-century Theosophical and psychological astrology. Why did the Hubers reinterpret the seven rays?[3] Chapter 4 shows how the Moon Node chart can unravel the past, and explains why Huber astrologers work with natal, nodal, and house charts, using those of the author and her mentor Alan Deyermond as examples. Transpersonal and chaosmic astrology are considered in chapter 5. Moving on from assessment of Huber astrology as a twentieth-century model emerging in the wake of World War Two and blossoming in the 1960s, consideration is given to contemporary trends away from scientific materialism in favour of a more organic interpretation of

---

2. Bruno and Louise Huber, *Astrology and the Seven Rays: Interpreting the Rays through the Natal Chart*, 2nd edn rev., transcribed from workshop at Beacon Centre, Exeter (1998), with additions, trans. by Heather Ross, and ed. by Barry Hopewell (Knutsford: HopeWell, 2006), p. 17.

3. To avoid confusion between Reformation Christian theosophy and the Theosophical Society (TS) founded in 1875 by Helena Petrovna Blavatsky and Henry Steel Olcott, the latter and its derivatives are capitalized. Similarly, pagan refers to ancient religions and Pagan with capital 'P' to modern religions.

life in our interconnected world, aligning astrological psychology with the resurgent interest in pilgrimage and humanity's salvational role.

About the Author

Following graduation with an honours degree in French and Spanish in 1972, I became a personal assistant and, in autumn 1977, I was introduced to astrology as an intricate psychological map interfacing with the cosmos. I enrolled as a student and was awarded a Diploma of the Faculty of Astrological Studies in 1981. My study, practice, and teaching of astrology ran parallel with an administrative career until 2009. In the early 1980s, I attended workshops of the Centre for Transpersonal Psychology (CTP) and briefly joined the Kabbalah group of Z'ev ben Shimon Halevi, which has its roots in the thirteenth-century school of Gerona. In 1987, encouraged by Alan Deyermond, I started investigating astrological symbolism in fifteenth-century Spanish poetry, eventually publishing a Paper of the Medieval Hispanic Research Seminar, in 1999.[4] Rekindling my enthusiasm for contemporary astrology and transpersonal psychology, I took a one-year Certificate training in transpersonal perspectives with CTP (1999) and a correspondence course leading to a Diploma of the Astrological Psychology Institute (2003)—now the Astrological Psychology Association (APA)—and I have been a tutor of the APA school since 2005.

In 2010, I enrolled at the University of Exeter Centre for the Study of Esotericism (EXESESO), graduating with an MA with Merit in Western Esotericism in 2012. During two years of immersion in this rich field of study, directed by Nicholas Goodrick-Clarke, I noted the absence of material referencing the connecting links between Western esotericism and astrological psychology that seemed to arise with great frequency in the course of my research,

4. Sue Lewis, *Astrology and Juan de Mena's 'Laberinto de Fortuna'*, Paper of the Medieval Hispanic Research Seminar, 21 (London: Department of Hispanic Studies Queen Mary and Westfield College, 1999).

so this volume aims to fill that niche, and to introduce this method into wider discussions of astrology in the twenty-first century.

My work is the fruit of subjective searching and objective investigation, intuitive knowing and meticulous attention to detail. The seeker and scholar viewpoints coexist in a text that covers broad perspectives, is well referenced, and reflects where I am coming from while also drawing attention to what other people are doing. Arising from my knowledge of Spanish but not German, the content extends beyond the activities of the British APA to the flourishing Spanish school in Barcelona, but is regrettably short of information on the German-speaking schools. It opens up a hitherto neglected field of astrology, sets it in a historical and philosophical context, as well as showing how it works, and reaches various conclusions in the final chapter.

One hallmark of the Huber tutor, lecturer and writer is the sharing of personal astrological chart data with students and readers and—in keeping with this tradition—my details are used as a case history in chapter 4. In the words of Jacob Needleman:

> The understanding of any level of esotericism, insofar as it embraces both the outer and the inner movement of the mind, requires that the seeker and the scholar each honour the other... in the study of the esoteric scholars need to allow the seekers *within themselves* to exist; and the seekers after esoteric knowledge must, for their part, allow within themselves the validity of the outward, analytic, or critical mind.[5]

---

5. Jacob Needleman, 'Introduction II', in *Modern Esoteric Spirituality (MES)*, ed. by Antoine Faivre, and Jacob Needleman (London: SCM, 1993), p. xxix.

Presentation, Explanation, and Glossary

When dealing with complex themes, it is often necessary to give explanations of the usage of certain words. As different writers attribute a variety of meanings to such terms as esotericism and occultism, I have incorporated definitions in context rather than in a separate glossary. Relevant pages are listed in the subject index, making them easy to locate, and the chapters have sub-section headings.

Although it is customary in scholarly works to cite the dates of historical figures when first referring to them, for convenience and to avoid splitting the text, I have put chronological data in the index of names. To help readers from different disciplines situate authorities I quote, I have included the positions of some of them at the time of writing.

As Huber astrology, also known as astrological psychology, is central to the text, I have merely indexed those references that apply specifically to the approach of one or other of the Hubers. For explanations of particular astrological techniques, readers are referred to the subject index and to specialist books by the Hubers and Joyce Hopewell.

Footnotes follow guidelines of the Modern Humanities Research Association. Books, papers, dictionaries, and principal websites consulted are listed in a comprehensive bibliography at the end.

This section closes with a glossary of glyphs, models, and seed thoughts, referred to from time to time in the course of the text. As not all diagrams are in colour, I end the textual part of this introduction with a brief explanation of colour co-ordinates in astrological psychology and then allow visual images to speak for themselves with minimal commentary.

The four elements, temperaments, humours, or triplicities of the Signs of the Zodiac are: choleric red fire; melancholic green earth; sanguine yellow air; phlegmatic blue water.

The three crosses, motivations, qualities, or quadruplicities are: cardinal red, urge for direct action; fixed blue, oriented towards security and harmony; mutable green, communicating through relationship and raising awareness. Red, blue, and green aspects express these motivations, while the orange conjunction merging two or more planets conveys the tension of seedling talent.

The glyphs for Sun, Moon, and Saturn are drawn in red on astrological charts to stand out as ego planets. The natal charts of Bruno and Louise Huber, and Roberto Assagioli are included in the first chapter with some commentary, and the three charts of Alan Deyermond and myself are considered in chapter 4.

The Five Levels of Astrological Psychology

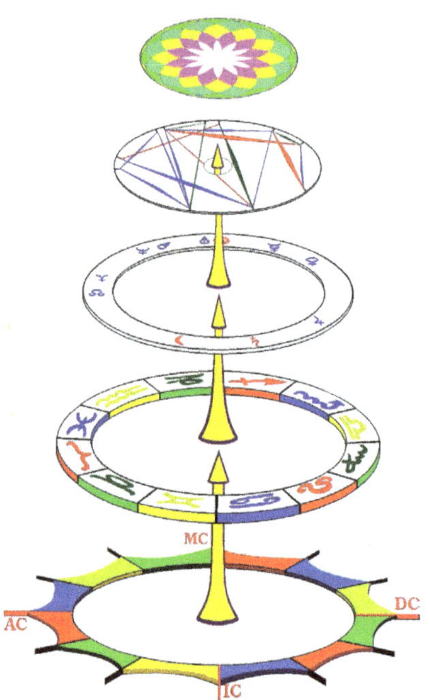

Central core, causal body, source of being, doorway to universal energies

Aspect structure, plane of inner motivation, potential to encounter, resolve, and move forward

Planets, driving energy -interactive, responsive

Signs, archetypal qualities, human inheritance

Houses show us where and how we interact with the environment and can do most for ourselves and the wellbeing of our world

Glyphs, Colours, Rulers, and Seed Thoughts

Signs	Traditional & Modern Rulers	Esoteric Rulers	Esoteric Seed Thoughts recorded by Alice Bailey
Aries ♈	Mars ♂	Mercury ☿	I come forth, and from the plane of mind I rule
Taurus ♉	Venus ♀	Vulcan √	I see, and when the eye is opened all is illumined
Gemini ♊	Mercury ☿	Venus ♀	I recognize my other self and in the waning of that self I grow and glow
Cancer ♋	Moon ☽	Neptune ♆	I build a lighted house and therein dwell
Leo ♌	Sun ☉	Sun ☉	I am That and That am I
Virgo ♍	Mercury ☿	Moon ☽	I am the Mother and the Child, I God, I matter am
Libra ♎	Venus ♀	Uranus ♅	I choose the Way that leads between the two great lines of force
Scorpio ♏	Mars ♂ Pluto ♇	Mars ♂	Warrior I am, and from the battle I emerge triumphant
Sagittarius ♐	Jupiter ♃	Earth ⊕	I see the goal, I reach the goal and see another
Capricorn ♑	Saturn ♄	Saturn ♄	Lost am I in light supernal, yet on that light I turn my back
Aquarius ♒	Saturn ♄ Uranus ♅	Jupiter ♃	Water of life am I, poured forth for thirsty men
Pisces ♓	Jupiter ♃ Neptune ♆	Pluto ♇	I leave the Father's home and turning back, I save

The 30-degree aspects of astrological psychology

with their Cardinal, Fixed, and Mutable Motivational Colours.

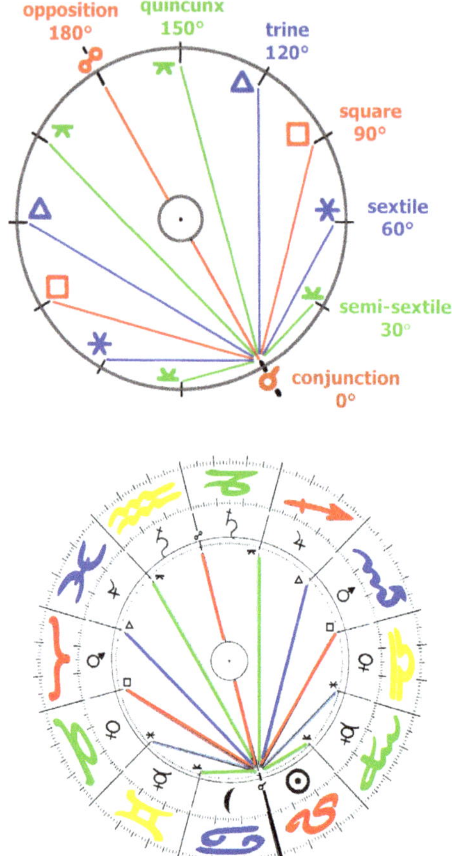

This arrangement of aspects, planets and signs, takes as its point of departure the Ptolemaic symmetry in which, following the conjunction of Sun and Moon each traditional planet has a day sign and a night sign.

However, Ptolemy only used the red and blue aspects, dismissing the green semi-sextile and quincunx as inconjunct aspects that disturbed the relationships within the circle. In Huber astrology the green aspects have a significant role to play in the raising of consciousness.

The Planetary Hierarchies and the Threefold Personality

DEVELOPING AREA ASPIRATIONS **SPIRITUAL GROWTH**	Spiritual level Superconscious realm	**CREATIVE INTELLIGENCE** MOTHER ♅ IMAGO Occultist Methodology Ideal of the perfect world Organising	**ALL – LOVE** (Christ) CHILD ♆ IMAGO Mystic Mediation Ideal of unconditional love Serving	**SPIRITUAL WILL** FATHER ♇ IMAGO Magician Metamorphosis Ideal of the perfect human being Creating
PERSONALITY (EGO) ROLES OF THE EGO Interests and Motivation	Personal level Daily awareness	**BODY** Self-Confidence ♄ **Immunity** housekeeping MOTHER **Security** closing heteronomous	**FEELING** You-awareness ☽ **Sensitivity** learning CHILD **Sympathy** opening ambivalent	**MENTALITY** Self-awareness ☉ **Vitality** growing FATHER **Mental capacity** radiating autonomous
Drive-Instinct = Achievements **LIFE-SUSTAINING FUNCTIONS**	Animal level Unconscious realm	**Enjoying** AESTHETIC ♀ **Assimilation** **Selection** Woman Fruitfulness	**Learning** DEDUCTIVE ☿ SENSORY ♃ **Formulation** **Information** **Evaluation** **Perception** Human Receptivity	**Achieving** MOTOR ACTIVITY ♂ **Achievement** **Activity** Man Potency

The Axis Crosses in the House System

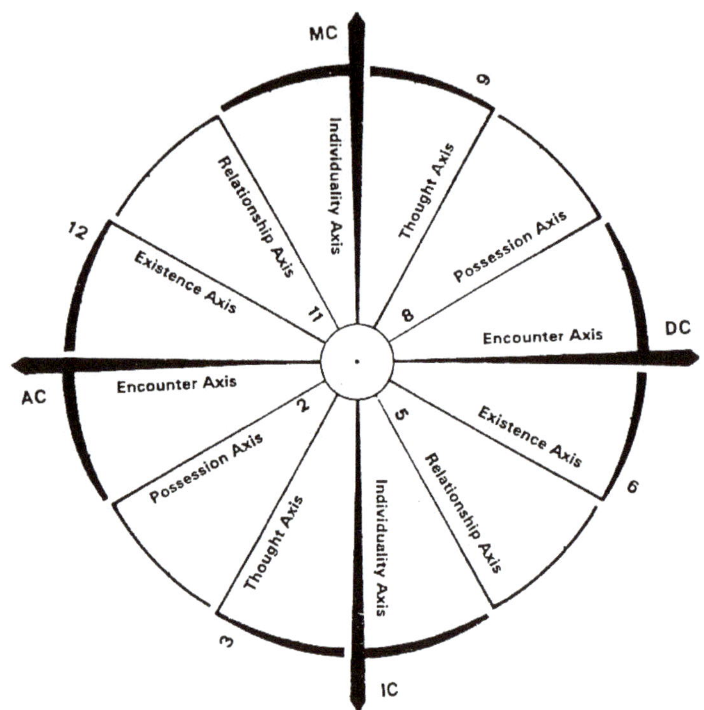

Cardinal Cross

Ascendant/Descendent, Houses 1/7—I-YOU Encounter Axis
Medium Coeli/Imum Coeli, Houses 4/10—Individuality Axis

Fixed Cross

Houses 2/8—Possession Axis
Houses 5/11—Relationship Axis

Mutable Cross

Houses 3/9—Thought Axis
Houses 6/12—Existence Axis

The Four Quadrants

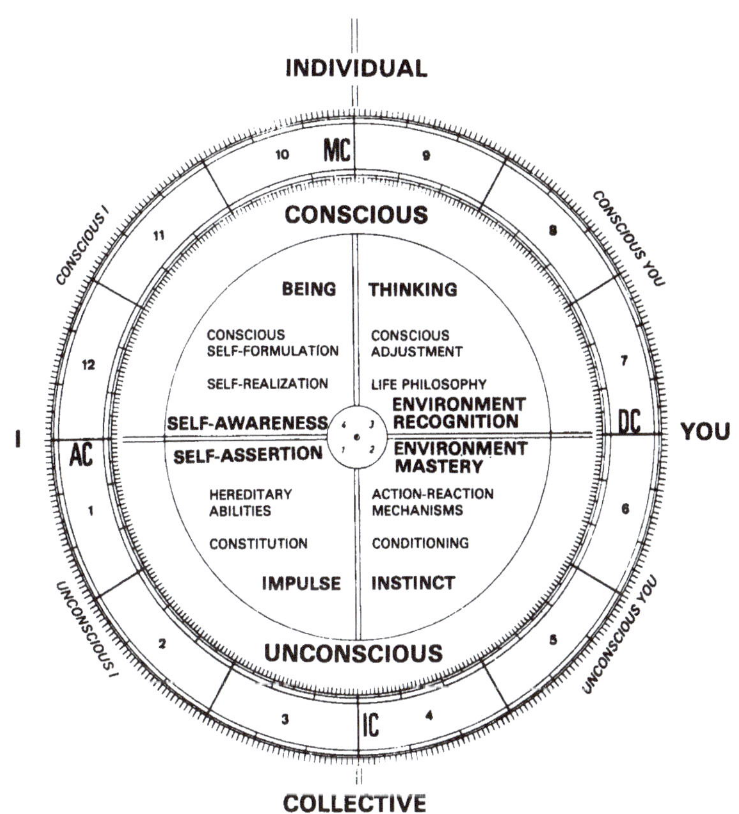

The Intensity Curve

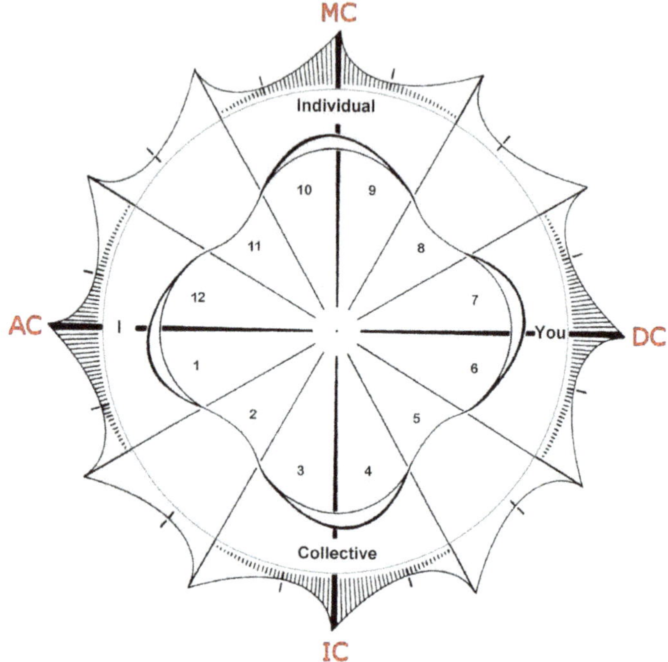

Low points of fixed houses are most indrawn; the angles of cardinal houses are most accessible.

Intensity Curve within a house:

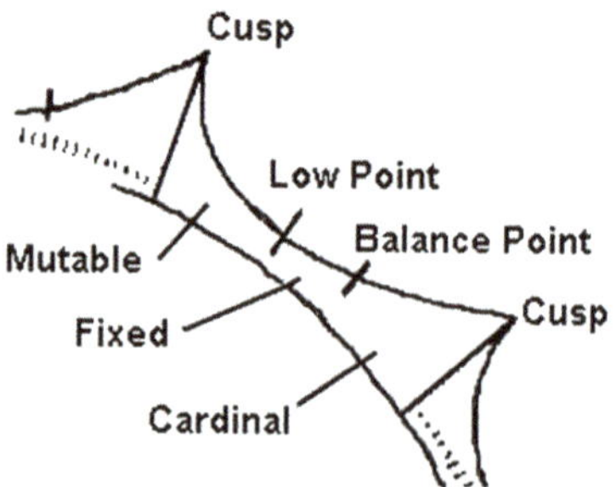

Assagioli's Egg Diagram

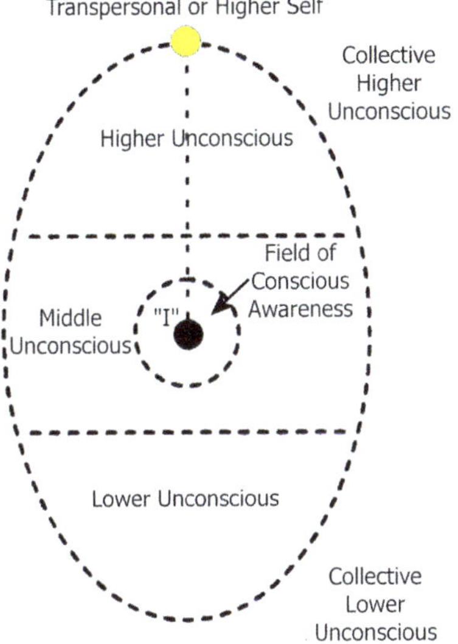

Bruno Huber's Amphora

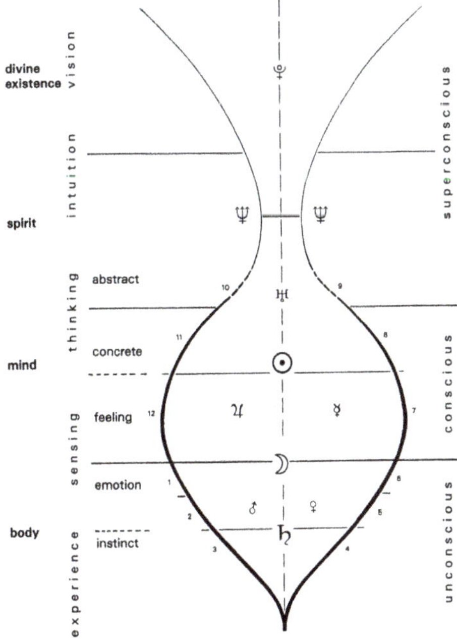

Combining an Astrological and a Psychological Model

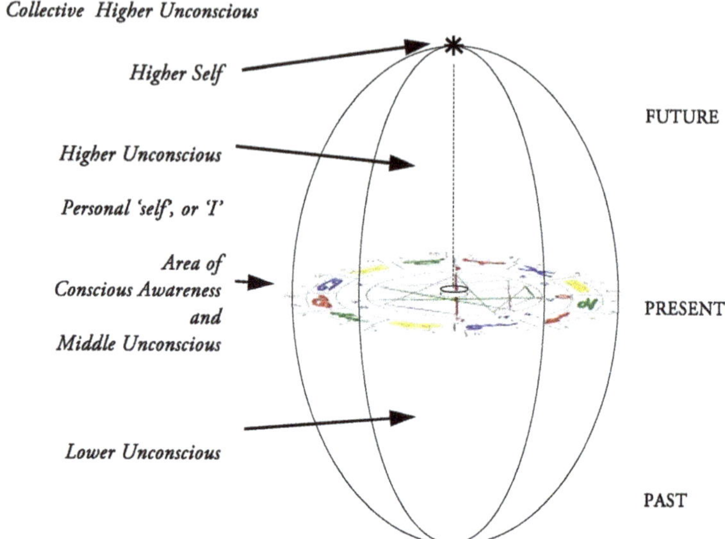

1. The Genesis of Huber Astrology

1.1 Germany: 1946-52

In 1946, twenty-two-year-old Louise lived with her first husband in Stuttgart, immersing herself in the spiritual life while recovering from the trauma of World War Two. Alternative mediumistic, psychological, and spiritual practices were widespread in pre-war Germany, offering an antidote to disenchantment engendered by the greater emphasis on intellectual rationalisation arising from scientific and technological advance, but—notwithstanding some evidence of the alignment of Ariosophy and Wotanism with Nazi racism, and interest in astrology among such high-ranking Nazis as Rudolf Hess and Heinrich Himmler—most alternative belief systems, including Mazdaznan, were banned in the 1930s. After the war, many Germans, including Louise and her husband, adopted the Neo-Zoroastrian, non-sectarian religion of Mazdaznan, whose teachings promote vegetarian diet, healthy exercises, and self-responsibility.[6] Louise took courses in philosophy and astrology—for which she had a natural gift—and, with the eagerness and naivety of idealistic youth, she set up a consultancy with the aim of helping her fellow Germans to reconstruct their broken lives. This was a harrowing venture, as she later recorded:

---

6. Louise Huber, 'The Development of an Astrologer—36 years of API', trans. by Heather Ross, in Bruno and Louise Huber, *The Development of Astrological Psychology (DAP)*, trans. by Agnes Shellens and Heather Ross (Knutsford: API [UK], 2006), pp. 15, 17; Nicholas Goodrick-Clarke, *The Occult Roots of Nazism: Secret Aryan Cults and their Influence on Nazi Ideology*, 3rd edn (London: Tauris Parke Paperbacks, 2005), pp. 17-55; Corinna Treitel, *A Science for the Soul: Occultism and the Genesis of the German Modern* (Baltimore and London: Johns Hopkins UP, 2004), pp. 56-80, 210-29; 'Karl Emil Maximilian "Max" Weber (1864-1920)' <en.wikipedia.org/wiki/Max_Weber> [accessed 24 April 2014]; <en.wikipedia.org/wiki/Mazdaznan> [accessed 10 November 2013]; <www.mazdaznan.info> [accessed 10 November 2013]; Alex Owen, *The Place of Enchantment: British Occultism and the Culture of the Modern* (Chicago and London: University of Chicago Press, 2004), pp. 10-11.

There were wives and mothers who wanted to know if their husbands, fathers and sons were still alive, if they were in prison and when they would be coming home. There were calls for help from refugee camps from people wanting to know when they would finally find a home. There were questions from war invalids, who wanted to know if they would still be able to find work without a right arm...

Sometimes I had sleepless nights... I needed to know both my own limits and those of traditional astrology. I had to admit that I could not answer such questions with a good conscience, and I closed my office immediately.[7]

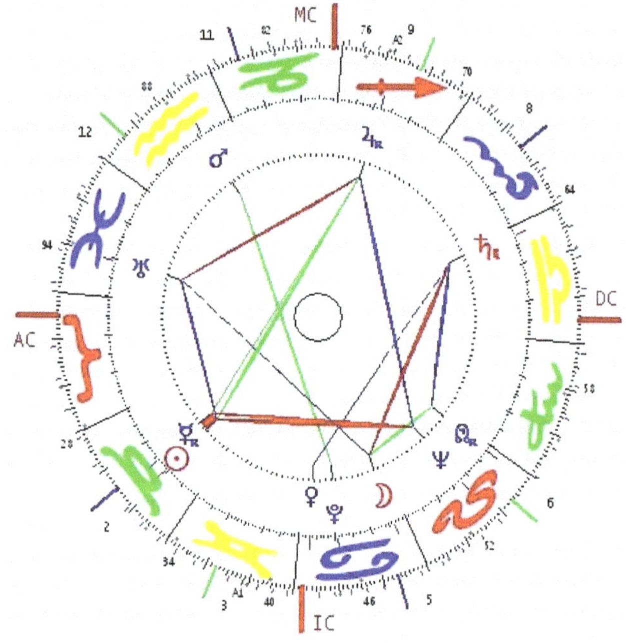

Louise Huber
b. 10 May 1924, 03:15 Bamberg, Germany (RR: A)

7. *DAP*, pp. 15-16.

If we look now at the four-sided and three-coloured aspect figure of a trapeze with Jupiter in high profile, dignified in Sagittarius in the 9th house at the top of Louise's chart, and at the quincunx between cardinal action planets Mars and Pluto that escape containment in the dominant structure rising like a poplar reaching for the skies, we can see that Louise needed her work to be constructive and meaningful. So, in 1948, she turned away from traditional predictive and horary methods of astrology, embarking on a correspondence course of the Arcane School, founded by the Theosophist Alice Bailey, in 1923, to 'bring the New Age into being', and transmit the esoteric teachings of her Tibetan Master Djwahl Khul (DK).[8] Louise's mentor, Frau Anny Huber-Wuhrmann, based in Zürich, Switzerland, was the mother of Bruno, whom she would meet in 1952 and marry in 1953. His enthusiasm for a non-predictive astrology that encouraged psychological growth and spiritual enrichment rekindled her latent interest in reading the planetary cycles as guiding lights to human purpose and transcendence:

> Bruno's ideas and comments fascinated me, for they were completely different from those that I had hitherto read in books and I already suspected that they contained significant astrological innovations for the New Age.[9]

1.2 Switzerland: 1947-57

Born and brought up in Zürich, Bruno initially read physics at university, where his astronomy tutor took every opportunity to denigrate astrology. Bruno related his adverse reaction to such deliberate criticism of a traditional way of interpreting the interface between cosmos and earth to the challenging square

8. Nicholas Campion, *Astrology and Popular Religion in the Modern West: Prophecy, Cosmology and the New Age Movement* (Farnham: Ashgate, 2012), p. 32; DAP, p. 7; William A. Meader, *Shine Forth: The Soul's Magical Destiny* (Mariposa, CA: Source, 2004), p 1.

9. *DAP*, p. 16.

between Saturn and Uranus in his horoscope. As a result, he changed courses to read psychology and began studying astrology in 1947, aged seventeen, starting with the Swiss astrologer Alfred Fankhauser, and extending his reading to include such classical writers as Ptolemy, Maternus, and Manilius, as well as modern authors with a Theosophical perspective like Alan Leo.[10] Although his mother's interests in Rosicrucianism and Theosophy had introduced him to an esoteric perspective at a young age, Bruno was keen to understand practical psychology, the history of astrology, and earlier and later interpretations of the workings of the universe outside the Theosophical spectrum.[11] Nevertheless, he did not take long to conclude that:

> It was the ancient wisdom which provided me with the most fruitful approach to research into astrology. Esotericists explore the underlying structure and the intent which underpin the outward phenomenal appearance of life. That's how they hope to gain a glimpse of the pattern and purpose of nature's ways.[12]

In 1952, Bruno met his mother's student, Louise, in Stuttgart, where their mutual attraction was sustained by a wealth of shared objectives, expressed astrologically by the conjunction of Louise's Jupiter with Bruno's Sagittarian Sun and Mercury. Whether we subject their charts to traditional sign synastry, in which case his Mercury and her Jupiter fall within 18-19 degrees of Sagittarius, or to house clicks which bring his Sun and her Jupiter together in the 9th house of research and travel, their ideological and adventurous minds stimulated each other and cemented a creative and lasting relationship. They married on 21 March 1953, and embarked on two years of intellectual and spiritual exploration in Zürich, attending lectures, groups, meditations, and all-night discussions

---

10. Verena Bachmann, 'Si tiene que ver con el ser humano, debe tener sentido', Interview with Bruno Huber (1930-1999), on 30 July 1999 in Adliswil, pub. in *Astrologie Heute*, 82 (December 1999/January 2000) and trans. into Spanish by Joan Solé i Girbau, p. 1; Bruno Huber, 'When someone makes a journey... forty years of exploring astrology', trans. by Agnes Shellens, in *DAP*, p. 3.

11. Bachmann, p. 2.

12. *DAP*, p. 5.

on diverse topics such as Dante's *Divine Comedy*, Blavatsky's *Stanzas of Dyzan*, and Szondi's tests of character and destiny.[13]

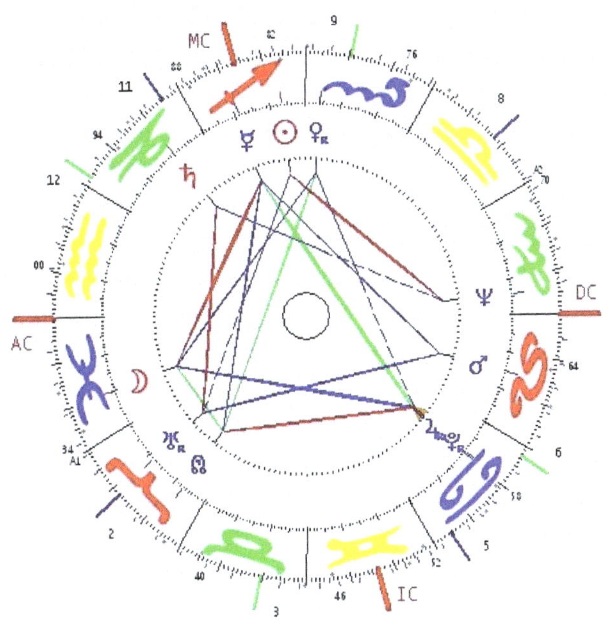

Bruno Huber
b. 29 November 1930, 12:55, Zürich, Switzerland (RR: A)

Six months after the birth of their son Michael Alexander, on 9 August 1955, the family moved to Geneva to administer the new European centre of the Arcane School. This venture began well, and Bailey's *Esoteric Astrology* greatly influenced the conception of Huber astrology. The shift of emphasis from personality-centred astrology to the transpersonal or esoteric plane, as participants

13. *DAP*, pp. 6, 16; Helena Petrovna Blavatsky, *The Secret Doctrine: The Synthesis of Science, Religion, and Philosophy*, 1, Cosmic Evolution, 1st edn 1888 (Forgotten books, repr. 2008), pp. 44-231; <en.wikipedia.org/wiki/ L%C3%A9pold_Szondi> and <en.wikipedia.org/wiki/Szondi_test> [accessed 10 November 2013].

access higher levels of awareness, becoming motivationally directed towards humanitarian service and spiritual practice, inspired the meditations and initiations of Louise, in particular, and is fundamental to Huber practice.[14] Bailey's assertion that 'astrologers will eventually find it necessary to cast three horoscopes' has been actualized in their use of natal, nodal, and house charts for a full interpretation, a practice that is explored in depth in chapter 4.[15] However, Bruno was dissatisfied with the ethos of Geneva's Arcane School in the mid-1950s with its top-heavy spiritual programme, emphasis on detachment, and discouragement of grounding psychotherapeutic exchanges.[16] Although he would revisit Bailey's seven rays forty years later, during the gestation of their astrological psychology his primary concern was with finding an astrological method that would assist the fragmented personality to recover its wholeness and integrity. Using the metaphor of the mountain that reflects the supercelestial world of God, unity and eternity at its summit and the earthly world of action and formation at its base, Bruno the psychologist—whose natal chart image depicts a chain of mountain peaks—understood that 'seeing reality as a whole means seeing the top and bottom together'.[17] His needs for more practical psychological engagement and analytical rigour would be met by Roberto Assagioli, the father of psychosynthesis who, while representing Bailey's Arcane School in Italy, nevertheless recognized that the 'healing of childhood trauma and development

14. Louise Huber, *Reflections and Meditations on the Signs of the Zodiac*, trans. by Moray Patterson (Tempe, AZ: American Federation of Astrologers, 1984); Bruno and Louise Huber, *The Planets and their Psychological Meaning: Capabilities and Tools of the Personality*, trans. by Heather Ross, and ed. by Barry Hopewell (Knutsford: HopeWell, 2002), pp. 239-84.

15. Alice A. Bailey, *A Treatise on White Magic or The Way of the Disciple* (New York and London: Lucis, 1951), p. 439.

16. *DAP*, p. 7.

17. Gregory Szanto, *The Marriage of Heaven and Earth: The Philosophy of Astrology* (London: Arkana, 1985), p. 136; see combined model, p. 14.

of a healthy ego were necessary aims', and prerequisite to spiritual progress.[18]

In 1930—the year of Bruno's birth—Assagioli and Bailey had been the key speakers at a summer school organized by Olga Fröbe-Kapteyn in Ascona, on the banks of Lake Maggiore in Southern Switzerland, a precursor to the Eranos conferences that would make the Swiss psychiatrist and psychotherapist Carl Gustav Jung their leading light, from 1933-51, and record an alternative intellectual history of twentieth-century European thought.[19] The ethos of Eranos, captured by its former head, the Swiss biologist Adolf Portmann, expresses well the landscape of the esoteric astrologer:

> The Eranos meetings have always aimed to serve the life that exists within the mesocosm. Their exploration of archaic traditions of thought has not been for the sake of irrationality per se nor because of any fundamental opposition to the existence of rational attitudes. The reason for cultivating this archaic world view was because it offered a domain where a richer and purer form of harmony exists between rational and irrational experience, and because here the creative powers can bear forceful witness to the vastness of the inner, spiritual realms and to things that have the power to make us whole, things which we are in danger of losing...[20]

This mesocosm is the celestial realm linking the microcosm of humanity on earth and the macrocosm of divinity. It is the 'world of the Intermediate, transmitting and receiving between levels of being', where the philosopher—lover of knowledge—sought for 'that which is higher than oneself'. Plato named this longing *eros*, and the spiritual forces of love transmitting guiding messages from

18. *DAP*, pp. 7-8; John Firman and Ann Gila, *Psychosynthesis: A Psychology of the Spirit* (Albany, NY: SUNY, 2002), p. 10.

19. Hans Thomas Hakl, *Eranos: An Alternative Intellectual History of the Twentieth Century*, trans. by Christopher McIntosh with Hereward Tilton (Montreal and Kingston: McGill University Press, 2013), pp. 28-30, 57, 188.

20. Adolfo Portmann, *Eranos Jahrbuch*, 30 (1961), in Hakl, pp. 11, 295 n. 32 and 33.

the supercelestial realm of divinity are *daemons*—angels in Judaism and Christianity.[21]

'Multi-levelled Platonic cosmology', love of knowledge as an ethical path, and the 'idea of the threefold nature of man and the universe diversely expressed throughout' are fundamental to astrological psychology's interpretation of the planetary drives in the chart of an individual, and psychosynthesis is similarly triadic, representing resolution through synthesis of problems posed by duality.[22] In addition, Assagioli—a seminal influence on Huber astrology—placed great emphasis on the will as helmsman, finding inner resources when danger threatens, navigating skilfully to balance a fragile boat, wisely choosing the good paths of harmony and synthesis, and acknowledging cosmic responsibility.[23]

1.3 Working with Assagioli in Italy: 1958-62

In 1958, Assagioli invited the Hubers to a summer school in the Tuscan hills. For financial reasons, Bruno travelled alone to Italy on his motorbike, where Assagioli was so impressed by his enthusiasm and talent he offered him the post of research assistant, tasked with compiling a textbook on psychosynthesis for an American publisher. Early in 1959, the Hubers moved to Florence for three years. There, Louise and Bruno also provided pastoral care and group therapy for visiting clients, who had travelled long distances for daily sessions of fifty minutes with the maestro, and their predicaments and case histories were excellent source material for astrological analysis and statistical testing.[24]

21. Jacob Needleman, *The Heart of Philosophy*, 2nd edn (New York, NY: Tarcher/ Penguin, 2003), pp. 13-14.

22. Wouter J. Hanegraaff, *Western Esotericism: A Guide for the Perplexed* (London: Bloomsbury, 2013), p. 5; Needleman, *Heart*, p. 14; J. E. Cirlot, *A Dictionary of Symbols*, trans. by Jack Sage, 2nd edn (London and Henley: Routledge and Kegan Paul, 1983), p. 232.

23. Roberto Assagioli, *The Act of Will: A Guide to Self-Actualization and Self-Realization*, 2nd edn (Woking: Platts, 1999), pp. 7-18.

24. *DAP*, pp. 7-9.

Whereas Assagioli's enthusiasm for combining astrology and psychology may have been stirred by Bailey or his own extensive reading, an additional stimulus was Dane Rudhyar's assimilation of astrological principles with Jungian analytical psychology and Eastern and Western philosophies in a book dedicated to Bailey, and brought out by her publisher Lucis, in 1936.[25] The two men clearly had much common ground, and their first meeting in New York, in May 1937, was followed up when Rudhyar joined Assagioli in Florence later that year.[26] In psychotherapy and astrology their objectives were to help clients achieve synthesis, and Rudhyar complimented Assagioli on his search 'to integrate depth psychology with the modernized expression of the occult'.[27]

Rudhyar's use of 'occult' needs further clarification, given the pejorative connotations of a word that falls into a category of 'tainted terminologies'.[28] Firstly, Rudhyar defines the devotee, whose yearning for unity 'takes the form of a longing for the glorious and spiritual past, for the Golden Age which is the first period of the cycle, when the "first-born"—the divine Ancestors—lived, still bathed in the glowing remembrance of the One'. Then he defines the scientist/psychologist/philosopher, who studies the cyclical process in an attempt 'either to bring order into its apparent confusion or to help men go safely through it until the end is reached'. Bridging the two:

> The occultist, if he be a true one, is a combination of devotee and scientist. Because he knows in varying degrees the reality and form of the One-in-the-beginning or Monad, he can also know the result of the process which will have for its consummation the integrated sum

25. Dane Rudhyar, *The Astrology of Personality: A Re-formulation of Astrological Concepts and Ideals, in Terms of Contemporary Psychology and Philosophy*, 3rd edn (Garden City, NY: Doubleday, 1970).

26. Deniz Ertan, *Dane Rudhyar: His Music, Thought, and Art* (Rochester, NY: Rochester UP, 2009), p. xxiv.

27. Rudhyar, *Personality*, p. 7; Dane Rudhyar, *Astrology and the Modern Psyche: An Astrologer Looks at Depth Psychology* (Davis, CA: CRCS, 1976), p. 77; collected articles originally published in 1930s and 40s.

28. Wouter J. Hanegraaff, *Esotericism and the Academy: Rejected Knowledge in Western Culture* (Cambridge: Cambridge University Press, 2012), pp. 177-91.

> total uniting in an organic synthesis the successful fruits of the entire process.[29]

From this definition, it is evident that Rudhyar understands the qualities of the occultist as synonymous with those of the esotericist, as do some other scholars, notably Corinna Treitel in *A Science for the Soul: Occultism and the Genesis of the German Modern.*[30] Nevertheless, it is helpful to differentiate between the perceived spiritual knowledge of the esotericist and the practical experiments of the occultist. To give a graphic example, Yeats was expelled by Blavatsky from the Esoteric Section of the TS because he set up occult experiments in an effort to prove esoteric truths and, to this day, any unwitting scholar who addresses a Theosophical gathering as occultists may be gently rebuked and told that Theosophists are esotericists.[31] The late Theosophist and scholar John Gordon took a comprehensive look at these subtle differences of meaning:

> Esotericism involves the study of the essential nature and interrelationships between all aspects or expressions of existence, whereas occultism—whether conscious or not—concerns itself with understanding the associated energies and forces of the omniverse [space] and the manner of their natural implementation, hence with the law of cause and effect.[32]

Gordon then explains how esoteric philosophy and occult science might operate together:

> Esoteric philosophy deals not only with the perception as to the widely varying interrelationships between subtle organisms and beings at every possible level of objective or subjective existence but also their causes. Occult science, however, deals very specifically not only with the characteristic nature of all the energies and forces in the universe... but also the techniques by which they work or can be controlled. The

29. Rudhyar, *Personality*, p. 151.

30. Dane Rudhyar, 'Foreword to the Third Edition', *The Planetarization of Consciousness*, 3rd edn (New York, NY: ASI, 1977), p. v.

31. W. B. Yeats, *Autobiographies*, rev. edn (London and Basingstoke: Macmillan Papermac, 1980; repr. 1987), pp. 173-88.

32. J. S. Gordon, *The Path of Initiation: Spiritual Evolution and the Restoration of the Western Mystery Tradition* (Rochester, VT: Inner Traditions, 2013), p. 30.

> former, while not exactly theoretical, does not concern itself with quite the practical 'hands-on' involvement of the latter. This distinction is highly important and needs to be kept in mind, as does the fact that esotericism and occultism, if properly practised, work hand in glove with each other as the expression of intelligent purpose.[33]

Seen from this perspective, Rudhyar correctly pinpointed Assagioli's synthesis of occult sciences—meaning hidden forces of the universe emerging from the ancient wisdom narrative—with modern advances in depth psychology, and similar deductions can be made about astrological psychology insofar as, like psychosynthesis, it advocates development of the will and methods of self-transformation to facilitate more fruitful alignment between body and soul, macrocosm and microcosm.[34] While recognizing that the perceived distinctions between esotericism and occultism are extremely subtle and their boundaries somewhat porous, given that most astrological psychologists, like most Theosophists, associate themselves more readily with the esotericist accessing spiritual wisdom than the occultist summoning magical powers, my focus is on the interface between esotericism and astrology, and I introduce occultism only in the context of relevant quotations such as Rudhyar's.

Rudhyar added that Assagioli took a 'Platonic-Hindu approach to man and God' in search of 'highly significant answers to the evident need of a confused and machine-haunted society', anticipating the term 'Platonic Orientalism' adopted by scholars to indicate that divine wisdom and philosophical knowledge originated in the East.[35] Evidence of Assagioli's appreciation of Rudhyar's work can be found in citations on the book jackets of his psycho-spiritual *Triptych*, first published in 1956—'Your new book, *An Astrological Triptych*, means for me all psychosynthesis...

33. Gordon, pp. 32-33.

34. Hanegraaff, *Esotericism*, p. 183.

35. Rudhyar, *Modern Psyche*, p. 77; Hanegraaff, *Esotericism*, pp. 12-17.

in its widest and highest sense'[36]—and more philosophical, *Planetarization of Consciousness*, published in the 1960s:

> I am particularly pleased because Rudhyar's whole trend of thought is in the spirit of psychosynthesis. From different starting points and using a different terminology he arrives at the same basic conclusions on important issues such as: harmonizing the opposites in individuals and society; the central importance of purpose; the need of a new humanistic psychology.[37]

Rudhyar's pioneering interpretation of the mystic rectangle in Assagioli's chart, with peace-loving outer blue walls containing tense red oppositions, is credited by the Hubers and assimilated into their aspect-pattern astrology.[38] The rectangle pinned by Venus in Aquarius opposition Saturn in Leo, and Jupiter in Sagittarius opposition Pluto in Gemini, forms a central figure across the relationship and possession axes that inspired Rudhyar to write:

> Rectangles of such a shape can be considered as 'altars' or 'chambers of initiation' in terms of archaic symbolism. They define a consecrated space within which a transcending process of integration and spiritualization takes place... the rectangle configuration of planets emphasizes the resolution of two conflicting natures into a dynamic effort toward a transcendent or sacrificial goal. [39]

Assagioli not only had a mystic rectangle with fire-air dynamics, but also what Rudhyar called a perfect square, more often referred to as a grand cross, and in Huber terminology as an efficiency or achievement square. This is pinned by Sun in Pisces on the *Medium Coeli* opposition full Moon in Virgo on the *Imum Coeli* across the individuation axis interacting with Jupiter and Pluto across the

---

36. Dane Rudhyar, *An Astrological Triptych: Gifts of the Spirit; The Way Through; The Illumined Road*, 3rd edn rev. (New York, NY: ASI, 1978), back cover.

37. Rudhyar, *Planetarization*, back cover.

38. Rudhyar, *Modern Psyche*, pp. 79-80; Bruno, Louise and Michael Alexander Huber, *Aspect Pattern Astrology: A New Holistic Horoscope Interpretation Method*, trans. by Heather Ross, and ed. by Barry Hopewell (Knutsford: HopeWell, 2005): for Assagioli's chart, pp. 258-63 (p. 260); for righteousness or mystic rectangle, pp. 162-66, and Joyce Hopewell, *Aspect Patterns in Colour* (Knutsford: HopeWell, 2010), pp. 22-23.

39. Rudhyar, *Modern Psyche*, pp. 79-80; see axis cross, p. 10.

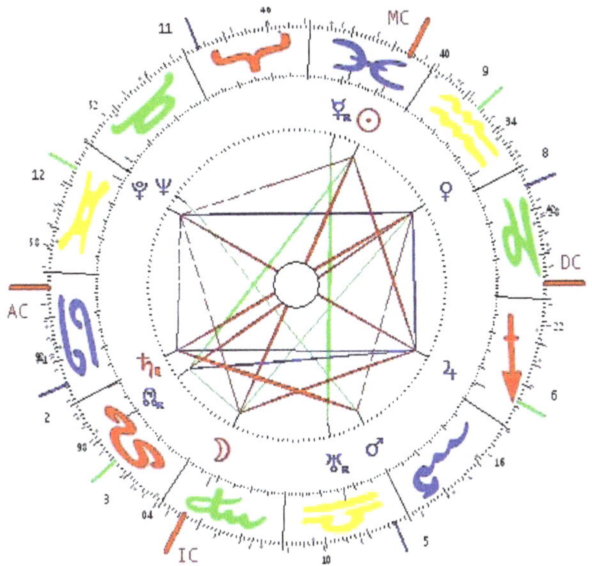

Roberto Assagioli

b. 27 February 1888 12:03, Venice, Italy (RR: AA)

relationship axis, and incorporating all four elements in mutable signs. According to Rudhyar:

> the very pressure of this unusually varied and inclusive potential upon Assagioli's consciousness, and the very challenge of a personality structure able to stand so many lines of stress and creative projection is discernible in the ideal of psychosynthesis which he described.[40]

In Assagioli's chart, the interaction of personal mind (Sun), emotional heart (Moon), sensorial evaluation (Jupiter), and transpersonal will (Pluto) in a mutable cross epitomizes 'the postmodern situation' requiring 'a new sort of learning' to cope with 'a creative explosion of possibilities'.[41] He rose to this challenge, setting out a four-stage path to psychosynthesis:

---

40. Rudhyar, *Modern Psyche*, pp. 80-81; *Aspect Pattern*, pp. 141-46; Hopewell, *Pattern*, pp. 10-11.

41. Gerry Goddard, 'The Mutable Cross and the Postmodern Ethos', in *Orpheus: Voices in Contemporary Astrology*, ed. by Suzi Harvey (Frome: Consider, 2000), pp. 107-56 (p. 113).

(1) a complete knowledge of one's personality;

(2) control of its various elements;

(3) realization of one's true self, or at least the creation of a unifying centre; and

(4) psychosynthesis: the formation or reconstruction of the personality around a new centre.[42]

Assagioli taught that:

> A seeker can attain self-realization by consciously emanating transpersonal qualities such as tranquillity, loving-kindness, eternity, detachment, generosity, gratitude, bliss, luminosity, mercy, silence, and wholeness... The Self, in its expression of the will, actively brings about changes in the personality and in our circumstances... The will possesses multi-spectral qualities...[43]

Besides the blue rectangle and the red square Louise draws attention to the large number of green quincunxes in his chart:

> The green-red aspects around the central core indicate a dynamic-creative potential, enabling Assagioli not only to activate his inner core but also to awaken the 'awareness of the soul' in others. His therapeutic treatment always began at the core personality. He had a special ability to take people back again and again to their inner core, with loving patience and wisdom—sometimes also with the gentle assistance of his bell-like voice... He called the core personality 'the higher self', which the person integrates into an active whole.[44]

Assagioli had the enthusiasm and flexibility to engage with the Hubers' ambition to create an astrological method based on psychosynthesis, and his experience with clients, thoughtful input, and wise counsel contributed significantly to their early experiments.[45] So any serious study of their system requires some understanding of his vast range of classical learning and spiritual insight, from the Neoplatonist vision of 'the human soul as a

---

42. Rudhyar, *Modern Psyche*, p. 83.

43. Greg Bogart, *Astrology and Spiritual Awakening*, 2nd edn (Tempe, AZ: American Federation of Astrologers, 2014), pp. 130-31.

44. *Aspect Pattern*, p. 259.

45. *DAP*, pp. 10, 17.

voyager..., seeking a path of ascent to its divine origins' to peak experiences described by Abraham Maslow, who gave humanistic psychology its language and contributed—with Assagioli—to the transpersonal movement of the 1960s, and from Kabbalah and Theosophy in the West to the *Bhagavad Gita* and the *I-Ching* in the East.[46]

The father of psychosynthesis was born in Venice into a cultured Jewish family where Italian, French, and English were spoken at home. He started learning German at the age of eight, did classical Greek and Latin at school, and Russian and Sanskrit at the University of Florence where he studied medicine and psychiatry. As a trainee, Assagioli sojourned at the Burghölzi Hospital in Zürich, prompting Jung, in 1909, to recommend him to Freud as 'a promising candidate to develop psychoanalysis in Italy'. By completion of his doctoral thesis in 1910, Assagioli had identified limitations in Freudian psychoanalysis. Disillusioned by Freud's preoccupation with libido, he compared it to 'the basement' of a building, shrouded in darkness away from the light.[47]

Psychosynthesis was conceived around that time, nine years before Bailey was first contacted by DK in 1919. Contemporary writers have emphasized the non-aligned nature of Assagioli's spirituality, backed up by citations from his own work, regarding psychosynthesis in general:

> Psychosynthesis does not attempt in any way to appropriate to itself the fields of religion and philosophy. It is a scientific conception, and as such it is neutral towards the various religious forms and the various religious doctrines, excepting only those which are materialistic and therefore deny the existence of spiritual realities. Psychosynthesis does not aim nor attempt to give a metaphysical nor a theological

46. Will Parfitt, *Psychosynthesis: The Elements and Beyond* (Glastonbury: PS Avalon, 2003), pp. 115, 118; John, trans. and ed., *The Neoplatonists*, trans. and ed. by John Gregory (London: Kyle Cathie, 1991), p. vii; Abraham H. Maslow, *The Farther Reaches of Human Nature*, 3rd edn (New York: Penguin-Arkana, 1993), pp. xv, 162-72; Firman and Gila, pp. 10-11.

47. Jean Hardy, *A Psychology with a Soul: Psychosynthesis in Evolutionary Context* (Arkana, 1987), pp. 11-14; Firman and Gila, pp. 9-12.

> explanation of the great Mystery—it leads to the door, but stops there.[48]

and transpersonal or spiritual psychosynthesis in particular:

> The specific therapeutic task... is that of arriving at a harmonious adjustment by means of the proper assimilation of the inflowing superconscious energies and their integration with the pre-existing aspects of the personality; that is, of accomplishing not only a personal but also a spiritual psychosynthesis.[49]

Such interpreters of psychosynthesis have been criticized for minimizing the underlying importance of spiritual hierarchy and levels of being evident in Assagioli's posthumous volume *Transpersonal Development* (1988), and for playing down his links with Alice Bailey.[50] According to Louise, Assagioli was a disciple of Kuthumi, one of Blavatsky's Masters of Wisdom, whose closest disciple was Bailey's Tibetan DK. Despite Assagioli's maintenance of a 'wall of silence' between his professional career as a psychotherapist and his spiritual journey, there is evidence of their interaction in his correlation of the seven cosmic rays of light with the seven psychological types, and his reinterpretation of them in turn changed the perspective taken by the Hubers in their reworking of Bailey's seven rays.[51]

---

48. Roberto Assagioli, *Psychosynthesis: A Manual of Principles and Techniques*, 2nd edn (Wellingborough: Turnstone, 1975), pp. 6-7; Firman and Gila, p. 16.

49. Assagioli, *Psychosynthesis*, p. 55; Firman and Gila, p. 179.

50. Kenneth Sørensen, 'Integral Psychosynthesis: Integral Perspectives on Psychosynthesis', MA thesis, Psychosynthesis and Education Trust (2008), rev. 2009, <www.psykosyntese.dk/a-198/> [accessed 17 June 2014] criticizes Firman and Gila, pp. 16, 20, 38, 195 n.8; Roberto Assagioli, Transpersonal Development: The Dimension beyond Psychosynthesis, ed. by Maria Luisa Girelli, 2nd edn (London: Thorsons, 1993), pp. 253-57.

51. *Astrology and the Seven Rays*, pp. 80-81; Roberto Assagioli, *Los siete tipos humanos y la psicosíntesis*, trans. by Lluïsa Sallés, and ed. by the API Escuela Española Huber de Astrología (Barcelona, 1994).

There is also ample evidence of the influence of William James, whose twenty lectures on *The Varieties of Religious Experience* were published in 1902 and described by Assagioli as 'a model for the impartial scientific investigation' of spiritual consciousness and the superconscious. James presented 'sex-theory' as 'profoundly uninstructive' to the interpretation of religious consciousness and, in his concluding lecture, he wrote:

> The farther limits of our being plunge... into an altogether other dimension of existence from the sensible and merely 'understandable' world. Name it the mystical region, or the supernatural region, whichever you choose. So far as our ideal impulses originate in this region... we belong to it in a more intimate sense than that in which we belong to the visible world, for we belong in the most intimate sense wherever our ideals belong. Yet the unseen region in question is not merely ideal, for it produces effects in this world.[52]

James initiated use of the word 'transpersonal', adopted in the second half of the twentieth century and applied to movements in psychology, astrology, and philosophy, incorporating psychosynthesis, whose aim, as Assagioli explained in a final interview, is to

> ...try to build an elevator which will allow a person access to every level of his personality. After all, a building with only a basement is very limited. We want to open up the terrace where you can sunbathe or look at the stars. Our concern is the synthesis of all areas of the personality.[53]

---

52. Assagioli, *Transpersonal*, p. 20; William James, *The Varieties of Religious Experience: A Study in Human Nature*, ed. by Jim Manis, <www2.hn.psu.edu/faculty/jmanis/wjames/varieties-rel-exp.pdf> [accessed 26 July 2013], pp. 21, and 498; Firman and Gila, p, 12.

53. Sam Keen, 'The Golden Mean of Roberto Assagioli', *Psychology Today* (December 1974), repr. <samkeen.com/interviews-by-sam/interviews-by-sam/the-golden-mean-of-roberto-assagioli/> [accessed 23 October 2013], p. 1; *Transpersonal Psychotherapy: Theory and Practice*, ed. by Nigel Wellings and Elizabeth Wilde McCormick (London and New York: Continuum, 2000), p. 1.

Having sketched in Assagioli's background and established his objective 'to create a scientific psychology which encompassed the whole of man—creativity and will, joy and wisdom, as well as impulses and drives', it is appropriate to outline some of the ways in which the psychosynthesis model has been assimilated into Huber astrology.[54] If we envisage Assagioli's egg diagram in three dimensions, the natal chart of the individual fits over the field of consciousness, stretching out across the middle unconscious to the periphery, with the personal 'I' at the centre of the egg corresponding to the central core of the chart.[55] Moving to the inner circle of aspect patterns made by the planetary aspects, attention is given to their motivational structures, the formulation of sub-personalities for managing situations, and the capacity to disidentify from those sub-personalities that have outgrown their usefulness, the development of learning figures, and the ability to live inwardly and outwardly to full potential. Released from the shackles of conditioning, the subject can find the freedom of will to act in the interests of self-realization and higher purpose.[56]

54. Hardy, p. 13.

55. APA Diploma Course in Astrological Psychology, module 1 unit 3 page 7; see egg, combined model, pp. 13-14.

56. Firman and Gila, pp. 24-25, and 36; Assagioli, *Will*, pp. 9, 17-18.

1.4 The Spiritual in Art

Bruno and Louise were bowled over by Florence, especially Bruno, who discovered the language of colour from the American Fulbright art scholars he met there. So he read Goethe's *Theory of Colours* (1810) and Wassily Kandinsky's *Concerning the Spiritual in Art* (1911), and observed colour tests developed by the Swiss psychotherapist Max Lüscher, in 1969. In Florence he started painting, producing an abstract every full Moon and one every new Moon.[57] Although Bruno chose to focus on astrology in preference to art, and executed only one series of paintings, this engagement with the visual medium is demonstrated in the arrangement of the chart, showing the five levels fanning out from the central circle of the self, through the inner motivations represented by the aspect structure, to the driving planetary energies, outwards to the archetypal signs of the zodiac, and around the periphery are the mundane houses interacting with the environment.[58] The chart is a mandala whose colours and shapes enable the astrologer envisage the whole person whose chart is being read, so it is a truly esoteric space. Looking at the charts of Bruno and Louise, Bruno's might resemble a Himalayan mountain range, such as painted by the Theosophist Nicholas Roerich, with peaks and valleys, while Louise's opens out onto a broad plateau with tall poplars reaching for the heavens.

Although Kandinsky acknowledged Blavatsky as a torchbearer, the first art historian to publicly recognize the influential part played by Theosophy in twentieth-century art was Sixten Ringbom with an article in 1966, followed up by a seminal work, *The Sounding Cosmos* (1970).[59] Ringbom claimed that Theosophy, especially its interpretations of colour aura and thought-forms by Annie Besant

57. *DAP*, pp. 9, and 11; Bruno and Louise Huber, *Transformation: Astrology as a Spiritual Path*, trans. by Heather Ross, and ed. by Barry Hopewell (Knutsford: HopeWell, 2008), pp. 151-59.

58. See intro., five levels, p. 6.

59. Wassily Kandinsky, *Concerning the Spiritual in Art*, trans. by Michael Sadler, 1st edn, 1914 (Mineola, NY: Dover, 1977), p. 13.

and Charles Webster Leadbeater, together with the colour theory and aesthetics of Goethe edited and promoted by Rudolf Steiner, had significantly influenced Kandinsky's abstract approach to painting and widely circulated manifesto of the Blue Rider Group of artists, and there is supporting evidence that he purchased a copy of *Thought Forms* in 1908 and joined the TS in 1909.[60] Subsequently, the late American scholar and art historian, Peg Weiss, drew attention to the influence of folklore and shamanism on Kandinsky's use of bright colours, and identified the Blue Rider as the Russian folk hero St George—a Christian saint with shamanic powers, who rode to other worlds on his magic horse. The symbolism is explicit in the choice of the Blue Rider as signature of the group of exhibiting artists led by Kandinsky and Franz Marc, and their almanac of 1912 contained illustrations of ethnic objects used for shamanic healing to transmit the message that new art was a metaphor for cultural healing and salvation.[61] Affinities between Theosophy and shamanism are unsurprising, given the Russian background of Blavatsky, and this combination of esoteric sources of inspiration in no way detracts from the acknowledged influence of Kandinsky's work on the Hubers. Recent research shows that Kandinsky was not the first abstract artist, and it has also been suggested that the influence of Theosophy on art has less to do with abstraction than with intentional focus on the picture, gazing inwards to access the soul and divine nature without reference to external context.[62]

60. Sixten Ringbom, 'Art in "The Epoch of the Great Spiritual": Occult Elements in the Early Theory of Abstract Painting', *Journal of the Warburg and Courtauld Institutes*, 29 (1966), pp. 386-418.

61. Peg Weiss, 'Kandinsky and "Old Russia": An Ethnographic Exploration', *Syracuse Scholar*, 7 (1986), repr. <surface.syr.edu/suscholar/vol7/iss1/5> (2013).

62. Massimo Introvigne, 'Theosophy and the Visual Arts: The Nordic Connection', International Conference on Theosophical History, London, 20-21 September 2014.

If we consider Kandinsky's assertion that, 'colour provides a whole wealth of possibilities of her own, and when combined with form, yet a further series of possibilities', all of which will be 'expressions of inner need', in the light of the Platonic solids, in particular the tetrahedron with four triangular surfaces, we can see the alignment of the triangle with elemental fire and spiritual growth. Kandinsky describes the triangle of humanity as moving 'forwards and upwards', becoming, in its three-dimensional form, 'a spiritual pyramid which will some day reach to heaven'. Unsuitable combinations of form and colour are 'not necessarily discordant but may, with manipulation, show the way to fresh possibilities of harmony'.[63] A key innovation of the Hubers is the three-coloured learning triangle, combining challenging red, harmonizing blue, and searching green in a mutable pattern of growth, working towards synthesis and higher purpose. A similar connection can be made between the cube representing the earth, rootness, and fixity, and the four-sided fixed square emphasizing a preoccupation with security.

Paul Klee exhibited with the Blue Rider Group in 1912, becoming a close colleague of Kandinsky's after in World War 1, and for several years both artists worked at the Bauhaus and lived in adjacent houses. Although Klee's ghoulish *Astrological Fantasy Portrait* might imply a lack of sympathy towards some kinds of astrology, his way of taking alternative perspectives to make visible hidden forces that initially appear chaotic before assuming a shape of their own was undoubtedly influential, and the emergence of coherent patterns from abstract forms is replicated in the presentation and visualization of horoscopes. The Hubers' debt to Klee's subtle manipulation of colour and shape to depict movement is made evident by their inclusion of his *Jumper* in *The Planets* to illustrate Mercury.[64]

63. Kandinsky, pp. 6, 20, 29, 33.

64. *Planets*, p. 51.

In my opinion, Klee's building-blocks of picture-making may have been applied to *Aspect Pattern Astrology*. They provide a guiding key to the changing nature of linear energies as connecting lines turn into triangles or squares, and outer contours containing inner energies impact on one another. Klee selected colour tones and geometrical forms to reveal hidden perspectives such as when a dark Sun hovers behind a castle or a full Moon lights up the sky. His paintings of the full Moon have all the dynamic energy conceived of by Leo when he wrote, 'Full Moon, the opposition of the two luminaries, represents the personality illuminated by the Sun, or spirit, and throwing its borrowed light upon the earth, physical consciousness'.[65]

The image created during the astrologer's initial focus on the pattern formed by the inner circle, and drawn from its overall shape and predominating colours, gives the Huber astrologer an astrological signature for that chart. Thereafter the sphere of vision extends outwards to incorporate astrological significators into an emerging picture of the whole person. According to my understanding of the vocabulary of hermeneutic astrology set out by Geoffrey Cornelius, the Huber astrologer's 'take' on the chart engages the creative imagination at the outset, thereby lessening dependence on keyword interpretations of planets, signs, and houses.[66]

---

65. Alan Leo, *Esoteric Astrology* (Rochester, VT: Destiny, 1983), p. 3.

66. Geoffrey Cornelius, *The Moment in Astrology: Origins in Divination*, 2nd edn rev. (Bournemouth: Wessex Astrologer, 2003), p. xxiii.

1.5 Founding of the Huber schools: 1964-90

The Hubers returned to Switzerland, in 1962, with much tested data aligning their astrological method with psychosynthesis, and a clear vision of how best to present a chart representing the spectrum of life They launched the Astrologisch-Psychologisches Institut (API) in Adliswil, near Zürich in 1964, an educational programme in 1968, and a publishing house in 1974. There was an enthusiastic response among German-speakers, their courses and books proved popular, and their journal *Astrolog*—whose articles cover global cosmology, as well as astrological techniques, psychological interpretation, and spiritual enquiry—enjoyed wide circulation. In 1982, they held their first international conference in Zurich and, in 1984, Bruno signed the document setting out 'The Basic Principles of Astrological Associations' in German-speaking countries.[67] After his death, in 1999, *Astrolog* was taken over by Internationaler Fachverband für Astrologische Psychologie based in Munich, whose President, Wolfhard König is a depth psychologist using astrological psychology in therapy. A number of articles from *Astrolog* have been translated into English, collated in two books, published in *Conjunction* or on the astrological psychology blog. API Adliswil was co-run by Louise and her son Michael until 2012.[68] Several small astrological institutes have been created in German-speaking Europe to spread Bruno's 'ideas and unique holistic horoscope interpretation technique... in line with his own (and Roberto Assagioli's) expressed desire to disseminate the theory in different ways throughout the world'.[69]

67. DAP, pp. 9, 13-14, 17-18; <www.astro.com/astro-databank/Huber,_Louise> [accessed 24 April 2014]; Kocku von Stuckrad, Astrología: Una historia desde los inicios hasta nuestros días, trans. by Roberto H. Bernet (Barcelona: Herder, 2005), pp. 407, 412.

68. <wiki.astro.com/astrowiki/de/Louise_Huber> [accessed 24 April 2014]

69. Wolfhard König, 'In memory of Bruno Huber 1930-1999', trans. by Heather Ross, Astrolog (October/November 2014) repr. <astrologicalpsychology.org/in-memory-of-bruno-huber-1930-1999/> [accessed 23 January 2015].

The English Huber School, now known as the Astrological Psychology Association (APA), was founded in 1983 by Pamela Tyler and Richard Llewellyn, launched distance learning Foundation and Diploma courses in 1985, and is a member of the Advisory Panel for Astrological Education (APAE). Its journal, *Conjunction*, comes out three times a year. The establishment of HopeWell publishers, in 2004, has made English translations of Huber manuals widely available and saw publication of *The Cosmic Egg Timer*, a lucid, and entertaining, illustrated introduction to the method by Joyce Hopewell and Richard Llewellyn, now in a kindle edition.[70] Joyce has written three more books, referred to from time to time and listed in the bibliography. APA's website holds back issues of *Conjunction* for members, and links with its blog, bookshop, videos by Joyce on YouTube, and Twitter.

The Escuela española Huber de Asesoramiento Astrológica, formed in Barcelona in 1990 by Rosa Solé-Gubianes and Angela Wilfart, initially used the English model for developing its correspondence course, and started publishing books in 1994.[71] The Spanish school has an evolving programme of courses and workshops, with online teaching as well as an online journal and an active presence on Facebook, Twitter, and YouTube. In 2014, Rosa wrote a new manual in memory of Bruno and to commemorate Louise's ninetieth birthday.[72]

There are worldwide networks of Huber astrologers, in Norway, Sweden, South Africa, Australia, North and South America, and elsewhere.

70. Joyce Hopewell and Richard Llewellyn, *The Cosmic Egg Timer: Astrological Psychology: An Introduction to the Huber Method*, ed. by Barry Hopewell and illustr. by Annabel Burton (Knutsford: HopeWell, 2004).

71. Escuela Huber de Psicología Astrológica, Calle Roger de Llúria, 5, 6o, 3a, Barcelona, Catalonia 08010, Spain; <www.escuelahuber.org> < www.psicologiaastrologica.es>

72. Rosa Solé Gubianes, *Psicología Astrológica: Bases prácticas del método Huber* (Barcelona: Sincronía, 2014).

1.6 Differences between Astrological Psychology and Psychological Astrology

The discipline of astrology evolved from human observation of the planets in the celestial sphere, or mesocosm, an intermediary place of dialogue between the macrocosm or supercelestial sphere of unseen divinity and the microcosmic realm of humanity. In ancient civilizations, the astrologer might have been a priest, whereas in our postmodern era the astrologer is more likely to combine the interpretation of horoscopes with psychotherapeutic and counselling skills. Experiences of spiritual gnosis, meaning immediate 'knowledge of divine things' are no longer the exclusive domain of religious faith, and guided meditation performs a similar role to devotional prayers, enabling the devotee to realize the 'timeless in the present moment'.[73] Both rituals enable the individual to transcend the personal and acknowledge the 'existence of a unifying centre', whether this transpersonal centre is defined as 'Self or Atman', or as God, or an aspect of the Deity.[74]

The Western esotericist, Wouter Hanegraaff has expressed the blurring of edges between psychology and religionism in terms of 'double dialectics':

> the increasing psychologization of the sacred is paralleled by an increasing sacralisation of psychology. This means that in much of modern and contemporary esotericism, authors and practitioners can talk about divine realities while really meaning their own psyche, and about their own psyche while really meaning the divine.[75]

He connects this trend with contemporary preference for adjectives like 'spiritual' or 'transpersonal'. Although potentially interchangeable, the two words are used differently. 'Spiritual' features widely in discussion of esoteric and New Age movements,

73. Arthur Versluis, *Theosophia: Hidden Dimensions of Christianity* (Hudson, NY: Lindisfarne, 1994), pp. 9, 13.

74. Ian Gordon-Brown, with Barbara Somers, *The Raincloud of Knowable Things: A Practical Guide to Transpersonal Psychology: workshops; history; method*, ed. by Hazel Marshall (Dorset: Archive Publishing, 2008), p. 59.

75. Hanegraaff, *Guide*, pp. 10-14, 135-38 (p. 137).

so I have contained its vagaries by categorizing its usage in the index. A transpersonal experience involves 'detachment from immediate human concerns and the taking of a cosmic perspective', transcendence of the little ego so that 'the person is centred in a larger whole', and relates to a particular branch of psychology and philosophy.[76] In astrology, transpersonal planets are located beyond the orbit of Saturn outside the field of consciousness.

The pioneering transpersonal psychiatrist Stanislav Grof coined the word holotropic to describe states 'characterized by a specific transformation of consciousness associated with perceptual changes in all sensory areas, intense and often unusual emotions, and profound alterations in the thought process'. Holotropic experiences are enormously varied. They may be induced by 'technologies of the sacred', such as drumming, ritual chanting, rhythmic dancing, fasting, and breathing techniques used in yoga and meditation, or by the use of mind-altering substances, or psychological techniques like biofeedback. Or else they may occur spontaneously, in all probability against the conscious will of the individual, triggering a spiritual emergency. Giving practical examples of holotropic experiences that cover similar ground to Hanegraaff's 'double dialectics', Grof explains:

> They are the key for understanding the spiritual life of humanity from shamanism and sacred ceremonies of aboriginal tribes to the great religions of the world. But, most important, they provide invaluable guidelines for a rich and satisfying life strategy that makes it possible to realize to the fullest our creative potential.[77]

His view that this 'emerging alternative approach to existence will integrate science and spirituality and introduce important elements of the ancient wisdom into our technological world' could potentially build an interdisciplinary bridge between Western esotericism, transpersonal philosophy, astrological psychology, and the new paradigm of science, and this concept will be given further

---

76. Gordon-Brown and Somers, *Raincloud*, p. 59.

77. Stanislav Grof, *The Cosmic Game: Exploration of the Frontiers of Human Consciousness*, 2nd edn (Dublin: Newleaf, 1998), pp. 5, 7-9.

consideration in the final chapter. Enduring experiments from the 1960s have evolved into a kind of practical mysticism in which spiritual love is 'accompanied by intelligent thought and practical skill in action', becoming a spur to enlightened humanity to act 'in harmony with the evolutionary intention of the Cosmos' instead of being 'driven by the quest for power, conquest and control and the appropriation of the Earth's resources for the benefit of the few'.[78] Consciousness of our connectivity to earth and cosmos, an ongoing thread in the esoteric tradition fuelled by greater urgency in recognition of our need to treat them with respect instead of plundering their resources, is common to the ethos of many schools of astrology, as well as environmental organizations and forward-thinking scientific networks and is fundamental to the concept of salvation in its modern interpretation.

Notwithstanding similarities of purpose on both sides of the Atlantic, transpersonal psychology and astrology took alternative routes in post-war America and continental Europe, and both streams operated in Britain. Ultimately, the Eranos conferences, which acted as an incubator of esoteric spirituality in early twentieth-century Europe, had more influence on the American model, emphasizing 'religion, myth and symbolism' as presented by Eliade and Jung, reinforced by Joseph Campbell and James Hillman, and resurfacing in the archetypal astrology of Richard Tarnas, Keiron Le Grice and others, which reunites psyche and cosmos in the postmodern myth. German-speaking post-war Europe, by contrast, 'declared taboo' anything related to mythological inflation, retaliating against possible but questionable links between the 'myths, symbols, and fantasies' of Ariosophists

78. William Meader, 'Practical Mysticism: The Way of the Future' (2007), <meader.org/articles/practical-mysticism-the-way-of-the-future> [accessed 4 April 2014]; Anne Baring, The Dream of the Cosmos: A Quest for the Soul (Dorset: Archive Publishing, 2013), p. 536.

and *völkisch* movements, the rise of Nazism, and Fascism more generally.[79]

In 1978-79, the Centre for Transpersonal Psychology (CTP), founded in 1973 by Ian Gordon-Brown and Barbara Somers, joined Liz Greene to form a Centre for Transpersonal Astrology that ran a series of workshops in London. Participants were introduced to the psychological models of Jung and Assagioli, Jung's four functions were linked to sign elements, and Bailey's esoteric rulerships of signs contrasted with the exoteric rulerships of traditional astrology. Greene—always more comfortable with the Jungian model—soon parted company with CTP to set up the Centre for Psychological Astrology (CPA) with Howard Sasportas, an award-winning astrologer of great insight with a diploma in psychosynthesis. Several CTP facilitators and trainee therapists took the CPA Diploma in Psychological Astrology while others—notably Joan and Reynold Swallow—favoured the Huber method.

Although the relationship between the four elements or temperaments of astrology and Jung's psychological functions had significant input in both astrologies, whereas his map of the psyche is the starting point for chart analysis by CPA, APA's chart interpretation begins with the three qualities—cardinal, fixed, and mutable—which combine to form an image of the psyche represented by an aspect structure indicative of coherence, inner motivation, and evolving sub-personalities. Sub-personalities are related more directly to planets in signs and houses in CPA interpretations than to the aspect patterns they form.[80]

CPA's engagement with mythology is evident in its manuals, portrayal of Mercury as Jung's archetypal trickster, and speedy

79. Hanegraaff, *Esotericism*, pp. 307-08, 352; Goodrick-Clarke, *Occult Roots*, pp. 1, 51-55; Treitel, p. 26; Robert Ellwood, *The Politics of Myth: A Study of C. G. Jung, Mircea Eliade, and Joseph Campbell* (New York, NY: SUNY, 1999), pp. 1-35; Mark Sedgwick, *Against the Modern World: Traditionalism and the Secret Intellectual History of the Twentieth Century* (New York: Oxford UP, 2004), pp. 95-117.

80. APA psychosynthesis workshop facilitated by Richard Llewellyn and Joyce Hopewell, Knutsford, May 2000; Wrekin Trust workshop facilitated by Howard Sasportas, Swanwick, Derbyshire, November 1982.

adoption of Chiron into its pantheon.[81] 2060 Chiron, a minor planet discovered in 1977 making an eccentric orbit between Saturn and Uranus, was named after the centaur parented by Cronos (Saturn) disguised as a stallion and the nymph Philyra. Born immortal and raised by the gods, Chiron became a teacher and healer. When accidentally wounded by Heracles' arrow, he was unable to heal himself and wanted to end his suffering in death, a wish that was eventually granted to him when Prometheus became immortal in his place.[82] Greene connects Chiron with the 'irredeemable flaw':

> Something has crippled us, and because of that injury we must take a different path in life, one which often we feel we would not have chosen if we had been left 'intact'.[83]

Whereas he is often referred to as the 'wounded healer', she makes the point that 'we cannot heal unless we understand the nature of our wound'.[84] Bruno was aware of ephemerides for Chiron circulating in America as early as 1978, but chose not bring the centaur into the Huber method. It is difficult to see how the Chiron myth might have been assimilated into an astrological psychology that does not use mythological archetypes as its point of departure. The kinds of collective wounds that Greene associates with Chiron can be found in the Huber moon node chart, covered in chapter 4. When writing about Chiron, in 1985, Bruno raises the question as to how many newly discovered astronomical bodies to include in a

81. Liz Greene, *Star Signs for Lovers* (London: Arrow, 1980), and *The Astrology of Fate*, 2nd edn (London: Unwin, 1985) are full of myths as is Howard Sasportas, *The Gods of Change: Pain, Crisis and the Transits of Uranus, Neptune and Pluto*, 2nd edn (Bournemouth: Wessex Astrologer, 2007); Carl Gustav Jung, *Four Archetypes: Mother, Rebirth, Spirit, Trickster*, trans. by R. F. C. Hull, 4th edn (London: Routledge Classics, 2003), pp. 159-79.

82. Pierre Grimal, *A Dictionary of Classical Mythology*, trans. by A. R. Maxwell-Hyslop (Oxford: Blackwell, 1986) pp. 100-01.

83. Liz Greene, *Barriers and Boundaries: The Horoscope and the Defences of the Personality* (London: CPA, 2002), p. 163.

84. Greene, *Barriers*, p. 165.

horoscope, discussed in chapter 5, and anticipates the demotion of Pluto to dwarf planet status.[85]

While placing primary emphasis on the three qualities, the Huber method also draws on Jung's four functions of consciousness, linking the elements not only with signs and houses—as does Greene—but specifically with its four sensory planets, in this respect giving a different slant to interpretation: Mars represents fire as 'spontaneous fusion'; Jupiter as earth is the summation of the senses, 'understanding of the nature of reality'; airy Mercury expresses the argumentative ideas person; and watery Venus the aesthetic individual seeking ideal form.[86] Of these, only choleric Mars corresponds to traditional medical psychology linking planets to elements and humours, as set out by Galen of Pergamon.[87] The connection between Jupiter and earth might seem unusual, given its traditional rulership of Sagittarius and Pisces, exaltation in Cancer, detriment and fall in the earth signs Virgo and Capricorn, and esoteric rulership of Aquarius corresponding to the Galenic association with sanguine air. However, Alan Leo related Jupiter to 'the magnetic aura that surrounds every living creature and rules its four divisions in the triplicities of fire, earth, air, and water', and this perception of Jupiter's physical vitality and capacity to fulfil 'practically achievable ideals' is reiterated by Stephen Arroyo with reference to Jupiter and earth.[88] Given the emphasis placed on growth of planetary seeds, forming sub-personalities to support survival and motivation, and on learning

---

85. Bruno Huber, 'Is Pluto a Planet?' 1st pub. in *Astrolog* (1985), repr. in Bruno and Louise Huber, et al, *Astrolog 1: Life and Meaning*, trans. by Heather Ross, and ed. Barry Hopewell (Knutsford: HopeWell, 2008), pp. 61-62.

86. 'Air-Thinking; Water-Feeling; Earth-Sensation; Fire-Intuition', in Liz Greene, *Relating: An Astrological Guide to Living with Others on a Small Planet*, 2nd edn (New York: Weiser, 1978), pp. 52-90; Bruno Huber, *Astrological Psychosynthesis: The Integration of Personality, Love, and Intelligence in the Horoscope*, 2nd English edn (York Beach, ME: Weiser, 1996), pp. 81-88.

87. 'Sanguine-Air-Jupiter; Choleric-Fire-Mars; Phlegmatic-Water-Moon; Melancholy-Earth-Saturn', in Frances Yates, *The Occult Philosophy in the Elizabethan Age*, 4th edn (London and New York: Routledge Classics, 2008), pp. 59-60.

88. Alan Leo, *The Art of Synthesis*, 6th edn (New York: Astrologer's Library, 1978), p. 80; Stephen Arroyo, *Exploring Jupiter: The Astrological Key to Progress, Prosperity and Potential*, ed. by Barbara McEnerney (Sebastopol, CA: CRCS, 1996), p. 100.

through experience to build confidence and banish fear, opening the way to psychosynthesis and spiritual purpose, it is unsurprising that Jupiter —Leo's 'Uplifter'—should play a leading role in the Huber method, whose main objectives are synthesis, renewal, and regeneration.[89]

Astrological psychology also relates the elements to the four quadrants of the horoscope, starting with fire as impulse in the lower left-hand corner of the unconscious hemisphere of the chart, followed by earth as instinct in the lower right-hand corner, air as thinking in the upper right-hand corner of the conscious hemisphere, and water as being in the upper left-hand corner. These are perceived as phases of growth operating sequentially through age progression round the life cycle, although emphasis differs, depending on the distribution of planets in an individual's chart. Within each quadrant there is potential for physical, emotional, mental, and spiritual development. Comparisons have been drawn between the Huber method and the transpersonal philosopher Ken Wilber's 'all-level, all-quadrant' transformative practice for 'implementing a more integral vision'.[90]

Instead of invoking mythological gods, Bruno connects Mercury, Jupiter, and Saturn with intelligent functions, Saturn with memory, Mercury with information-gathering, language, and correlation, and Jupiter with sense-perception, vision, and comprehension. Too much emphasis on Mercury facilitates information transfer lacking depth of thought, and the mind needs a well-developed Jupiter to make wise choices. Saturn is an ego planet concerned with defence and security, and an overactive Saturn can hold back progress by keeping the individual incarcerated in past memories. Sun and Moon as ego planets interact with the intelligent functions, Sun expressing vitality and self-awareness and Moon our emotional nature. Uranus adds creative intelligence, Neptune intuitive

89. Richard Llewellyn, 'The Carter Memorial Lecture, Astrological Association Conference 2001', *The Astrological Journal*, 43 (November/December 2001), 8-17 (pp. 11-17); Leo, *Synthesis*, pp. 80-87; see quadrants, p. 11.

90. Ken Wilber, *A Brief History of Everything*, 2nd edn, (Dublin: Gateway, 2001), pp. 310-11; Catharine Collier, *Celebrating the Quality of Four: The Human Condition as the Fourth Kingdom in Nature* (Knutsford: API [UK], 2004); Barry Hopewell, 'Beauty, Truth and Goodness', *Conjunction*, 49 (2010), pp. 18-20.

imagination, and Pluto intelligent will. Aspects between planets form motivational patterns, expressing how we think.[91]

The search for wholeness through synthesis advocated by Assagioli is translated into an astrology that emphasizes triangular growth. According to Pythagorean number theory, one and two are principles, and three becomes

> the first real number... having beginning, middle, and end. By virtue of the triad, unity and diversity of which it is composed are restored to harmony... Perhaps the best definition of the triad is perfect unity as it is comprehensible to human experience by virtue of 'form'. For this reason, it is referred to by Plotinus... to the soul.[92]

Huber astrology's triadic nature manifests in its 30-degree red, blue, and green aspects, the interplay of cardinal, fixed, and mutable motivations, three tiers of sensory, ego, and transpersonal planets in three columns, the threefold evolution of each planetary quality in character from sleeping automatic reactivity, through wakening awareness and conscious learning to fully awakened gnosis facilitating alignment of personality and soul[93] Comprehensive interpretation uses the natal (or radix), moon node, and house charts, with supplementary click charts to focus on specific questions. This emphasis on three with its growth potential contrasts sharply with 'Self-Knowledge through Cosmobiology', pioneered in early twentieth-century Germany by Alfred Witte and Reinhold Ebertin, employing only hard oppositions, squares, and semi-squares, using their midpoints to deconstruct the psyche, and presenting its findings as experimental science.[94] Bernadette Brady has traced back Ebertin's attempt to create a scientific

---

91. *Astrological Psychosynthesis*, pp. 42-62.

92. Vincent Foster Hopper, *Medieval Number Symbolism: Its Sources, Meaning, and Influence on Thought and Expression*, Columbia University Studies in English and Comparative Literature, 132 (New York: Columbia University, 1938; repr. Mineola, NY: Dover, 2000), pp. 41-42; Plotinus, *The Enneads*, trans. by Stephen MacKenna, abr. and ed. by John Dillon (London: Penguin, 1991), v.1.10.

93. See planet hierarchies, p. 9.

94. Reinhold Ebertin, *The Combination of Stellar Influences*, trans. by Alfred G. Roosedale and Linda Kratzsch, 4th edn (Tempe, AZ: American Federation of Astrologers, 1972), p. 11.

astrology using midpoint trees to the 'linear rational astrology' proposed by the thirteenth-century Majorcan theologian, Ramon Llull.[95] Cosmobiology was popularized in London around 1980, when Reinhold's son Baldur gave workshops enthusiastically promoted by Charles Harvey—one of the most inspiring teachers and presenters of astrology in the late twentieth century—so I duly calculated my midpoints, subjected them to keyword diagnoses given in *The Combination of Stellar Influences*, and concluded that if I took much notice of the results I would condemn myself to a life sentence in the Freudian basement! Whereas I acknowledge the personal nature of my reaction and am aware that midpoints have been widely adopted as an additional technique yielding useful insights, I was astonished to find the Ebertins' attempt to create a modern scientific astrology set alongside the Hubers' astrological psychology, based on psychosynthesis and deriving from ancient wisdom, by Kocku von Stuckrad, who places both under the umbrella of astrologies evolving from romantic *Naturphilosophie* and working with karma. Von Stuckrad unusually accords space to Huber in a general history of astrology and recognizes the significant contribution of the moon node chart discussed in chapter 4. Baldur is nowadays a practising psychotherapist using regression therapy more than cosmobiology, and the friendship between the Ebertins and the Hubers appears to have deterred them from criticizing each other's work.[96]

Both CPA and APA draw on the Neoplatonic astrology of Ficino, the Theosophical astrology of Leo, and the humanistic astrology of Rudhyar. CPA interacts primarily with Jungian psychology. Astrological psychology melds with psychosynthesis, with additions from Bailey's esoteric astrology and Jungian models. Jung's library contained many books by Leo, and his autobiography, *Memories, Dreams and Reflections* (1961), provided the Hubers

95. Bernadette Brady, *Cosmos, Chaosmos and Astrology: Rethinking the Nature of Astrology*, Sophia Centre Master Monographs, 1 (Ceredigion: Sophia Centre Press, 2014), pp. 63-66.

96. Stuckrad, *Astrología*, pp. 413-16; in conversation with Baldur Ebertin, Kepler Conference, London, 16 November 2013.

with useful examples of how primary and secondary personalities might be identified in chart structure and age progression aligned with the rhythms of an eventful inner and outer life.[97]

As efforts to align twentieth-century astrology with advances in astronomy fell out of fashion, from 1985-97 there was a revival of traditional astrological methods, and psychological astrology attracted much criticism.[98] In *Jung and Astrology* (1992), Maggie Hyde praises Jung for retrieving the imagination from the unconscious but is highly critical of the way in which psychological astrologers have adopted his methods:

> The borrowing of archetypes from Jung has, therefore, become associated with a loose and undisciplined approach and has led to a distinct polarity between traditional methods and current psychological astrology. This has been compounded by the adoption of the Jungian technique of amplification... employing fairy tales and mythical associations to elaborate symbols, images and situations produced by the analysand.[99]

Myths are powerful connectors with suppressed material hidden deep in the unconscious, but they may distort the individual narrative, and they can be rewritten. The Huber school has its own methods and checks, and Greene's acknowledgement that interpretations may be 'hopelessly mixed herein with fairy tales,

---

97. Liz Greene, 'Receiving the "Messengers": The Astrology of Jung's Liber Novus', in *Sky and Symbol: The Proceedings of the Ninth Annual Conference of the Sophia Centre for the Study of Cosmology and Culture, University of Wales, Trinity St David, 4-5 June 2011*, ed. by Nicholas Campion and Liz Greene (Ceredigion: Sophia Centre Press, 2013), pp. 257-99 (p. 271); C. G. Jung, *Memories, Dreams, Reflections*, ed. by Aniela Jaffé, and trans. by Richard and Clara Winston, 3rd edn (Glasgow: Collins Fount, 1977), pp. 81-103; *Astrological Psychosynthesis*, pp. 23-26; Bruno and Louise Huber, *LifeClock: The Huber Method of Timing in the Horoscope*, trans. by Haloli Q. Richter, Transcript, and Agnes Shellens, vols 1 and 2, 2nd edn rev. (York Beach, ME: 1994), 2, pp. 173-204.

98. Nicholas Campion, 'The Traditional Revival in Modern Astrology: A Preliminary History', <astrologyfoundation.org.nz/2004/08/03/the-traditional-revival-in-modern-astrology> [accessed 10 November 2013].

99. Maggie Hyde, *Jung and Astrology* (London: Aquarian, 1992), pp. 64, 91.

myths, dreams and other oddities' is not generally applicable to Huber, which Hyde did not consider in her book.[100]

Some scholars have aligned Greene's psychological approach with Ficino and Neoplatonic astrology without extending their interest to Huber.[101] It could be argued that Huber astrologers have contributed to the neglect of their branch of astrology in scholarly circles by emphasizing only the experiential and holistic nature of their work. This volume shows that behind its conception and practice lies an esoteric tradition that is psychologically transformative, spiritually sensitive, culturally mature, and of ongoing relevance in the world today.

---

100. Greene, *Fate*, p. 14, cited by Hyde, p.92.

101. *Marsilio Ficino*, Western Esoteric Masters Series, ed. by Angela Voss (Berkeley, CA: North Atlantic Books, 2006), pp. 51-52; Roy Willis and Patrick Curry, *Astrology, Science, and Culture: Pulling Down the Moon* (Oxford and New York: Berg, 2004), pp. 72-73.

2. Defining Western Esotericism

2.1 Esotericism as a Form of Thought

The pioneering study, *Giordano Bruno and the Hermetic Tradition* by Frances Yates, published in 1964, revived interest in the esoteric traditions underpinning Renaissance thought and, in 1965, François Secret—a specialist in Christian Kabbalah—was appointed to a new chair in the History of Christian Esotericism at the Sorbonne. He was succeeded, in 1979, by Antoine Faivre, who specialized in Christian theosophy and modernized the title of his chair to the History of Esoteric Currents in Modern and Contemporary Europe.

Faivre began attending Eranos conferences in 1967, and joined their speaking elite in 1973. In those days, Fröbe gave mere participants no question time, taking the ungenerous view that 'most questioners only wanted to assert themselves and hear their own voices'. He challenged this opinion, noting the absence of young people at these prestigious conferences, but his 1975 petition fell on deaf ears in Ascona, whose organizers failed to establish a round table until the 1990s. Meanwhile, Faivre's appointment to the chair at the Sorbonne gave him scope to define Western esotericism, in a way that would not only shape the emerging discipline but also enable a wider number of interested students to access its mysteries through a coherent framework of reference.[102]

In 1992, Faivre published his four intrinsic and two optional characteristics of the Western esoteric form of thought. Until the appearance of Hanegraaff's *Western Esotericism: A Guide for the Perplexed* (2013), textbooks on Western esotericism usually began with these criteria, approaching the subject through Faivre's methodological lens, supplemented by modifications proffered by other experts in the field. Notwithstanding criticism of this

102. Hakl, pp. 234-36.

'checklist approach to Western esotericism', and difficulties caused by this discipline's inception in the esoteric currents of the Christian Renaissance and expansion into contemporary spirituality non-aligned with any particular faith, in my view, Faivre's defining characteristics usefully classify complex ideas emerging from ancient wisdom whose relationship with dogmatic theology and rational philosophy is ambiguous, establishing an effective gateway to hidden knowledge for seekers and scholars whose historical, cultural or theological background may be somewhat patchy.[103] So I am beginning my task of assigning Huber astrology a place in the Western esoteric tradition by setting out Faivre's criteria and assessing their relevance to astrological psychology. The four essential components are: correspondences, living nature, imagination and mediations, and transmutation; the optional extras are the praxis of concordance and transmission.[104] So, how well does astrological psychology fit this pattern?

Firstly, like all astrology, it resonates to the correspondences inherent in the hermetic maxim 'as above, so below', the reflection of macrocosm in microcosm and vice versa, revealing a myriad of similarities and interconnections between the material world of humanity and the invisible celestial and supercelestial spheres above the horizon.

Regarding the second criterion, Bruno Huber was drawn to esoteric astrology 'to gain a glimpse of the pattern and purpose of nature's ways'.[105] The 'perception of the natural world as a living and mysterious whole' was fully acknowledged by Louise and Bruno, and homage duly paid to its rhythmic laws:

103. Hanegraaff, *Esotericism*, pp. 11, 360.

104. Antoine Faivre, 'Introduction 1', in *MES*, pp. xi-xxii; Antoine Faivre, *Access to Western Esotericism* (Albany, NY: SUNY, 1994), pp. 10-15.

105. *DAP*, p. 5.

> The essential rhythms that determine life on our planet are regulated by laws of nature... We know the obvious rhythms of day and night, the changes of seasons, and the growth of the individual from childhood to youth, then maturity, and finally old age. Within a larger framework, the human being is also subject to cosmic time units, cycles, and epochs that correspond to planetary changes... These cycles carry life through its highs and lows like the waves of an ocean.[106]

The question as to whether all esotericists viewed nature as a living entity, posed by Jane Williams-Hogan with reference to Emanuel Swedenborg, drew the negative conclusion that for Swedenborg, 'the natural world is the world of appearances' and 'essentially dead'.[107] Hanegraaff extended her line of enquiry and its implications, bearing in mind that Faivre's 'four intrinsic characteristics of traditional esotericism mutually imply each other in the context of one integral worldview of correspondences', and concluding that, notwithstanding subtle changes to the God-Humanity-Nature relationship over the years, the philosophy of nature, *Naturphilosophie*, remained fundamental to the esoteric form of thought:

> Essential to the character of esotericism as a modern *Naturphilosophie* is the additional perception that divinity is immanent in nature itself. Accordingly, a salvational gnosis is obtained... in the very perception of the natural world as a living and mysterious whole, permeated by a secret 'fire' and held together by a web of correspondences.[108]

The torch of Romantic *Naturphilosophie*, carried into the twentieth century by Jung, is central to the modern Pagan 'holistic worldview

106. *LifeClock*, 1, pp. 105-07.

107. Jane Williams-Hogan, 'The Place of Emanuel Swedenborg in Modern Western Esotericism', in *Western Esotericism and the Science of Religion: Selected Papers presented at the 17th Congress of the International Association of the History of Religions, Mexico City 1995* (*WESR*) (Leuven: Peeters, 1998), ed by Antoine Faivre and Wouter J. Hanegraaff, pp. 201-52 (pp. 220-23).

108. Wouter J. Hanegraaff, *New Age Religion and Western Culture: Esotericism in the Mirror of Secular Thought* (Albany, NY: SUNY, 1998), p. 427.

of correspondences, organicism and many levels of reality'.[109] Like Jung and Steiner, the Hubers were inspired by Goethe. As well as his colour theory, the concepts of 'polarity, synthesis, and resolution' fundamental to Goethe's 'private religion' are intrinsic to their system of interpretation.[110] The Huber method embraces a contemporary holistic worldview, with natal horoscopes depicting five layers of existence for analysis at physical, emotional, mental, and transpersonal levels, and two further charts providing insights into the ancestral past and identifying obstacles, stimuli, and expectations in the surrounding environment.[111] Whereas Swedenborg may have substituted 'mechanistic science resting on Cartesian premises' for *Naturphilosophie*, in our twenty-first century of global warming and extremes of climate, where we witness apparently sound, man-made buildings and sophisticated transport systems collapse in the wake of tsunamis, volcanic eruptions, high winds, searing heat, and relentless floods, it is inconceivable that any esotericist minded to serve the cause of humanity would discount the elemental forces of the natural world or fail to pay them due respect.[112] The significance of salvation, which occurs frequently in esoteric literature, is usefully explained with reference to Eranos:

---

109. Hanegraaff, *New Age*, p. 497; Wouter J. Hanegraaff, 'Magic V: 18th-20th Century', in *Dictionary of Gnosis and Western Esotericism (DGWE)*, ed. by Wouter J. Hanegraaff, Antoine Faivre, Roelof van den Broek, and Jean-Pierre Brach (Leiden: Brill, 2006), pp. 738-44 (p. 743).

110. Bruno and Louise Huber, *Astrology and the Spiritual Path: The Spiritual Significance of Age Progression* (York Beach, ME: Weiser, 1990), p. 7; Nicholas Goodrick-Clarke, 'The Hermetic Harvest of Goethe's Alchemical Retreat', EXESESO Study Conference, 18 October 2009, p. 18.

111. *Aspect Pattern*, pp. 12-13 and 55; Joyce Hopewell, *The Living Birth Chart: Astrological Psychology: A Practical Workbook* (Knutsford: HopeWell, 2008), pp. 183-214; see intro., five levels, p. 6.

112. Hanegraaff, *New Age*, p. 427.

> Understanding and existential awareness were not to be pursued for purely intellectual reasons but because they made possible salvation in this world and from this world.[113]

This non-denominational interpretation, carefully worded to avoid aligning salvation with any particular theology, applies to psychosynthesis, astrological psychology, and other New Age movements, anticipating the drive towards active participation in 'heroic communities' aware of their 'crucial role in the postmodern world' as builders of 'a framework of values or a vision of the true and the good', as proposed by Tarnas, while retaining 'the God/Human/Nature triangle', identified by Faivre as characteristic of theosophy.[114]

The third compulsory trait, imagination and mediations, relates to the mesocosm, the realm of intermediaries situated between microcosm and macrocosm, which Henry Corbin—philosopher, theologian, professor of Islamic Studies at the Sorbonne, and another giant of Eranos—called the *mundus imaginalis* or the imaginal world:[115]

> Corbin considers the word 'Oriental' as primarily a symbolic term signifying the realm of light... 'Oriental philosophy' means the journey of the realm of the spirit and away from the prison of sense or matter... it is a form of wisdom or a 'theosophy' which has for its purpose the deliverance of man from this world of imperfection to the 'world of light'. It is non-Greek in the sense that the specific genius of the Greeks of the historical period was dialectical. They even hid the Egyptian, Orphic and Babylonian mysteries, upon which Pythagoreanism was based, under a veil of dialectics. The 'Oriental philosophy' removes this veil and seeks to present the *philosophia perennis* not as something to satisfy the need for thinking but as a guide, or at least a doctrinal aid, for the illumination of man which arises from the inner experience

113. Hakl, p. 52.

114. Richard Tarnas, 'The Carter Memorial Lecture, Astrological Association Conference 2013: Role of Astrology in a Civilization in Crisis', *The Astrological Journal*, 56 (January/February 2014), 27-34 (p. 31); Antoine Faivre, *Theosophy, Imagination, Tradition: Studies in Western Esotericism*, trans. by Christine Rhone (Albany, NY: SUNY, 2000), p. 7.

115. Hakl, pp. 161-63.

> of its author. Its language is therefore primarily symbolic rather than dialectical even if it begins with Aristotelian logic and employs some of the cosmological ideas of the Peripatetic philosophers.[116]

The adjective imaginal, drawing a 'distinction between the imaginary, which is utopian and unreal, and the imagination, which is cognitive and creative' usefully describes the world where the esotericist dialogues with intermediaries on the path of initiation.[117]

Faivre differentiates the esotericist's encounters with daemons, angels, or guides from the spiritual gnosis of the mystic, for whom such interventions are unnecessary. For Arthur Versluis, this distinction is artificial, since visions recorded by the Lutheran theosophist Jacob Boehme could fall into either category, while in transpersonal work oceanic unity is quite rare and illumination is more frequently achieved in relationship with a guide or by working with symbols.[118] This is also true of the astrological psychologist, for whom the planets and the geometrical patterns they create act as mediators.

Transmutation, the fourth compulsory characteristic, is an alchemical term, meaning metamorphosis, or rebirth following pursuit of an illuminative path to higher knowledge. This transformation can be achieved over time, whilst studying for a Diploma in Astrological Psychology that involves extensive self-examination. There are specific exercises both for shifting emphasis from the ego planets, Saturn, Moon, and Sun to their transpersonal or spiritual counterparts, Uranus, Neptune, and Pluto, and for

---

116. Seyyed Hossein Nasr, *An Introduction to Islamic Cosmological Doctrines*, 2nd edn rev. (London: Thames and Hudson, 1978), pp. 190-91.

117. Jérôme Rousse Lacordaire, 'Corbin, Henry, b. 14.4.1903 Paris, d. 7.10.1978 Paris', in *DGWE*, pp. 271-73 (p. 272).

118. Arthur Versluis, 'What is Esoteric? Methods in the Study of Western Esotericism', Esoterica, 4 (2002), <www.esoteric.msu.edu/VolumeIV/ Methods.htm> [accessed 12 December 2011], pp. 1-15 (p. 3); Faivre, Access, pp. 12, 27; Gordon-Brown and Somers, Raincloud, pp. 59-64.

alleviating stressed planets through a process of compensation, sublimation, and transformation.[119]

In the context of alchemical transmutation, Mary Anne Atwood expressed the opinion that:

> Man... is the true laboratory of the Hermetic art; his life the subject, the grand distillatory, the thing distilling and the thing distilled, and Self-Knowledge... at the root of all Alchemical tradition.[120]

Her depiction of the alchemist as both distiller and distilled can equally well be applied to the astrological psychologist, whose perception is refined through increasing self-knowledge, synthesis, and alignment, as the scales fall away to reveal a picture of the soul hidden behind outer appearances. Astrological psychology emphasizes Jupiter's visionary and sensory functions, combining expansion and depth, 'opening our inner awareness'.[121] A parallel can be drawn with Klee's evaluation of abstract art in his 'Creative Confession' (1920): 'Art does not reproduce the visible, rather, it makes visible'.[122] He shared with his students the process of creating pictorial relationships to elicit the energy within:

> Analyzing first the basic building blocks of all picture-making, Klee traces the plane back to its source as a point that moved to a line, thence to many lines that configured the plane; he compares the character of the linear energies that resolve into a triangle with those that result in square or circle; then he further pursues the concept of the outer contour as a result of the inner energies of the form; and vice versa.[123]

---

119. *Planets*, pp. 91-117; *Transformation*, pp. 43-78; see planet hierarchies, p. 9.

120. Mary Anne Atwood, A Suggestive Inquiry into the Hermetic Mystery and Alchemy (London: Trelawney Saunders, 1850), repr. <www.archive.org/details/suggestiveinquir00atwo> [accessed 10 February 2014] p. 153; Hereward Tilton, 'Spiritual Alchemy and Transfiguration', EXESESO Study Conference, 27 March 2011, pp. 5-6.

121. *Astrological Psychosynthesis*, p. 32.

122. Matthew Gale, 'Carefully ordered confusion', in *The EY Exhibition—Paul Klee: Making Visible* (London: Tate, 2013), pp15-31 (p. 24).

123. Deborah Rosenthal, 'A transparent world: the notebooks of Paul Klee', *The New Criterion* (1993), pp. 33-38 (p. 35).

Similarly, the student of Huber astrology is introduced to houses, signs, planets, and aspects as 'building blocks' of the chart, and learns how to join up aspects to create linear, triangular, and quadrangular figures expressing cardinal, mutable, and fixed motivational energies. Having assembled and memorized these details with Mercurial dexterity and Saturnian rigour, the apprentice astrologer is then asked to set them aside, focus on the big picture of the aspect structure and, using free association

> catch a glimpse of a deep inner world of subconscious potency not accessible to superficial investigation, but open to be gleaned by our deeper mind, our intuition, our sensitive awareness.[124]

Astrologers of other schools find it difficult to assimilate the techniques of astrological psychology, and Huber astrologers often struggle to read the charts of other schools, because the horoscope is a mandala whose inner circle is a crucible, and the reading of Huber charts requires a fundamental change of vision.

The optional praxis of concordance is not generally applicable to Huber astrologers, whose processes of self-initiation, self-regulated psychological growth, and spiritual progress are neither underpinned by the Renaissance quest for a *prisca theologia*—meaning ancient God-given theology or unitary wisdom tradition that is the source of truth and inspiration of all other religions—nor by the purism of more recent Traditionalists seeking a 'treasury of wisdom and gnosis' that humanity has allowed 'to be dispersed and diluted' in our dark age of Kali Yuga.[125] Notwithstanding their use of a term from Hindu cosmology to describe our fallen world, Traditionalists do not promote initiation into Indian mysteries by Western esotericists, but encourage disciples to enter the inner circle of their authentic faith as preparation for receiving the 'primordial Tradition'. One of the major exponents of Traditionalism, also known as Perennialism and described as 'the secret intellectual

124. *Astrological Psychosynthesis*, pp. 32-33.

125. *Planets*, p.106; Faivre, *Access*, p. 14; Nicholas Goodrick-Clarke, *The Western Esoteric Traditions: A Historical Perspective* (New York, NY: Oxford University Press, 2008), p. 7.

history of the twentieth-century', was the French metaphysician, René Guénon, who lived as a Sufi in Cairo. The Romanian historian of religion Mircea Eliade has been dubbed a 'soft' Traditionalist with a more covert approach, who also drew on other sources.[126] In contrast to this purist approach, Faivre has identified a historical path in contemporary esotericism that includes the TS, whose three objects are: (1) to form a nucleus of the Universal Brotherhood of humanity without distinction of race, creed, sex, caste or colour.; (2) to encourage the study of comparative religion, philosophy and science; and (3) to investigate unexplained laws of nature and the powers latent in man.

Arising from both currents, a 'humanist path... touches upon transmutation of ourselves'.[127] For the astrologer at least, is important to differentiate the word 'humanist' referring to the humanistic psychology of Maslow and the human potential movement—as Faivre does here—from the body of non-believers, whose 'Objections to Astrology' were published in *The Humanist* journal in 1975.[128] Rudhyar, shifting from his early allegiance with Theosophy to a more Maslovian, person-centred approach, set up an International Committee for Humanistic Astrology, in 1969, and published his major philosophical work, *The Planetarization of Consciousness*.[129] Humanistic psychology sought 'to help and guide individuals regarded as developing, aspiring, self-actualizing persons who at times may reach moments of exalted spiritual consciousness in "peak experiences"', and may be drawn to 'a cause outside their own skin... some calling or vocation in the old sense, the priestly sense'.[130] The redemptive and transmutative strands of this evolutionary current echo the visualizations of heavenly

126. Faivre, *Access*, pp. 37-38; Sedgwick, pp. 73-83, 98-117 (p. 111); Jean Borella, 'René Guénon and the Traditionalist School', in *MES*, pp. 330-58; Hans Thomas Hakl, 'Some additional remarks on Julius Evola and Aleister Crowley, in Marco Pasi, *Aleister Crowley and the Temptation of Politics* (Durham: Acumen, 2014), pp.141-52.

127. Faivre, *Access*, pp. 39-40.

128. Cornelius, pp. 22-23.

129. Ertan, p. xxvii.

130. Rudhyar, *Personality*, p. xi; Maslow, p. 42.

palaces, or *heikhalot*, ascending to the divine chariot, or *merkavah*, of early Jewish mystics, while also opening up a spiritual dimension for future humanity 'not to be reduced to any single interpretation of universal truth or any single path'.[131] In this context, Faivre cites Needleman, who describes 'real philosophy' as

> one of the influences that orient men and women toward the path that leads to becoming fully human... by seeding awakening ideas into the world which further the process of inner questioning, a process that ultimately opens the heart and mind to a new experience of one's Self.[132]

Rudhyar places this awakened Self at the centre of the globe and calls upon humanity to make 'one vast creative effort'.[133] Despite some blurring of boundaries, differences between backward-looking and forward-seeking esoteric currents are made increasingly apparent in subsequent chapters, and astrological psychologists are among those who believe in the ability of enlightened humanity to use creative imagination constructively and change some fundamental things for the better.

Regarding Faivre's second optional characteristic of Western esotericism, transmission, education in astrological psychology takes place through the international teaching schools, their books, websites, and mass media presence. Faivre's specialist use of the word transmission, meaning 'esoteric teaching... transmitted from master to disciple following a pre-established channel, respecting a previously marked path', is applicable only to courses taught by schools.[134] A student registering to take a Diploma in eight modules with the British APA is assigned a tutor, with whom he or she will work closely, interpreting the tutor's chart as well as his or her own

---

131. *The Early Kabbalah*, trans. by Ronald C. Kiener, and ed. by Joseph Dan (Mahwah, NJ: Paulist, 1986), pp. 7-8; Keiron Le Grice, *The Archetypal Cosmos: Rediscovering the Gods in Myth, Science and Astrology* (Edinburgh: Floris, 2010), p. 37.

132. Faivre, *Access*, p. 40; Needleman, *Heart*, pp. xi-xii.

133. Rudhyar, *Planetarization*, pp. 308-09.

134. Faivre, *Access*, pp. 14-15.

as part of the learning process, and receiving carefully considered feedback. There are four assessed assignments, marked by two tutors and moderated by the school, each one expecting the student to display not only more knowledge of astrological techniques but also greater ability to visualize the whole picture with empathy and awareness of the soul's journey. Teaching methods are changing rapidly, with many seekers self-educating on the Internet, so it is unsurprising that Faivre gave transmission optional status.

2.2 Identities and Discourse

In a bid to tighten up its defining characteristics, Hanegraaff has suggested that

> Western esotericism is ultimately grounded in a historiographical concept, rather than in a common philosophical or religious worldview, a specific approach to knowledge or a 'form of thought'. However, because the Renaissance narrative of ancient wisdom was itself derived from Platonic Orientalism, the philosophical worldviews and salvational epistemologies basic to late antique phenomenon certainly become central to it.[135]

Platonic Orientalism refers to the light of ancient wisdom transmitted by the Persian sage Zoroaster as well as legends of meetings between Pythagoras with Chaldean astrologers and the Egyptian sage Hermes Trismegistus who supposedly predicted the birth of Christ. Plato, too, is said to have travelled to Egypt, Babylon, Persia, and India to study with priests and sages. Neoplatonism imbued Platonism with theurgic purpose, and texts lost to the West were recovered from the Eastern Orthodox city of Constantinople by Florentine scholars in the fifteenth century, translated and assimilated into the Christian narrative.[136] The detailed chronicling of a perception of history in the Renaissance that has since been discredited may enhance the dialogue with

135. Hanegraaff, *Esotericism*, pp.11, 73, 360.

136. Hanegraaff, *Esotericism*, pp. 12-17; Goodrick-Clarke, *Western Esoteric*, pp. 16-18; Paolo Lucentini, 'Hermes Trismegistus II: Middle Ages', in *DGWE*, pp. 479-83.

other schools of Renaissance studies, but this linear approach has more relevance to those esoteric currents that 'show a consistent tendency to try to establish common denominators between two different traditions or... among all traditions' than to experiential currents, like astrological psychology, that do not conform to the praxis of concordance.[137]

This approach, which emphasizes the Christian story, is justified by Hanegraaff on the grounds that Faivre was doing for Christianity what Gershom Scholem had done for Jewish mysticism and Corbin for esoteric Islam, and that his four intrinsic characteristics emerged from 'a Christian and religionist notion of "true" esotericism'.[138] By tracing the link between Neoplatonism and the Florentine Renaissance solely through the Christian apologists, Hanegraaff omits earlier cultural flowering, between the eleventh and early thirteenth centuries, centred on the Spanish city of Toledo, where 'a dramatic intellectual encounter between scholars in the Latin West... and the rich intellectual traditions of the Islamic world', made available many significant cosmological texts as well as works by Aristotle.[139] Besides, surely, when Faivre changed the title of his chair to the History of Esoteric Currents in Modern and Contemporary Europe, he intended to broaden the scope of this research?[140] Western esoteric currents were no longer being presented as exclusively Christian and might encompass developing interest in the study of comparative religions since the founding of the TS (1875), twentieth-century 'secularization of esotericism', as in psychosynthesis and astrological psychology, and syncretic spirituality, merging diverse traditions into 'a powerful

137. Faivre, *Access*, p. 14.

138. Hanegraaff, *Esotericism*, pp. 308, 354.

139. Nicholas Campion, *The Medieval and Modern Worlds: History of Western Astrology*, 2 (New York, NY: Continuum, 2009), pp. 29-30.

140. Faivre, *Access*, p. ix; Hanegraaff, *Esotericism*, pp. 348-49.

system of guidance that can enhance our minds and bodies and show us how to manage our spirits within the world'.[141]

A controversy has arisen as a result of Faivre's presentation of Christian Kabbalah as an esoteric current, and his exclusion of Jewish Kabbalah. Intellectuals like Giovanni Pico della Mirandola and Johann Reuchlin learned Kabbalah from Jewish scholars expelled from Spain, thereafter adapting its exegetical techniques to Christian speculation.[142] Their work was researched by Yates, and Secret made impressive contributions to scholarship in the field that became known as Christian Kabbalah, showing just how influential kabbalistic methods were in rewriting the 'narrative of ancient wisdom' during the Renaissance.[143] Nevertheless, as Greene has demonstrated, most Jewish kabbalistic texts from Europe exhibit all the required characteristics of an esoteric form of thought. Moreover, her invaluable research provides evidence that the Kabbalah of the nineteenth-century occult revival, with its widespread influence on New Age psychological and spiritual paths, derives largely from Jewish sources.[144] This perspective is supported by Marco Pasi, writing about Kabbalah in the context of the TS and the breakaway Hermetic Society of Anna Kingsford and Edward Maitland:

141. *Helena Blavatsky*, ed. by Nicholas Goodrick-Clarke, Western Esoteric Masters Series (Berkeley, CA: North Atlantic Books, 2004), p. 18; Hanegraaff, *Esotericism*, p. 354; Caroline Myss, *Anatomy of the Spirit: The Seven Stages of Power and Healing* (London: Bantam, 1997), p. 91.

142. Antoine Faivre, 'Questions of Terminology Proper to the Study of Esoteric Currents in Modern and Contemporary Europe', in *WESR*, pp. 1-10 (p. 4); Moshe Idel, Introduction to Johann Reuchlin, *On the Art of the Kabbalah: De Arte Cabalistica*, trans. by Martin and Sarah Goodman, 2nd edn (Lincoln and London: University of Nebraska Press, 1993), p. vii.

143. Frances Yates, *Giordano Bruno and the Hermetic Tradition*, 3rd edn (London and New York: Routledge, 2009), 90-129; François Secret, *Les Kabbalistes Chrétiens de la Renaissance*, 3rd edn rev (Milan: Archè, 2006), p. xxxiv; Hanegraaff, *Esotericism*, p. 74; Liz Greene, *Magi and Maggidim: The Kabbalah in British Occultism, 1860-1940*, Studies in Cultural Astronomy and Astrology, 3 (Ceredigion: Sophia Centre Press, 2012), pp. 30-31, 457.

144. Greene, *Magi*, pp. 14-15.

> With the 'Hermetic reaction' that develops in occultism as a response to Blavatsky's emphasis on the 'Eastern' sources of esoteric wisdom, the idea of a specifically 'Western' esoteric tradition takes shape. Jewish Kabbalah plays a crucial role in this process. Whereas Mme. Blavatsky tends to devaluate Jewish Kabbalah by considering it an inferior form of older 'Oriental' traditions..., later 'Hermetic' occultists come to perceive it as one of the pillars of a distinctly 'Western' esoteric tradition together with phenomena such as Rosicrucianism, alchemy, and the tarot.[145]

As he points out:

> Whereas Christian kabbalists saw Kabbalah as a means to prove Christian truths by using the esoteric wisdom of the Jews..., Blavatsky does the opposite. She uses Kabbalah in order to disprove the truths of Christianity, especially in its dogmatic and institutional forms.[146]

Consequently, Christian Kabbalah appears to add little to our understanding of contemporary esoteric practice and is omitted from subsequent chapters.

Any scholar of esotericism not brought up in the Jewish tradition and with little knowledge of the Hebrew language must tread warily when referring to Jewish mysticism and acknowledge that some readers may object to her discussing it at all. Even so, the tradition of Kabbalah has been such a formative influence on many psycho-spiritual models we use today that this debt must be acknowledged. In her monumental work, *Dream of the Cosmos,* Anne Baring identifies the Shekinah, meaning 'Presence of God in the world' as

> the most complete image of the feminine aspect of spirit to have survived from the ancient past. She restores the missing connective cosmology of the soul that the three major patriarchal religions... had lost... Because the tradition of Kabbalah makes the association

145. Marco Pasi, 'Oriental Kabbalah and the Parting of East and West in the Early Theosophical Society', in Kabbalah and Modernity: Interpretations, Transformations, Adaptations, ed. by Boaz Huss, Marco Pasi, and Kocku von Stuckrad (Leiden and Boston: Brill, 2010), pp. 151-66, repr. <www.academic.edu>, p. 162.

146. Pasi, 'Oriental Kabbalah', p. 161.

> between the feminine aspect of the godhead, Divine Wisdom, and the Holy Spirit, it showed me how Christianity, in its definition of the Holy Spirit as the Third Person of a male Trinity, had lost the ancient and connective mythology of spirit as a great web of life... I understood that the mystical tradition of Kabbalah offers us one of the major missing links between the participatory experience of the great lunar cultures of the Bronze Age and our own age... What we have lost and what this extraordinary tradition has preserved for us is the image of a sacred Earth as well as an unseen web of relationships connecting the life of our planet with the life of the Cosmos.[147]

This is a powerful statement that has relevance for Huber astrology. The Hubers reflected on the importance of cultural evolution in their concept of the family model, assigning the nomadic culture to the Moon as child, 'mobile and spontaneous', the matriarchal culture to Saturn, as protective parent accentuating security as key to survival, and the patriarchal culture to the Sun, as leader making a mark on society, while recognizing that 'all people possess both male and female qualities'. Their controversial assignment of Saturn to mother—based on research showing that when Saturn was the highest ego planet in the chart the client had usually been 'brought up in a fairly pronounced matriarchal family atmosphere'—breaks ranks with the alchemical marriage of Sun and Moon, emphasizes the interface between Sun and Earth, and corresponds to the Shekinah.[148] She is identified both with the lowest sefirah, Malkhut representing Earth, body, and the trunk of the Tree of Kabbalah and with Binah, the sefirah of understanding, passive intellect and mother represented by Saturn on the left-hand pillar, as the 'one who brings forms into being'.[149]

147. Baring, pp. 36-38.

148. *Astrological Psychosynthesis*, pp. 122-29.

149. Arthur Edward Waite, *The Holy Kabbalah: A Mystical Interpretation of the Scriptures* (New York, NY: Citadel, 1995), p. 147; Z'ev ben Shimon Halevi, *Astrology and Kabbalah: a rewrite of The Anatomy of Fate* (London: Urania Trust, 2000), pp. 18, 44, 174; Z'ev ben Shimon Halevi, *Kabbalah and Psychology* (Bath: Gateway, 1986), p. vii; Brian L. Lancaster, *The Essence of Kabbalah*, 2nd edn (London: Arcturus, 2006), p. 84.

The backbone of planets in Bruno's amphora resembles the middle pillar with Saturn in the Malkhut position at the base, and there are links between the psychosynthesis egg and the three levels of the soul in kabbalistic thought: *nefesh*, meaning bodymind, *ruach* meaning psyche, and *neshamah*, the divine soul. As Les Lancaster writes:

> The emphasis on synthesis, and on the psychological means of promoting it, leads to some stimulating parallels between Assagioli's school of therapy and Kabbalah... There is a profound psychological edge to Kabbalah, which gives it especial value in the quest for self-betterment.

Nevertheless:

> For all its potential relevance to matters of psychological insight and therapeutic transformation, the real objectives of Kabbalah are considerably larger in scale. The ultimate challenge is that of bringing the dynamics of the Godhead into their proper conformation, thereby promoting *tikkun olam*, the healing of the world.[150]

This ideology is shared by many groups today and transformation of self is the first step.

Mindful of the plurality of traditions, Kocku von Stuckrad takes the view that the

> many overlapping and competing ideologies, worldviews, and identities that have given shape to Western culture can only be appreciated by giving serious attention to the role that esoteric discourse has played in the history of the West.[151]

Applying the term discourse, as outlined by Michel Foucault, to refer to 'the totality of certain thought systems that interact with societal systems in manifold ways', in his *Brief History of Secret Knowledge*

---

150. Lancaster, pp. 39-41; see egg, amphora, p. 13.

151. Hartley Lachter, review of Kocku von Stuckrad, Locations of Knowledge in Medieval and Early Modern Europe (Leiden: Brill, 2010), <www.h-net.org/reviews/showrev.php?id=31482> [accessed 6 November 2013]

(2005), Stuckrad cites an example of significant historical events and their incorporation into a doctrine of salvation:[152]

> While Shiites in the Middle Ages related the astrological doctrine of so-called Great Conjunctions to the date of the return of the Hidden Imam, Jews could relate the same doctrine theologically to their expulsion from Spain in 1492 and to the exile, which would soon give way to a messianic era. Christians again used this doctrine in terms of apocalypticism and eschatology to escalate the confessional tensions of the sixteenth and seventeenth centuries... One could speak of an apocalyptic, redemptive or even an astrological field of discourse.[153]

The Great Conjunctions of Jupiter and Saturn, elaborated by the ninth century Islamic astrologer Abū Ma'shar and extended to include the interacting cycles of Uranus, Neptune, and Pluto, reference moments of transition in cross-cultural history, as effectively demonstrated by Tarnas, and Stuckrad accords astrology a seminal role in the esoteric traditions, because its primordial cosmic principles—signs of the Zodiac and planets—can be applied in multiple ways.[154] However, his more recent redefinition of esoteric discourse as 'a secretive dialectic of concealment and revelation which is concerned with perfect knowledge' presents an exacting ideological concept, dissociating from most of what we call esoteric astrology.[155]

---

152. Kocku von Stuckrad, 'Esoteric Discourse and the European History of Religion: In Search of a New Interpretational Framework', <ojs.abo.fi/index.php/scripta/article/viewFile/398/1176> [accessed 8 October 2014], p. 221.

153. Kocku von Stuckrad, *Western Esotericism: A Brief History of Secret Knowledge*, trans. by Nicholas Goodrick-Clarke (London: Equinox, 2005), pp. 6-7.

154. Kocku von Stuckrad, '*Astrologia Hermetica:* Astrology, Western Culture, and the Academy', in *Hermes in the Academy: Ten Years' Study of Western Esotericism at the University of Amsterdam*, ed. by Wouter J. Hanegraaff and Joyce Pijnenburg, eds (Amsterdam: Amsterdam UP, 2009), pp. 51-58 (p. 54); Dane Rudhyar, *The Astrology of Transformation: A Multilevel Approach* (Wheaton, IL: Quest, 1980), pp. 73-74; Alexander Ruperti, *Cycles of Becoming: The Planetary Pattern of Growth* (Davis, CA: CRCS, 1978), pp. 171-258; Richard Tarnas, *Cosmos and Psyche: Intimations of a New World View* (New York, NY: Viking, 2006); Stuckrad, *Astrología*, p. 25.

155. Stuckrad, *Locations*, p. 67; Hanegraaff, *Esotericism*, p. 364.

In an effort to combat biased historiography, Stuckrad has devised an intellectual construct that loses touch with the pragmatic intent of the contemporary esotericist, whose scope extends well beyond self-development in a quest to peel back hidden layers of meaning and do something useful for humanity and our planet. Astrology—albeit recognized as 'an important element in European cultural history'—is no longer put to astrological use:

> If we conceptualize esotericism as a discourse of perfect knowledge that addresses a dialectic of concealment and revelation, astrology can serve as a means to unlock the hidden knowledge of the universe and to grant the human being perfect understanding of the ultimate meaning of the world and its history... However, we should not forget that the best astrologers have never claimed that astrology offers perfect understanding or knowledge; rather, astrology has usually been understood to be conjectural or probable knowledge. We can conclude that the use of astrological conjecture in discourses of perfect knowledge in not necessarily an astrological use any more.[156]

As a consequence, Stuckrad suggests that

> in the future we study astrology as part of philosophy, science, mathematics, medicine, historiography, art, and religion; only when it comes to hidden, perfect knowledge by means of astrological methods does it make sense to talk of esoteric astrology.[157]

Notably, in an earlier book, Stuckrad drew attention to the Huber assertion that their astrological path to spiritual growth has much in common with esoteric thinking, even if he did not quote Bruno's categorical statement that it is 'the foremost expression of esoteric thinking', and Faivre agrees that some levels of astrology can be considered esoteric:[158]

---

156. Stuckrad, '*Astrologia Hermetica*', pp. 53-54.

157. Stuckrad, '*Astrologia Hermetica*', p. 55.

158. Stuckrad, *Astrología*, p. 412; *Astrology and the Seven Rays*, p. 17.

> Astrology still responds to a more or less conscious need to find once more in our uncentred and fragmented world the *unus mundus*, the unity of mankind and the universe, through an integral language based on the principle of similitude. When this need is conscious, when it opens out upon a reflection—on a veritable hermeneutics of 'signs'—which integrates a praxis and a gnosis, then we may speak of 'esoteric' astrology.[159]

In my view, the dismissal of esoteric astrology on grounds of imperfection distorts the original meaning of the Greek word *ἐσωτερικός* pertaining to inner knowledge, which may be revelatory, connective, and transmutative, but not necessarily perfect, and perfection is an ideal not an esoteric current of thought.[160] Regarding singular or plural identities, neither the historiographical concept of Hanegraaff, nor the religious discourse of Stuckrad captures the esotericism of the postmodern syncretist.

2.3 Seeker and Scholar

When considering esoteric currents the reader benefits from knowing the ideological position of the writer, and Needleman addresses this issue in his introduction to *Modern Esoteric Spirituality*, which he jointly edited with Faivre. He contrasts the motivational directions of the seeker, on a passionate quest for perceived truths, participating in an intensely subjective experience, and the scholar whose ambition is to frame the object of study and support his research with philosophical arguments and authoritative references. Whereas the seeker looks inwards and upwards towards what Jung termed individuation and Assagioli psychosynthesis, in preparation for the attainment of spiritual gnosis, the scholar moves horizontally, from 'I' to 'you', disengaging from personal beliefs and prejudices to marshal evidence backing up a thesis directed at an audience and preparing his conclusions for acceptance by the academy. Both are driven by a love of knowledge. Needleman acknowledges their

159. Faivre, *Access*, p. 95.

160. J. T. Pring, *The Pocket Oxford Greek Dictionary*, 3rd edn rev. (Oxford: Oxford University Press, 1995), p. 71.

distinct movements, while speculating on their reconciliation as 'a central defining characteristic recognized and even emphasized by the teachings that may authentically be termed esoteric'.[161] An astrologer may assess whether a chart has a predominantly vertical or horizontal focus, although the meaning may shift register on the vertical axis from spiritual to worldly ascent, and on the horizontal axis from didactic projection to intimate partnership, once again ideally reconciling the two.

The prevailing academic discipline of Western esotericism has replaced the stereotypes, 'seeker' and 'scholar', used by Needleman in the early 1990s, by the adjectives 'emic' and 'etic'—coined from the school of anthropology—with emic qualifying the viewpoint of the seeker or believer, and etic the objective position of the scholar researching the topic.[162] Hanegraaff's assertion that 'a continuing (self-) critical dialectics of emic material and etic interpretation... is the indispensable foundation for an empirical study of esotericism' has been countered by the argument put forward by Versluis that 'a sympathetic empiricist perspective may well be indispensable for understanding the work one is investigating', and modified by Hanegraaff's own observation that 'the emic/etic distinction is not static and closed' and that 'all terminology, etic as well as emic, is contextual'.[163] This modification accords better with quantum physics, which has 'uncovered an underlying level of reality, a deeper supersensible order permeated by patterns of interconnection', and Werner Heisenberg's uncertainty principle, which has demonstrated that

> It is impossible for a human being to act as an impartial, objective observer in scientific experiments, for the very expectations and posture adopted by the experimenter actually influence the nature of

161. Jacob Needleman, 'Introduction 2', in *MES*, pp. xxv-xxvi.

162. Goodrick-Clarke, *Western Esoteric*, p. 10.

163. Wouter J. Hanegraaff, 'On the Construction of "Esoteric Traditions"', in *WESR*, pp. 11-61 (p. 13); Versluis, 'What is Esoteric?' p. 4; Hanegraaff, *Esotericism*, pp. 156-57, n.12.

> the phenomena under scrutiny. Human beings are part and parcel of the universe they seek to observe.[164]

The findings of quantum physics, as well as Jung's interpretation of synchronicity and archetypes, and the power of mythology as expounded by Campbell, underpin the approach of archetypal astrology, whose mission is to show how well the postmodern holographic paradigm accommodates astrology in which psyche and cosmos are both active participants.

The next section explores further ways in which an astrological method applying visualization and imagination to interpretation might be researched and presented to a scholarly audience.

2.4 Using Symbolism and Imagination

Before Copernicus published *De revolutionibus orbium coelestium* (1543), establishing that the Sun, not the Earth, was at the centre of our solar system, astronomy and astrology were used synonymously to refer to observation and reading of the 'wandering stars'. Shakespeare almost always used the word astronomy when referring to astrology. Since the sixteenth century, the gulf between the science of astronomy and the art of astrological interpretation has steadily widened, as new bodies have been located in space and others redesignated. The demotion of Pluto from full planet to dwarf planet status, in 2006, has, if anything, enhanced the transformative impulse attributed to this small astronomical body making its eccentric orbit at the frontier of our solar system and the multiverse beyond. Keiron Le Grice quoting Grof has associated Pluto with the process of 'pyrocatharsis: the burning out and destruction of a psychological complex or pattern of behaviour by driving it to its extreme'.[165] Meanwhile, astrologers ponder over how many more cosmic objects might reasonably be introduced

164. Le Grice, *Archetypal Cosmos*, pp. 102, 139.

165. Keiron Le Grice, 'The Archetypal Dynamics of Individuation', in *Astrology, The New Generation: Essays from 14 Rising Stars of Astrology*, ed. by Demetrius Bagley and Nan Geary, (London: Flare and London School of Astrology, 2012), pp. 298-325 (pp. 316-17).

into a busy horoscope and consider what they might mean.[166] The symbolic power of the hermetic maxim, 'as above, so below', is as strong as ever but the umbilical cord linking astronomy and astrology in any literal sense has become increasingly tenuous.

Over recent years, in the words of André Barbault, astrology has frequently been misrepresented by the application of rational scientific criteria to an interpretive method that uses a language of analogy to build 'a bridge in the dialectic between the astronomical exterior and the human interior'.[167] His discussion of the 'psychoanalytical key' to astrology contains arguments of relevance to all modern astrology, emphasizing how important it is for anyone who wishes to explain this art to a readership of widely differing views to approach the subject from an inner as well as an outer perspective. Just as evidence of the workings of the universe recorded by human observers from time immemorial has generated a 'stable and rigorous system of numerical, spatial, and temporal relationships', providing a model for medicine and psychology, in turn, psychology has furnished astrology with a language of the unconscious with which to express the inner life of the soul, thus enabling an astrologer to read a client's chart 'like a psychoanalyst interpreting a dream'.[168]

The movement away from direct observation of the stars and simple definitions of planets in signs and houses in favour of deeper exploration of their psycho-spiritual meaning has led to extensive and often vague references to symbolism, and consequent discussion of its application to astrology. Greene traces the power of the visual image through the ages, from ancient sigils to Leo's exposition of 'the symbols of the planets', both as a pictorial

166. Harald Zittlau, 'Pluto and the Transneptunian Planets', 1st pub. in *Astrolog* (2007), repr. in *Astrolog 1*, pp. 53-60.

167. André Barbault, *The Value of Astrology from ancient knowledge to today's reality*, trans. by Kate Johnston, and ed. by Roy Gillett (London: Astrological Association, 2014), p. 169.

168. Barbault, pp. 160-84 (pp. 162, 170, 175).

representation and as an embodiment of the thing portrayed.[169] Nicholas Campion observes that 'the notion of symbol as glyph... occurs throughout astrological literature', adding that, 'for a Platonic astrologer symbols were necessarily embedded in the cosmos, simply because everything was interconnected and interdependent', taking us back to Faivre's first criterion of correspondences as essential to the esoteric current of thought.[170] Campion regrets the lack of theory and inconsistency between theory and practice accompanying contemporary astrologies that have adopted Platonism as transmitted by Blavatsky or Rudhyar, so he asks whether astrology is a symbolic language and, if it is, what form it takes. Like Barbault, Cornelius describes astrological interpretation as 'an exercise in analogy'.[171]

With reference to the Platonic model, Cornelius moves on to Faivre's third category of imagination and mediations to explain that 'imagination is the mode of perception granted to the soul' and that it occupies the symbolic realm 'between the material world known to the physical senses, and the divine intellectual principles'.[172] This hierarchy evolved into a 'fourfold hermeneutic of medieval Christianity', which Geoffrey Cornelius and Angela Voss have adapted to astrological interpretation. Literally, astrological data is presented as a straightforward, horizontal discourse. The allegorical level uses established astrological metaphors. At the tropological level, the astrologer becomes an active participant in the interpretation. Beyond, at the anagogic or mystical level, the theurgical diviner is, according to the Neoplatonist Iamblichus, 'suspended from the gods, spontaneous and inseparable from

169. Liz Greene, 'Signs, Signatures, and Symbols: The Language of Heaven', in *Astrologies: Plurality and Diversity: The proceedings of the eighth annual conference of the Sophia Centre for the Study of Cosmology and Culture, University of Wales, Trinity Saint David, 24-25 July 2010*, ed. by Nicholas Campion and Liz Greene (Ceredigion: Sophia Centre Press, 2011), pp. 17-45; Leo, *Esoteric*, p. 5.

170. Nicholas Campion, 'Is Astrology a Symbolic Language?' in *Sky and Symbol*, pp. 9-46 (p. 12).

171. Geoffrey Cornelius, 'Astrology, Imagination, and the Imaginal', *The Astrological Journal* (January/February 2014), 12-16 (p. 14).

172. Cornelius, 'Astrology, Imagination', p. 15.

them'.[173] As Plotinus wrote, 'the wise man is the man who in any one thing can read another' and Voss suggests that, for students of astrology,

> the four levels hermeneutic enables them to move in a process of interiorization so that they can enter into, rather than simply learn about, the meaning of a symbol. This surely has profound implications, for it may just begin to revolutionize the assumptions of an academic method which separates knowledge from knower, thought from being, conception of reality from its experience.[174]

At a recent conference, Pasi proposed a fourfold classification of esotericism in art: at the representational level, esoteric images or symbols express a visual language; at the talismanic level, the artistic object becomes a magical tool; the artistic work may be created as a means to achieve mystical experience; or else the work of art may be the outcome of inspiration coming from another dimension.[175] This conference on 'Visions of Enchantment', at the University of Cambridge in March 2014, adds to the evidence in academic circles of increasing interest in researching ways of seeing and communicating that defy rational quantification and require more flexible methodologies.

In the opinion of Cornelius, 'natal astrology, especially applied with psychological insight, is strongly tropological because it offers a powerful means for the individual to turn his or her life meaning around' and 'from the time of Alan Leo, the mainstream of Western natal astrology has been striving for this sense of the

173. Cornelius, *Moment*, pp. 278-84; Iamblichus, *On the Mysteries*, I.iii, trans. by T. Taylor (Frome, 1999), in Angela Voss, 'From Allegory to Anagoge: the Question of Symbolic Perception in a Literal World', in *Astrology and the Academy*, ed. by Nicholas Campion, Patrick Curry, and Michael York (Bristol: Cinnabar Books, 2004), pp. 1-9 repr. <www.skyscript.co.uk/allegory.html> [accessed 6 September 2010], p. 5.

174. *Enneads*, II. 3. 7; Voss, 'Allegory to Anagoge', p. 8.

175. Marco Pasi, 'Western Esotericism and Artistic Creativity: Searching for a New Interpretive Method', *Visions of Enchantment—Occultism, Spirituality and Visual Culture*, University of Cambridge, 18 March 2014.

symbol'.[176] Although this accords with the view of Barbault, in a recent article in the *Astrological Journal*, Cornelius implies that contemporary psychological and archetypal astrologers are still presenting 'objective and empirical correlations as the source of astrological perception' in preference to more imaginative analogical interpretation.[177] By contrast, the Huber method actively encourages astrologers to develop their imagination, using 'the Jupiterian function of sensing and visualizing', so that the horoscope's 'graphic structure, the colours, the shapes, the size of the picture combine to create pictorial associations in our mind'.[178] So astrological psychology opens the way into the tropological zone—which is the imaginal world of Corbin—and it often defies astrological convention.

Starting from the imaginal gnosis of Corbin and the sympathetic engagement deemed essential to esoteric understanding by Versluis, Voss has adapted the fourfold hermeneutic into a 'methodology of the imagination', which requires that 'the metaphorical mode is honoured as a primary means of investigation' and eradicates its hierarchical structure to allow 'free-flowing movement' between levels of seeing, facilitating 'transformative research... in which the researcher feels something is at stake for his or her life and is impelled to get to the bottom of it'.[179] Recognition of levels of interpretation and the ability to move seamlessly from one level to another are essential to the Huber astrologer, who not only approaches the chart through creative visualization but also needs to tune into the level at which a client or student is most receptive. Voss draws on the work of the transpersonal theorist, Jorge Ferrer, reminding us that '*tropos* means a turning, and this is the point at which apprehension turns back to acknowledge its

176. Cornelius, *Moment*, p. 243.

177. Cornelius, 'Astrology, Imagination', pp. 13-14.

178. *Astrological Psychosynthesis*, pp. 32-33.

179. Angela Voss, 'A Methodology of the Imagination', *Eye of the Heart: A Journal of Traditional Wisdom*, 3 (2009), 1-15 (pp. 4, 7, 11).

own implication in the knowing process'.[180] Ferrer's 'participatory turn', represents 'a radical shift from intersubjective experiences to participatory events in our understanding of transpersonal and spiritual phenomena'.[181]

Having established astrological psychology as an esoteric current methodologically, chapter 3 examines historical origins and affiliations, chapter 4 shows what an effective tool it can be, and the final chapter takes forward thoughts about transpersonal philosophy and participation that have seeped into the final section of this chapter.

---

180. Voss, 'Methodology', p. 13.

181. Jorge N. Ferrer, *Revisioning Transpersonal Theory: A Participatory Vision of Human Spirituality* (New York, NY: SUNY, 2002), p. 184.

3. Astrology and Esotericism: From Ancient Mesopotamia to 20th Century Europe

> Our astrology is pure esotericism, clearly based on the esoteric sources and on the ever-true values of esotericism in all cultures, going way back to the early human cultures.[182]

This assertion, made by Bruno Huber, is explored from historical and cultural perspectives in roughly chronological order by selecting periods of innovation and cultural interchange, highlighting landmark movements, and drawing out salient themes pertinent to the evolution of astrological psychology as an esoteric current.

3.1 Esotericism as a Third Pillar of Western Culture

Esotericism has been described as the third pillar of Western culture, alongside, drawing on, and in contention with pure Greek rationality and doctrinal Biblical faith. This contrasting pillar portrays 'an organic view of the world that assumed a strong internal coherence of the whole universe, including an intimate contact between both its spiritual and its material elements'.[183] The quest for a golden age of truth and purity that 'gave honour to good faith and righteousness' was recorded by Ovid in the opening book of *Metamorphoses*, and—according to Florentine scholars—the torch of a *prisca theologia* underpinning all religious wisdom was carried by such hallowed figures as the Persian prophet

182. *Astrology and the Seven Rays*, p. 3.

183. 'Preface' by Roelof van den Broek and Wouter J. Hanegraaff, eds., *Gnosis and Hermeticism from Antiquity to Modern Times* (Albany, NY: SUNY, 1998), pp. vii-viii.

Zoroaster, among whose sages were the magi who followed the Star of Bethlehem, Moses, the Biblical Lawgiver, Pythagoras, whose school 'conducted philosophy and science in a framework permeated by the beliefs of the mystery religions, especially Orphism', and Hermes Trismegistus, believed by Renaissance humanists to have lived shortly after Moses and to have predicted the birth of Christ.[184] In 1614, the classical scholar Isaac Casaubon produced linguistic evidence that texts comprising the *Corpus Hermeticum* and attributed to the thrice-great hybrid of Egyptian Thoth and Greek Hermes were written by various people in the second and third centuries CE, thus discrediting their pedigree and prophetic significance. Yet their message has withstood the course of time:[185]

> The philosophical assumption common to both the *Hermetica* and to modern times is the absence of absolute ontological dualism. In the treatise *Nous to Hermes*, the former instructs the latter to reflect the universe in his own mind, to grasp the divine essence of nature and engrave it within his psyche, which is made possible by the fact that humans possess a divine intellect. This theme of the 'mirror', on which 'speculating' never stops, is connected to a major common denominator of esotericism, namely, the idea of the universe seen as a book to be read or to decipher. God is known by contemplation of the world; and since the universe is a forest of symbols, it is natural to become interested in everything within it.[186]

Hermeticism is given further consideration later in this chapter.

Initially, I am exploring the provenance and intention of Bruno's statement that:

---

184. Ovid, *Metamorphoses*, trans. by A. D. Melville and ed. by E. J. Kenney (Oxford: Oxford UP, 1987), p. 3; Richard Tarnas, *The Passion of the Western Mind: Understanding the Ideas That Have Shaped Our World View* (New York: Ballantine, 1991), p. 23.

185. *Hermetica: The Greek 'Corpus Hermeticum' and the Latin 'Asclepius' in a new English translations with notes and introduction*, ed. by Brian P. Copenhaver, (Cambridge: Cambridge UP, 1992; repr. 2000), pp. xlviii-l; Goodrick-Clarke, *Western Esoteric*, pp. 19-20.

186. Antoine Faivre, 'Ancient and Medieval Sources of Modern Esoteric Movements', in *MES*, p. 5.

> Astrology is an expression, and I would say the foremost expression, of esoteric thinking. There is no other discipline that comes near to that complete usage of esoteric thinking that astrology does.[187]

Does such an assertion stand up to scrutiny? How do we define esoteric astrology in general, and relate this definition to astrological psychology in particular? To what extent does astrological psychology draw inspiration from the earliest stargazers? How does it fit into astrological history and esoteric tradition? This chapter attempts to answer these questions with the help of some historical background.

Since the sixteenth century, astrology, alchemy, and magic have been bracketed as the three main 'occult sciences', and sometimes they act together.[188] Insofar as astrological psychology can be transmutative, it is attuned to alchemy, and Bruno's amphora can be envisaged as an alchemical flask. Although the boundaries separating astrological divination, psychological healing, and natural magic—as opposed to black magic or *goetia*—are somewhat porous, the ancient Greeks made a distinction between divination or *manteia*, whose practitioners might advise people in high places, and magic, which was a fringe activity often carried out by itinerant charlatans.[189] In his 'notion of esotericism' as it applies to astrology, Faivre discounts the purely judicial or predictive practice—which is outside the scope of this work, as astrological psychology is non-predictive—and elaborates on 'a hermeneutics of "signs"; a type of reflection in which astrological practice is integrated with a gnosis', which he sub-divides as follows:

(a) a mantic art, a procedure of divination;

(b) a vision of the world and a gnoseological or soteriological practice; and

187. *Astrology and the Seven Rays*, p. 17.

188. Wouter J. Hanegraaff, 'Occult Sciences', in *DGWE*, p. 887.

189. Peter T. Struck, 'A World Full of Signs: Understanding Division in Ancient Stoicism', in *Seeing with Different Eyes: Essays in Astrology and Divination*, ed. by Patrick Curry and Angela Voss (Newcastle upon Tyne: Cambridge Scholars Publishing, 2007), pp. 3-20 (pp. 4-5); see amphora, p. 13.

(c) the particular and varied aspects which this practice and this vision of the world take on in the specific context of modern Western esotericism'.[190]

How well astrological psychology fulfils these criteria becomes clear in subsequent sections. Whereas manuals on Western esotericism often start with the confluence of cultures in Alexandria in late antiquity, I am beginning with the earliest recorded stargazers of ancient Mesopotamia.

3.2 Mesopotamian Cosmology

Interest in Mesopotamian cosmology was heightened when the Mul.Apin star tablets were deciphered, and Werner Papke published *Die Sterne von Babylon* (1989), describing the astrology underpinning the epic of Gilgamesh. From his interpretation of the tablets, he devised a star map showing the paths of Anu, Enlil, and Ea, and dated it around 2340 BCE. This early date, alluded to by Bruno Huber, has been disputed by scholars, and opinion favours a later date around 1000 BCE.[191] These tablets depict a holistic worldview, outlining the Sumerian system of reading the stars, divining their omens and how to work with rather than against them. It is said Gudea of Lagash, ruler of Sumer ca. 2144-2124 BCE, described 'how gods showed him in a dream which planet constellations were most favourable for the planned building of a temple'.[192] Hence, the ancient civilizations of Mesopotamia devised an all-embracing system of astrology that helped them

190. Faivre, 'Questions of Terminology' *WESR*, pp. 1-10 (p. 7).

191. Werner Papke, Die Sterne von Babylon: Die geheime Botschaft des Gilgamesch—nach 4000 Jahren entschlüsseit (Lübbe, 1989); Andis Kaulins, 'The "Text" and Interpretation of the MUL.APIN Tablets', <www.lexiline.com/ lexiline/ lexi179.htm> [accessed 17 November 2014]; Bruno Huber, 'When and Where did Astrology really begin?' 1st pub. Astrolog, 101 (1997), in The History of Astrology, trans. by Heather Ross (Knutsford: API [UK], 2007), pp. 12-14.

192. Gustav-Adolf Schoener, 'Astrology: Between Religion and the Empirical', trans. by Shane Denson, *Esoterica*, 4 (2002), 29-60 (p. 31); Nicholas Campion, *The Dawn of Astrology: A Cultural History of Western Astrology*, 1: *The Ancient World* (London and New York: Continuum, 2008), pp. 56-57.

make political decisions and played a key role in their religious rituals.[193] Whereas the orchestration of this system by scribes and priests working for the king might seem divorced from the journey of the contemporary individual, these early diviners, basing their interpretations on observation of the cosmos and learning its language, were true esotericists, who progressed from omen to zodiac astrology, opening the way to horoscope astrology.[194]

Mul.Apin, tablet 86378 describes thirty-three stars on the path of Enlil, god of the wind, twenty-three stars on the path of Anu, god of the sky, and fifteen stars of the path of Ea, the organizing intelligence.[195] In his article, Bruno reproduced Papke's map and wrote:

> These paths were the spheres of influence of three abstract superior deities, who were never physically represented: the divine trinity. They were the spheres of the material world (Ea), the human world (Anu), and the divine world (Enlil). Through these three belts meandered the 'road of the Moon' (Charranu), which was also the path of the planets: the zodiac. Thus part of the zodiac lies in the path of Enlil (the summer signs), part in the path of Anu (the spring and autumn signs), and part in the path of Ea (the winter signs).[196]

Previous tablets referred to only eleven signs. Mul.Apin describes how Libra was 'formed from the pincers of Scorpio... to designate the beginning of the harvest'.[197]

---

193. Stuckrad, *Astrología*, p. 55.

194. *Astrology and the Seven Rays*, p. 17; Nicholas Campion, *Astrology and Cosmology in the World's Religions* (New York and London: New York UP, 2012), pp. 124-25; Bruno Huber, 'Astrology—History and Development', 1st pub. *Astrolog*, 60 (1991), in *History*, pp. 2-5; Michel Gauquelin, *Neo-Astrology: A Copernican Revolution*, trans. by Stella Tomašević (London: Arkana, 1991), pp. 53-54.

195. Kaulins; Norman Cohn, *Cosmos, Chaos and the World to Come: The Ancient Roots of Apocalyptic Faith* (New Haven and London: Yale University Press, 1993), pp. 33-34.

196. *History*, pp. 13-14.

197. *History*, p. 14.

These priestly seers had a participatory approach to the cosmos. Unlike later readings by classical astrologers applying guidelines for predictions, theirs was a mantic, or divinatory art in which the human diviner was also an active participant:

> Despite the inexorable, if paradoxical, fulfilment of major prophecies, nevertheless in the particular circumstances in which men find themselves there can be no guaranteed or absolute destiny beyond human influence, or independent of man's participation. It may change from moment to moment, from omen to omen. Men find courage and invoke the gods: destiny is negotiable. The right attitude in ritual and divination may itself be part of the initiative.[198]

Mesopotamian cosmology is a field of wide and ongoing research and, were he still alive, Bruno would be at the forefront of these activities. With Sun in Sagittarius in the 9th house, he constantly sought ways to extend his knowledge and transmit an increasingly meaningful system of interpretation to his followers.[199] As he said, 'we live in a time that has completely lost orientation, because it thinks too much only in symptoms, in superficial values, in material values'. By contrast, when we look back to the astrology developed by the Sumerians, and at such images as the 'Queen of the Night' in the British Museum, we encounter a worldview where 'life forms and nature were blended, interlinked or interwoven'.[200] These people 'engaged in a dialogue with destiny', and from them we can learn what it means to live in harmony with nature and cosmos.[201] Around the fourth century BCE, Mesopotamian astrology was absorbed and transformed by the Greeks into cosmologies that 'were important to the constructions of the universe in the

198. Cornelius, *Moment*, pp. 131, 133.

199. Bruno Huber, 'Sol Sagitario y signos en el AC', ed. by Rita Keller for Astrolog 124, 125, and 126 (2001-02), and trans. by Joan Solé <www.escuelahuber.org/Private/Sol_Sagitario_signos_Ascendente_BH.pdf> [accessed 2 December 2014], p. 35.

200. *Astrology and the Seven Rays*, p. 27; 'The Queen of the Night' (1800-1750 BCE), Old Babylonian, British Museum, London; Brady, *Chaosmos*, pp. 23, 25.

201. Campion, *Dawn*, p. 57.

more mystical branch of astrology, associated with Hermetic and Gnostic texts'.[202]

3.3 Greek Philosophers, and a Confluence of Cultures in Alexandria

Two centuries earlier, the mathematician and mystic Pythagoras established the first philosophical school in Europe: 'Philosophy, literally "the love of wisdom,"... includes both heart and head, implying that one alone is not sufficient'.[203] At his school in Croton, Southern Italy, Pythagoras was an expert in metempsychosis, who reputedly remembered his previous incarnations, and this belief in the immortality of the reincarnating soul, adopted by Plato, accommodates Platonic Orientalism, bringing wisdom from Egypt, India, and Persia to the West, while also introducing 'a whole series mediating processes of which the planets and stars are the stages... characteristic of esoteric thought'.[204] Reincarnation, intrinsic to Hinduism and Buddhism, was deemed heretical by mainstream Christianity and resurfaced in the West in Allan Kardec's nineteenth-century school of spiritualism, gaining popularity through Theosophy.[205] The Hubers wrote: 'It seems so clear that we have lived more than once and that we shall live repeatedly until we reach our goal'.[206] Their esoteric 'vision of the world', incorporates a 'soteriological practice' that is attuned to

202. Tamsyn Barton, *Ancient Astrology* (London and New York: Routledge, 1994), p. 30.

203. Joscelyn Godwin, *The Golden Thread: The Ageless Wisdom of the Western Mystery Traditions* (Wheaton, IL: Quest, 2007), p. 32.

204. Carl Huffman, 'Pythagoras', *The Stanford Encyclopedia of Philosophy* (2014), ed. by Edward N. Zalta, <http://plato.stanford.edu/archives/sum2014/entries/pythagoras/> [accessed 4 December 2014]; Faivre, 'Ancient and Medieval Sources', p. 1.

205. Joscelyn Godwin, *The Theosophical Enlightenment* (Albany, NY: SUNY, 1994), pp. 340-02.

206. Bruno and Louise Huber, *Moon Node Astrology*, trans. by Transcript, (York Beach, ME: Weiser, 1995; repr. Knutsford: HopeWell, 2005), p. 139.

Kabbalah, and introduced into astrological interpretation through the moon node chart.[207]

According to tradition, Pythagoras ascribed the distances between the planets and earth to musical sequences, and he was credited by the Neoplatonist Proclus with discovery of the five solids assigned to the elements by Plato in the *Timaeus*: the tetrahedron of four triangular faces to fire, the hexahedron or cube to earth, the octahedron of eight triangular faces to air, and the icosahedron of twenty triangular faces to water. The dodecahedron with twelve pentagonal faces is associated with invisible ether or Akasha, as mind or medium between earth and heaven, and has been attributed to the celestial world of the twelve signs of the zodiac.[208] In this way, geometry became 'a symbolical key to understanding universal processes'.[209] The visual impact of geometrical forms and colours is fundamental to the Hubers' holistic method of aspect pattern astrology, in which the joined up aspects of a chart

> ...give a direct overview, a pattern, a model, whose very uniqueness makes them invaluable, without even considering the planets which form the pattern and their house and sign position.[210]

The astrologer's gaze then extends outwards to the planets and houses while retaining a vision of the interconnecting aspects and the original impression they made.

---

207. Faivre, 'Questions of Terminology', p. 7.

208. Campion, *Dawn*, pp. 154 and 157; Plato, *Timaeus*, trans. by Benjamin Jowett, in *The Collected Dialogues of Plato, including the Letters*, ed. by Edith Hamilton and Huntington Cairns, Bollingen 71, 2nd edn (Princeton, NJ: Princeton University Press, 1963), pp. 1151-1211, 31b-32c; Helena P. Blavatsky, *Isis Unveiled: Secrets of the Ancient Wisdom Tradition, Madam Blavatsky's First Work*, A New Abridgement for Today by Michael Gomes (Wheaton, IL: Quest, 1997), pp. 83-84; Phoebe Wyss, *Inside the Cosmic Mind: Archetypal Astrology and the New Cosmology* (Edinburgh: Floris Books, 2014).

209. Dane Rudhyar, *Person Centred Astrology*, 3rd edn (New York, NY: Aurora, 1980), p. 146.

210. *Aspect Pattern*, p. 69.

As well as preparing the way for Neoplatonism with its 'intermediaries and gradations', Pythagoreanism influenced Stoicism, which 'lasted for almost six centuries and also impregnated a part of the Gnostic and Hermetic currents'.[211] The question of whether or not Stoicism has a significant relationship with esoteric currents is complex, given that 'Aristotle and Stoics took a more physiological line' in contrast to 'Pythagoreans and Platonists who laid emphasis on the astral origin of the human soul'.[212] That is why I quote at length Faivre's case for its inclusion:

> The aspect of Stoicism which most heralds esoteric thought in the West is without doubt the accent it places on the necessity of knowing the concrete universe by combining wisdom and technique. Philosophy and wisdom are themselves considered practices... Stoicism thus teaches the necessity of concrete abilities; it refuses pure speculation and endeavours to understand the organic totality which guarantees the harmony between heavenly and earthly things.
>
> It was also open to popular religion, even to various types of divination. From Zeno to Posidonius, the Stoics defended such religion, for they were sensitive to whatever recalled the harmony and affinity joining the different parts of the universe together... The idea of a passage between opposing forces due to the discovery of intermediary forces assured the harmony of the soul with things. It was a monistic thought, which knew only a homogeneous universe all the parts of which were penetrated by breath... Western esotericism would remain... opposed to all forms of ontological dualism, while turning toward both the spiritual and the concrete. It would preserve this trait, which already was a part of Stoic thought—that is, the paradox consisting of conserving commonsense things by transmuting them into manifestations of universal reason.[213]

211. Faivre, 'Ancient and Medieval', p. 3.

212. Barton, p. 110.

213. Faivre, 'Ancient and Medieval', p. 3.

In Faivre's opinion, esotericism 'rests on the idea of mediation' and the use of an intermediary to counter opposing forces and bring about harmony is replicated in an exercise on working with the opposing axes in Huber astrology.[214]

During the second century CE, Claudius Ptolemy compiled the *Tetrabiblos* in Alexandria. With minor modifications, Huber astrologers draw on Ptolemy for their model of the traditional planets fanning out symmetrically from a conjunction at the cusp of Sun in Leo and Moon in Cancer, through Mercury, Venus, Mars, Jupiter, and Saturn, showing each planet domiciled in a day and a night sign with their multiples of 30-degree aspects corresponding to the distance from the conjunction of the greater and lesser lights. Whereas Ptolemy used only conjunctions, oppositions, squares, trines, and sextiles, the degrees of which divide equally into the 360-degree circle, he regarded the inconjunct 30-degree semi-sextiles between adjacent signs, and 150-degree quincunxes that do not divide the circle into equal parts as 'alien'.[215] By contrast, Huber astrologers treat semi-sextiles and quincunxes coloured green, 'the colour of transformation, the colour of earth in both Eastern and Western traditions', as awakening aspects with which to troubleshoot conflict by asking questions and learning lessons.[216] These inconjunct or ambivalent aspects were instated by Ficino to accord with the second and sixth notes in his music of the spheres, and they are aspects of growth in astrological psychology.[217] In Huber astrology, green semi-sextiles and quincunxes are linked with Mercury and Saturn as thinking planets that correlate information, ask questions and raise uncertainties, while Ficino

---

214. Faivre, 'Ancient and Medieval', p. 4; Bruno and Louise Huber, *The Astrological Houses: A Psychological View of Ourselves and Our World*, trans. by Haloli Richter, 3rd edn, rev. by Barry Hopewell (Knutsford: HopeWell, 2011), pp. 70-85; see axis cross, p. 10, aspects, p. 8.

215. Claudius Ptolemy, *Tetrabiblos*, trans. by F. E. Robbins, Loeb Classical Library, 435 (Cambridge, MA: Harvard UP, 1940, repr. 1994), pp. 73-83.

216. Barbara Somers, *The Fires of Alchemy: A Transpersonal Viewpoint*, ed. by Hazel Marshall (Morton: Archive Publishing, 2004), p. 42.

217. Voss, *Ficino*, pp. 184-86; see models of 30-degree aspects in intro.

associated Saturn with melancholy, and Shakespeare associated green 'not just with nature, innocence and jealousy but with—melancholy'.[218] This amendment might appear small, modernizing astrology to allow for evolutionary ways of thinking and being that are not all black and white but, insofar as it allows a discordant note to interfere with the perfect cosmic order Ptolemy sought to create, it changes everything philosophically.[219]

At least one academic astrologer is of the view that modern astrology has more in common with chaos theory than cosmic order, and Bernadette Brady makes illuminating comparisons between the chaotic creation myths of Egypt and Mesopotamia, chaotic attractors, and astrological patterns of unfoldment in time.[220] Her latest book links astrology to stoic sympathy with all things through a web of interlocking correspondences and 'a life lived in chaosmos' whose

> collisions produce the experience of life as a kaleidoscope of cyclic potentials, ideas, coincidences, and events which can fracture across a plethora of reflective surfaces as signs, omens, and coincidences, all of which deepen and enrich the individual's life.[221]

These ideas are explored in the final chapter.

A century after Ptolemy, Plotinus wrote *The Enneads* in defence of Plato, against the Gnostics, and to counter Aristotle's 'limited view of the human soul'.[222]

---

218. *Astrological Psychosynthesis*, p. 43; *Aspect Pattern*, pp. 33-34; Raymond Klibansky, Erwin Panofsky and Fritz Saxl, *Saturn and Melancholy: Studies in the History of Natural Philosophy, Religion and Art* (London: Nelson, 1964), pp. 232-59; Marsilio Ficino, *The Book of Life* trans. by Charles Boer, 2nd edn (Woodstock, CT, Spring, 1996), pp. 6-7; Iain McGilchrist, *The Master and his Emissary: The Divided Brain and the Making of the Western World* (Newhaven and London: Yale UP, 2010), p. 63, citing *Twelfth Night*, II.iv.111-16.

219. Bernadette Brady, *Astrology, A Place in Chaos* (Bournemouth: Wessex Astrologer, 2006), p. 46.

220. Brady, *Chaos*, pp. 13-16, 109.

221. Brady, *Chaosmos*, p. 10.

222. Gregory Shaw, 'Neoplatonism 1: Antiquity', in *DGWE*, pp. 834-37 (p. 834).

> Plotinus's emphasis on the creative emanation of the material universe from the thought of God was essentially cosmological. The idea was linked to the Ptolemaic view of the universe as a hierarchical system of nine concentric spheres, ranging from the outermost sphere of God as Prime Mover through the sequence of planetary spheres to the lowest sphere of earth.[223]

Whereas for Plotinus—whose writings were published by his student Porphyry—'salvation for the soul required an escape from material evil by withdrawing into its unfallen essence', Porphyry's student Iamblichus advanced the view that, 'the soul would not be saved by escaping an evil world, but by ritually transforming it in theurgy'.[224] Iamblichus dislodged the intellectualism of Plotinus 'in favour of a theurgy and theology that included all the mysteries, rituals, myths and deities of syncretistic paganism'.[225] 'Inductive divination' was inferior to the 'inspired divination' that 'bestows eternal and divine knowledge on those who utilize it'.[226] As theurgist, the philosopher or astrologer—using prayer, invocation, and symbolic or talismanic ritual—assumes the role of a high priest, in alignment with the spiritual forces and in receipt of divine inspiration.[227]

In the fifth century, Proclus of Byzantium developed an influential concept of polar opposites, accentuating 'the fruitfulness of antithetical principles'. He drew on Plato's perception of 'a non-empirical form of corporeality', anticipating Theosophical ideas concerning the 'vehicle', the 'subtle body', the 'garment of light', and the 'aura'. For Faivre, Proclus 'appears as one of the first representatives of Western esotericism in the sense that he was as concerned with transforming the sensible world as he was with purifying the soul.[228] Astrology was, for the later Neoplatonists,

---

223. Goodrick-Clarke, *Western Esoteric*, p. 23.

224. Shaw, pp. 835-36.

225. Israel Regardie, *The Tree of Life: An Illustrated Study in Magic*, ed. by Chic and Sandra Tabatha Cicero, 3rd edn (Woodbury, MN: Llewellyn, 2010), p. 26, n. 19.

226. Crystal Addey, 'Oracles, Dreams, and Astrology in Iamblichus' *De Mysteriis*', in *Seeing with Different Eyes*, pp. 37-38.

227. Goodrick-Clarke, *Western Esoteric*, p. 25; Voss, *Ficino*, p. 45.

228. Faivre, 'Ancient and Medieval', p. 11.

using practical ritual and theurgy, 'participatory as well as symbolic, and retained a strong sense that destiny is negotiable', not dissimilar to the perspective of the non-predictive astrologer who endeavours to bring opposing forces into balance and work towards synthesis.[229] This active engagement with the destiny would be developed by Ficino, who translated from Greek into Latin works of Plato, the Neoplatonists, and the body of texts attributed to Hermes Trismegistus, and whose *Book of Life* is considered later in this chapter.

The period of late antiquity is renowned for its confluence of cultures around Alexandria, the great centre of learning with its famous library in the Nile delta. Besides Neoplatonism, other esoteric currents emerging around that time are Hermeticism, Gnosticism, and the Jewish mysticism that would become Kabbalah in medieval Provence, Catalonia, and Castile—which I consider in the next section. The final part of this section is devoted to a comparison of Hermeticism and Gnosticism and what they mean for us today.

Firstly, it is useful to make a distinction between Gnosticism as a faith and the word 'gnosis' with a small 'g', which is frequently used by esotericists:

> Gnosis... is a spiritual and intellectual activity that can accede to a special mode of knowledge... gnosis is an integrating knowledge, a grasp of fundamental relations including the least apparent that exist among the various levels of reality, e.g., among God, humanity, and the universe. Gnosis is either this knowing in itself or the intuition and the certainty of possessing a method permitting access to such knowledge.[230]

Gnosticism, with reference to early Christianity, is the term applied to a heresy involving: 'the establishment of a dualism between spirit and matter; and, springing out of this, the doctrine that the world

229. Curry, 'Varieties', in *Astrology, Science, and Culture*, p. 67.

230. Faivre, *Access*, p. 19.

was created by some power different from the supreme God'.[231] This is in direct contrast to Hermeticism, which is non-dualistic. The following tabular comparison of Gnosticism and Hermeticism in antiquity, compiled by Clare Goodrick-Clarke and based on an article by Roelof van den Broek identifies salient differences.[232]

Gnostic	**Hermetic**
Dualist	Unified
World created by a demiurge	World is good and beautiful; its origin is divine: *as above, so below*
Soul is a 'divine spark' trapped in matter Mankind is in exile	Archetypal Man *chose* to dwell with Nature
Saving *gnosis* only means of attaining release from evil world—not available to all	Human capable of restoration through own efforts
Material world not a reflection of the higher	Can be an instrument of regeneration of Nature and self
Pessimistic	Optimistic

According to Nicholas Goodrick-Clarke, 'Gnosticism's chief legacy to the esoteric tradition consists in the rich variety of intermediaries which throng the pleroma'. Otherwise:

> Gnosticism is pessimistic and world-rejecting. Gnosticism regards the soul as an alien exile in matter, exaggerates the huge gulf separating the soul from the true God, and thus paints a tragic and humiliating image of humanity on earth. The Gnostic negation of the world is essentially at odds with the esoteric principle of continuous correspondences

231. George Salmon, 'Gnosticism', in *Dictionary of Christian Biography*, 2, ed. by W. Smith and H. Wace (London, 1877-87), p. 678, cited by R. A. Gilbert, *Gnosticism and Gnosis: An Introduction* (Bristol: Antioch Papers, 2012), p. 10.

232. Roelof van den Broek, 'Gnosticism and Hermetism in Antiquity: Two Roads to Salvation', in *Gnosis and Hermeticism*, pp. 1-20; Clare Goodrick-Clarke, 'The *Corpus Hermeticum*: A Founding Document of Western Esoteric Traditions', EXESESO Study Conference, University of Exeter, 15 October 2011.

> between the macrocosm and microcosm and the fundamental goodness of God's creation.[233]

Gnosticism resurfaced in nineteenth-century counter culture but the Gnostic Church of today is substantially different from its predecessor. With reference to Jung's adoption of the persona of the Gnostic teacher Basilides in his *Seven Sermons to the Dead* (1925), Robert Gilbert points out that, despite using Gnostic vocabulary:

> The text, however, is concerned with the unconscious mind. Jung does not preach Gnostic tenets, but emphasizes the need for individuation: self-realization here and now rather than escape from matter.[234]

Jung's *Sermons* predate his discovery of the Hermetic art of alchemy, on which he lectured in the 1930s and published a volume of his Collected Works in 1944, demonstrating how the alchemical process is a metaphor for individuation and the attainment of spiritual knowledge: 'it breaks down the original chaotic unity into the four elements and then combines them again in a higher unity'.[235]

The 'Law of Dualities' underpins twentieth-century Traditionalism, and Eliade lauded this 'more traditional and relatively unpopular form which "rejects the optimistic hope of cosmic and historic renewal without the preliminary catastrophic dissolution of the modern world"', while disparaging New Age anticipation of the Age of Aquarius as 'a popular form of occultism, which looks towards a brighter future and transformation of society'.[236] The term New Age, widely attributed to Bailey, contains

233. Goodrick-Clarke, *Western Esoteric*, p. 29.

234. Gilbert, p. 117-119.

235. C. G. Jung, *Psychology and Alchemy*, trans. by R. F. C. Hull, The Collected Works of C. G. Jung, 12, 2th edn (London: Routledge and Kegan Paul, 1980), p. 124.

236. Mircea Eliade, *Occultism, Witchcraft, and Cultural Fashions* (Chicago, IL: University of Chicago Press, 1976), quoted in Tim Rudbøg, *The Academic Study of Western Esotericism: Early Developments and Related Fields*, Introduction Series to Western Esotericism, 1 (Copenhagen: H-E-R-M-E-S Academic Press, 2013), p. 51; Whitall N. Perry, *The Widening Breach: Evolutionism in the Mirror of Cosmology* (Cambridge: Quinta Essentia, 1995), p. 3; Sedgwick, p. 111.

the idea that 'initiation ceremonies are being replaced by... self-initiation' through meditation and spiritual exercise to expand consciousness and facilitate personal growth.[237] Viewed in these contexts, Huber astrology is affiliated to the esoteric currents of Hermeticism and New Age.

3.4 Astrology and Kabbalah in Medieval Provence and Northern Spain

The reconquest of Toledo by the Christians, in 1085, opened the way for Christian scholars in Western Europe to meet and work with Islamic cosmologists in Spain and this was an important period for the development of astrology.[238] A horoscope could take five hours to calculate, so there was a need for tables of houses and ephemerides showing planetary positions. In the second half of the eleventh century, Islamic scholars produced the Toledan Tables and, in 1252, the Alfonsine Tables, compiled by Jewish scholars, were published in Toledo under the patronage of the Castilian king, Alfonso X, el Sabio.[239] Among the many texts that became available was *Ghayat al-Hakim* (*The Goal of the Sage*). Written in Arabic during the tenth century by an anonymous wizard, and attributed to a notable Sufi, it was translated into Spanish and Latin at Alfonso's court, in 1256, becoming widely known as *Picatrix*, and providing source material for Ficino's *Book of Life*. As well as magical philosophy:

> It contained an immense body of practical occult lore that had been gathered up among Arab occultists over the two centuries or so before its anonymous author put pen to paper. The practices of Neoplatonic theurgy contributed a great deal to the collection, and so did the astral magic of Mesopotamia; there are also workings in Picatrix that show

237. Hanegraaff, *New Age*, p. 95; *Planets*, p. 106; '*The New Age* was used as the title of a Journal of Christian liberalism and socialism, published as early as 1894, predating Bailey's use of the term', <en.wikipedia.org/wiki/Alice_Bailey> [accessed 10 December 2014].

238. Campion, *Medieval and Modern*, pp. 29-30.

239. Campion, *Medieval and Modern*, pp. 41-42.

close affinities with the magic practised in ancient Egypt, and others that are clearly borrowed from the Hindu tradition. [240]

Besides collaboration between the different ethnic and religious groups on scholarly and cosmological projects, evidence of complex, inter-religious and cross-cultural relations can be found in the Hispanic ballad tradition.[241] One of its many forms is *romance fronterizo*:

> a ballad set on or near the fourteenth- and fifteenth-century frontier between Christian Spain and Islamic al-Andalus and composed during the intermittent periods of trans-frontier warfare preceding the fall of the Kingdom of Granada in 1492.[242]

The Judeo-Spanish ballad evolved after 1492 among the Sephardim of the Eastern Mediterranean and Northern Morocco, becoming part of a living oral tradition of communities in exile.[243]

More than a millennium of Jewish mystical creativity preceded the emergence of Kabbalah in the late twelfth century with the composition of the *Sefer ha-Bahir*, defining the relationships between the *sefirot* of the Tree as primal principles of the universe, by Rabbi Isaac the Blind, or one of his school at Lunel in Provence. In addition:

---

240. John Michael Greer and Christopher Warnock, trans. and ed., *The Picatrix: Liber Viridis*, Green Magic edn (Iowa City, IA: Renaissance Astrology Adocentyn Press, 2010-11), pp. 11-12.

241. Alan Deyermond, *Points of View in the Ballad: 'The Prisoner, The Lady and the Shepherd', and Others*, The Kate Elder Lecture, 7 (1995), expanded (London: Department of Hispanic Studies, Queen Mary and Westfield College, 1996), pp. 62-63.

242. Şizen Yiacoup, *Frontier Memory: Cultural Conflict and Exchange in the 'Romancero fronterizo'*, MHRA Texts and Dissertations, 87 (London: Modern Humanities Research Association, 2013), p. 14.

243. Samuel G. Armistead and Joseph H. Silverman, 'The Judeo-Spanish Tradition', *Oral Tradition* (1987), 633-44.

> Rabbi Isaac was the first to present (in brief sayings that were preserved by his disciples) a Kabbalistic attitude toward communion with God (*devequt*), toward prayers and other Jewish rituals.[244]

Some of his disciples established a centre of Kabbalah in Gerona, northern Catalonia, but their prolific writing alarmed Rabbi Isaac, who forbad dissemination of secret teaching. Thereafter, kabbalistic writers exercised more caution by obscuring the underlying meaning of their esoteric perspective, but there remained an active interchange between philosophers and kabbalists, so that when *grado*—literally meaning degree—appeared in a poem, it was understood as a synonym for sefirah.[245]

As with the oral tradition of the ballad, kabbalistic wisdom was handed down through generations in the Sephardic diaspora. Colette Aboulker-Muscat, born in Algeria, was a descendant of Rabbi Isaac and Rabbi Jacob ben Sheshet, who practised the Kabbalah of Light in Gerona. The daughter of a neurosurgeon and a novelist, she added to the family's healing lineage modern techniques for working with the waking dream. Catherine Shainberg, who became her adopted daughter and successor, has recently run workshops for the Escuela Huber de Psicología Astrológica. In her book, *Kabbalah and the Power of Dreaming* (2005), Shainberg defines pure Kabbalah as 'that one "receives" from inner gazing', using experiential and contemplative practice, including *devequt*, rather than textual analysis, permutations of letters, or studying the Tree of Life. The revelatory and intentional dreaming techniques of Shainberg's School of Images, freeing the body of disabling memories and hidden agenda to encourage restorative *tikkun* and pro-active *kavanah*, share common ground with Huber astrology's association of Saturn with body and memory. *Tikkun*, or correction, reworks the unhappy memories we cling to, reversing fear and exonerating guilt, letting tears return to the ocean, and transforming sad

---

244. Dan, pp. 2, 7-8, 32; Peter Forshaw, 'Jewish Kabbalah', EXESESO module HISM 154 (University of Exeter, 2011).

245. Dan, pp. 34-35; Harvey J. Hames, 'Exotericism and Esotericism in Thirteenth Century Kabbalah', *Esoterica*, 6 (2004), 102-112.

narratives into luminous visions that can enrich the present.[246] The Huber moon node chart raises a mirror to the ancestral shadow, enabling integration and personal progress.[247] *Kavanah*, meaning will or intent, emphasizes the building a life plan in harmony with the spirit, as do psychosynthesis and Huber astrology.[248]

3.5 *The Book of Life* in Renaissance Italy

Several decades before the reconquest of Spain by the Christian kings in 1492, Constantinople fell to the Ottoman Turks in 1453, and Greek scholars fled to Italy with manuscripts yet to be translated into Latin. Ficino, son of a physician who tended Cosimo de' Medici—the wealthy banker who founded the Medici dynasty in Florence—transferred from a medical curriculum dominated by scholasticism to the study of Greek and Plato. As Greek texts arrived in Italy, Cosimo and his successors employed Ficino to translate them into Latin, and his Platonic academy became a focus of Renaissance philosophy and culture. Among the earliest translations he completed were fourteen books of the *Corpus Hermeticum* (1463) that Cosimo wanted to read before he died. Ficino, the astrologer, timed publication of Plato's *Dialogues* in Latin for 1484 to coincide with a Great Conjunction of Jupiter and Saturn in Scorpio. Meanwhile, Ficino the priest was ordained in 1473, while continuing to translate works by pagan Neoplatonists who influenced his understanding of interplay between macrocosm and microcosm and the music of the spheres. He moved between two languages, 'that of Christian orthodoxy and that of the symbolic imagination', in a guarded and sometimes contradictory style of writing.[249]

---

246. Catherine Shainberg, *Kabbalah and the Power of Dreaming: Awakening the Visionary Life* (Rochester, VT: Inner Traditions, 2005), pp. xvi, 146-60; <www.schoolofimages.com>.

247. *Moon Node*, pp. 141-51.

248. Shainberg, pp. 13, 170-72; Assagioli, *Will*, pp. 15-18; *Planets*, pp. 91-117.

249. Voss, *Ficino*, pp. xiii-xv, 15, 25.

His most daring publication, *De vita libri tres* (1489)—three treatises on life translated as *Book of Life* (1980) and sometimes referred to as three books on life—landed him in trouble with the papacy, obliging him to write a grovelling apology to the effect that he was only interpreting Plotinus, while camouflaging his greater debt to the theurgy of Proclus.[250] In his dedicatory letter to Lorenzo the Magnificent, he wrote:

> I, the least of priests, have had two fathers: the medical Doctor Ficino, and the Medici's Cosimo. From one I was born, from the other reborn. One commended me to Galen, first as a doctor, then as a Platonist; the other, however, consecrated me to the divine Plato. Both of them destined Marsilio for a doctor's life: Galen was a doctor of bodies, while Plato was a doctor of souls.[251]

A contemporary doctor of medicine might be more amused than impressed by his recipes and cocktails but, as a healer of souls he signalled the way for astrological psychology:

> There is well-established logic to Ficino's thought here: if human beings are a microcosm, a cosmos in miniature, and the planets are divine, then not only must they relate to the classical planetary deities, but these must have an internal presence. Jupiter, then, is not just outside but inside every human being, as are the other planetary gods and goddesses. The distinction with medieval cosmology is clear and radical: whereas Aquinas had reinforced the dogma that celestial influences were primarily on the material world, and that the soul was entirely independent of them, Ficino emphasized the contrary position, that the psychic and physical worlds were so intertwined that the planets were as alive in our minds and souls as in our bodies. It's for this reason that Ficino has been identified as a precursor of late twentieth-century depth psychology, especially Jungianism and its offshoots, with its adaptations of Platonic archetypes and celestial deities as internal psychological functions.[252]

---

250. Ficino, *Book of Life*, p. 186; Voss, *Ficino*, p 197; Don Cameron Allen, *The Star-Crossed Renaissance: The Quarrel about Astrology and Its Influence in England* (London: Frank Cass, 1966), p. 5.

251. Ficino, *Book of Life*, p. 1.

252. Campion, *Medieval and Modern*, pp. 90-91.

The first treatise, on 'Caring for the Health of Men of Letters', addresses the melancholia of scholars under the influence of Saturn, tuning into the intellectual face of Saturn as memory and karma. The second, on 'How to Prolong Life', invokes Venus for recapturing youth and advises a healthy diet. The final and most significant treatise, 'On Making Your Life Agree with the Heavens', shows how rays of light can empower gemstones and talismans, and how to draw down positive planetary qualities with skilful use of will and imagination, thereby countering negative influences. These activities involve natural or astral magic:[253]

> Natural magic refers to practices designed to employ the hidden virtues or qualities in all things, plants, gems, animals etc. The astrological is the system of those correspondences. Hence natural magic utilises astrology—and in European culture it is hardly conceivable to be a natural magician without being at the same time an astrologer.

The creation of talismans might be seen as stretching the limits of natural magic, bordering 'on the realms of celestial and daemonic Intelligences' and, in all probability, Ficino's musical arrangement of the *Hymns of Orpheus* incorporated ritual or ceremonial magic.[254] As a man of the cloth, he was treading dangerous waters.

Ficino's astral magic is central to Western esotericism and his widespread influence cannot be underestimated. The Elizabethan magus, John Dee, had 'the complete works of Marsilio Ficino and his translations and commentaries on Plato and Plotinus' in his famous library. His work features prominently in the *Three Books of Occult Philosophy* (1533) of the German occultist Henry Cornelius Agrippa von Nettesheim, and his concept of the magus as priest-physician was paramount to the vocation of the Swiss doctor Paracelsus:

253. Ficino, *Book of Life*, pp. 137-58.
254. Cornelius, *Moment*, pp. 3-4.

> His medical vocation absorbed the theory of two worlds and correspondences, the physician as magus, intervening as a transmuted soul in the spiritual hierarchy of nature. There is much textual evidence to support this interpretation of his worldview. In Ficino's *Apology* for his own attitude to astrology and medicine, we find the kernel of Paracelsian medical Neoplatonism.[255]

Notwithstanding his tangle with ecclesiastical authorities half a century earlier, Ficino's *Book of Life* was translated from Latin into Italian by Lucio Fauno, and circulated in a pocket edition by Michele Tramezzino, a publisher with presses in Venice and Rome, so *De le tre vite* (1548) was marketed as an everyday guide to healthy living with a glossary explaining each of the humours and their effects on health, physiognomy, and temperament.[256]

Over four centuries later, in *The Planets Within* (1982) inspired by his third treatise, Thomas Moore describes Ficino's astrology as

> ...a technique of enlivening imagination and memory. The signs and planets of astrology provide a means for ordering experience and inner movement, just as any system of imagery might help us to see through surface events to their fantasies.[257]

This use of astrological significators to make sense of experience is fundamental to my approach, as will become clear in the next chapter. Moore's critique is steeped in Jungian spiritual alchemy in which 'one finds reality to be a living system in which one participates, to which one contributes, and in which the boundaries between subject and object are fluid'.[258]

---

255. Goodrick-Clark, *Western Esoteric*, pp. 61-62, 80; Henry Cornelius Agrippa of Nettesheim, *Three Books of Occult Philosophy*, trans. by James Freake, and ed. by Donald Tyson (Woodbury, MN: Llewellyn, 2007), p. xli.

256. Sandra Cavallo and Tessa Storey, *Healthy Living in Late Renaissance Italy* (Oxford: Oxford University Press, 2013), pp. 18-19.

257. Thomas Moore, *The Planets Within: The Astrological Psychology of Marsilio Ficino*, 2nd edn (Hudson, NY: Lindisfarne, 1990), intro., p. 54.

258. Karen-Claire Voss, 'Spiritual Alchemy: Interpreting Representative Texts and Images', in *Gnosis and Hermeticism*', pp. 147-81 (p. 152).

3.6 Theosophy, New Age, and the Seven Rays

The TS was founded in 1875 by Helena Petrovna Blavatsky, Henry Steel Olcott and William Quan Judge. 'Theosophical', relating to God's wisdom, was chosen for the name of the society with reference to the 'eclectic theosophical' system of Ammonius Saccas, the pagan founder of the Neoplatonic School in Alexandria, in 193 CE.[259]

Blavatsky's first major publication, *Isis Unveiled* (1877)—presented as 'a plea for the recognition of the Hermetic philosophy, the anciently universal Wisdom Religion, as the only possible key to the Absolute in science and theology'—is steeped in the Hermetic philosophy of Egypt, while 'Oriental Cabala'—perhaps deriving from Zoroastrianism, but also aligned with the Hindu Sri-Yantra—'stands as a symbol for a repository of arcane truths, the hidden source of ancient wisdom'.[260] In her view, Pythagorean metempsychosis could supply the missing link in the chain of evolution, and Hermetic and Pythagorean cosmogonical doctrines—based on the formula that 'ether and chaos... were the two primeval and eternal principles of the universe'—represented the combination of intellect and matter common to microcosm and macrocosm.[261] In spite of her initial emphasis on Hermetic philosophy, India emerges as 'the cradle of humanity, the parent of all other nations, and the hotbed of all lost arts of antiquity', as she echoes the opinion of French writer Louis Jacolliot, introducing themes that would be expanded in her second two-volume opus.[262]

---

259. Goodrick-Clarke, Blavatsky, pp. 7-8; 'Great Theosophists: Ammonius Saccas', Theosophy, 25 (1936), 53-59, repr. <www.wisdomworld.org/setting/saccas.html> [accessed 1 March 2012].

260. H. P. Blavatsky, *Isis Unveiled: A Master-Key to the Mysteries of Ancient and Modern Science and Theology*, 1, Science, 2, Theology (Pasadena, CA: Theosophical University Press, 1976), 1, vii, 160, and 2, between pp. 258-59 and 265-73; *Isis* abridgement, p.xvii; Nicholas Goodrick-Clarke, 'H. P. Blavatsky and the Ambiguities of Orientalism: Western Esotericism and Eastern Religion in Theosophy', EXESESO Study Conference, University of Exeter, 29 January 2012, p. 8.

261. *Isis* abridgement, pp. 6, 83-84.

262. Blavatsky, *Isis*, 1, p. 584; Goodrick-Clarke, *Blavatsky*, p. 10.

The Secret Doctrine (1888)—structured as a commentary on the seven stanzas of the mysterious *Book of Dzyan*—connects the human condition with cycles of seven, karma and reincarnation, and with after-death states.[263]

Man's septenary constitution appeared in *The Theosophist* (1881) as teachings of Kuthumi received by Allan O. Hume, an outspoken civil servant in favour of Indian nationalism. The sacred seven featured in an article by Blavatsky and in volume 2 of *The Secret Doctrine*, where she stated that 'Number Seven, as a compound of 3 and 4, is the factor element in every ancient religion, because it is the factor element in nature'. Despite an apparent link with the chakras of kundalinī-yoga—'where soul and body...interpenetrate'—ancient Hindu and Buddhist systems mostly work with five, and seven is predominantly Western. Blavatsky's seven principles of man, comprising a triple aspect of the Deity equivalent to the upper triad of the sefirot and a quaternary, correlate most closely with the emanationist cosmology of Kabbalah, as she acknowledges herself:[264]

> To the metrological key to the symbolism of the Hebrews, which reveals numerically the geometrical relations of the Circle (All-Deity) to the Square, Cube, Triangle, and all the integral emanations of the divine area, may be added the theogonic Key. This Key explains that Noah, the deluge-Patriarch, is in one aspect the permutation of the Deity (the Universal Creative Law), for the purpose of the formation

263. Regardie, *Tree*, p. 29; Goodrick-Clarke, *Blavatsky*, p. 14.

264. Goodrick-Clarke, Blavatsky, p. 13, and Western Esoteric, pp. 220-21; 'The Mystery and Sacredness of Number Seven', from Collected Writings of H. P. Blavatsky, 2, p. 408, repr. <www.theosophical-society.org.uk/html/ insight_articles/ spring2005_mystery_seven> [accessed 16 February 2012]; 'Chakra' in The Rider Encyclopedia of Eastern Philosophy and Religion: Buddhism, Hinduism, Taoism, Zen, ed. by Ingrid Fischer-Schreiber, with Franz-Karl Ehrhard, and others, trans. by Rider (London: Rider, 1989), pp. 58-61 (p. 59); Lama Anagarika Govinda, Foundations of Tibetan Mysticism: According to the Esoteric Teachings of the Great Mantra 'Om Mani Padme Hum' (London: Rider, 1969), pp. 57, 184; Nicholas Goodrick-Clarke, 'Wheels of Fire: The Reception of Eastern Subtle Body Doctrines in the Western Esoteric Tradition', Scientific and Medical Network Conference, The Body and Beyond: Cross-Cultural Understandings of Subtle Energy, Bath Spa University, 22-24 August, 2008, pp. 6-7.

of our Earth, its population, and the propagation of life on it, in general.

> Now bearing in mind the Septenary division in divine Hierarchies, as in Cosmic and human constitutions, the student will readily understand that Jah-Noah is at the head of, and is the synthesis of the lower Cosmic Quaternary. The upper Sephirothal triad—of which Jehovah-Binah (Intelligence) is the left, female angle—emanates the Quaternary... symbolizing... the 'Heavenly Man', the sexless Adam-Kadmon viewed as Nature in the abstract, becomes a septenate again by emanating from itself the additional three principles, the lower terrestrial or manifested physical Nature, Matter and our Earth (the seventh being Malkuth, the 'Bride of the Heavenly Man'), thus forming, with the higher triad, or Kether, the Crown, the full number of the Sephirothal Tree—the 10, the Total in Unity, or the Universe. Apart from the higher Triad, the lower creative Sephiroth are seven.[265]

In this lengthy quotation, illustrated in *The Secret Doctrine* by a triangle over a square, we can see the origins of Huber planetary hierarchies, in which Venus, Mercury, Jupiter, and Mars form the quaternary base as sensory, life-sustaining functions supporting the threefold personality which, at the level of the ego is represented by Saturn, Moon, and Sun, and at the higher level of the individuated soul by Uranus, Neptune, and Pluto.[266]

Syncretizing East with West, Blavatsky used Hindu terminology to describe the seven principles comprising the esoteric body that are integral to Theosophical understanding of reincarnation and spiritual evolution. Starting with the highest, the upper triad are *Atma*, meaning universal spirit, *Buddhi*, the spiritual soul, and *Manas*, the human mind and soul, and the lower quaternary are *Kama-Rupa*, the animal soul, *Lingua Sarira*, the astral body, *Prana*, the life essence, and *Sthula Sarira*, the body.[267] She was careful to differentiate her portrayal of reincarnation from Kardec's

265. Helena Petrovna Blavatsky, The Secret Doctrine: The Synthesis of Science, Religion, and Philosophy, 2, Anthropogenesis, 1st edn 1888, repr. 2008 <www.forgottenbooks.org>, pp. 412-13.

266. See planet hierarchies, p. 9.

267. *Secret Doctrine,* 2, p. 413.

spiritualist interpretation since, in her view, mediums do not call up the 'reincarnating *Ego*', but elementary spirits, the 'double of the medium or someone present', or '*Kamalokic* shells'—astral remains improvising their former personalities.[268] The task Blavatsky set herself was not only to recover and synthesize lost wisdom, but also to form a study group to raise awareness and practise esoteric rituals in preparation for the new era.[269] Her seven principles morphed into Bailey's seven rays, Leadbeater's seven chakras, and many more New Age systems. In astrology, the three are identifiable with the astrological qualities forming the cardinal, mutable, and fixed crosses, and the three purposeful motivations manifest in four different temperaments corresponding to the elements of air, water, fire, and earth. Their importance is articulated by Leo, the esoteric side of whose work is taken forward by Bailey and the Hubers:

> It is upon the seven primary divisions of the Zodiac into Fire, Air, Earth, Water, Cardinal, Mutable and Fixed Signs, that the real meaning of every horoscope is fundamentally based.[270]

Theosophy 'paved the way for the study of comparative religion', expanding consciousness, promoting analogy and synthesis in preference to logic and analysis, inviting alternative approaches to seeing, thinking, and composing, exerting a significant impact on 'modern art, quantum physics and... New Age religion'. Theosophy's influence on spiritual as opposed to pop art is touched upon in the first chapter with reference to Kandinsky, Klee, and the evolution of Huber astrology, and its seminal role in art and music over the last century and a half is the subject of ongoing research. New Age

---

268. 'Letter 21 to Prof. Hiram Corson, dated 16 February 1875', in *H. P. Blavatsky Collected Writings: The Letters of H. P. Blavatsky*, 1, ed. by John Algeo (Wheaton, IL: Quest, 2003), pp. 85-87 (p. 87); Helena P. Blavatsky, *The Key to Theosophy: A Clear Exposition based on the Wisdom Religion of All Ages*, repr. of 1st edn (1889), with glossary of 2nd edn and new index (Pasadena, CA: Theosopical University Press, 1987), p. 28.

269. Campion, *Astrology and Popular Religion*, p. 23.

270. Leo, *Esoteric*, p. xiv.

refers both to the 'future spiritual era' of the Age of Aquarius, and to the culture and mindset built up around its various prophets.[271]

One significant expression of New Age religion is the channelling of spiritual teaching, following a line of continuity from Blavatsky's conversations with Mahatmas Morya and Kuthumi to Bailey's receipt of the esoteric teachings recorded in her books from the Tibetan Adept, DK, a disciple of Kuthumi.[272] Having joined the TS in 1917, Alice progressed quickly, becoming a member of its Esoteric Section in 1918. By 1919 she was receiving messages from DK. Thereafter, she and Foster Bailey—whom she married in 1921—had a falling out with the TS President and set about 'creating a group of individuals whose purpose was to bring the New Age into being'. They founded the Lucis Publishing Company in 1922 and the Arcane School for teaching by correspondence in 1923.[273] Steiner led another breakaway group, forming the Anthroposophical Society in January 1913, and he obliquely influenced the Hubers by bringing out an edition of Goethe's colour theory.[274] Leo was the Theosophist and astrologer who influenced Bailey directly.

Generally regarded as the father of modern astrology, Leo was a Theosophist who did not live to become a New Ager. He was introduced to the TS, in 1888, by Walter Old, whose astrological pseudonym was Sepharial. Although Old was a member of Blavatsky's Esoteric Section—her Astral Tramp—as an astrologer, he was best known for racing tips and financial forecasting. By contrast, Leo brought a Theosophical perspective to astrology and generated a market for personal horoscopes that placed more emphasis on psychological characteristics and spiritual development

271. Goodrick-Clarke, *Blavatsky*, p. 18; Ertan, p. 30; Campion, *Astrology and Popular Religion*, p. 33.

272. Hanegraaff, *New Age*, pp. 23-41; Gordon, 4-5.

273. <en.wikipedia.org/wiki/Alice_Bailey> [accessed 10 December 2014].

274. Nicholas Goodrick-Clarke, 'Rudolf Steiner and Anthroposophy', EXESESO module HISM 156 (University of Exeter, 2011), p. 105; Ringbom.

than predictions.[275] In 1915, he established the Astrological Lodge of London, which celebrates its centenary in 2015 but, although it meets on the premises of the TS it is no longer a part of it.

Two of Leo's books, *The Art of Synthesis* (1912) and *Esoteric Astrology* (1913), had a significant influence on Bailey and the Hubers. 'Every soul is a "Divine Fragment" with a long past history behind it', is the opening statement in *The Art of Synthesis*, which has 'An Astro-Theosophical Glossary' with clear definitions of Indian concepts that were quickly absorbed into twentieth-century astrological vocabulary, among which were 'Akasha: the subtle supersensuous matter which pervades all space,' and 'Akashic records: the permanent images of all past events which persist in the Akasha, and which may be seen by the exercise of a certain type of cultivated clairvoyance'.[276]

Leo's divine fragment is Blavatsky's deity, representing 'man's Atma' descending 'in its threefold aspect'. This unfolding of consciousness separates the divine fragment from the eternal self, as

> the personal man, descends into incarnation for the sake of gaining experience, and the horoscope shows in part the powers and characteristics of that ray on descent, the kind of experience it has come into the world to gain, and the work that lies before it to be done.[277]

Leo coined the phrase 'Character is Destiny' from the pre-Socratic philosopher Heraclitus to express the concept 'that understanding one's character and past, including past lives, was... to the control of one's future', and suggested that the Divine Fragment carrying this history be depicted 'as a small blank circle in the centre of every horoscope'.[278] Whereas he typically put a globe at the centre of his

---

275. Kim Farnell, The Astral Tramp: A Biography of Sepharial (London: Ascella, 1998), pp. ix, xiii, 14-36, 61; Kim Farnell, 'A Brief Biography of Alan Leo', <www.skyscript.co.uk/Alan_Leo.html> [accessed 19 April 2012], p. 8.

276. Leo, *Synthesis*, p. 256.

277. Leo, *Esoteric*, p. 241.

278. Leo, *Synthesis*, pp. 1, 134-41; Leo, *Esoteric*, p. 242; Campion, *Astrology and Popular Religion*, p. 57.

charts, the Hubers adopted his proposal of a small blank circle to represent the personal and transpersonal centre, and APA forbids their students to present charts put up on computer programmes that do not respect the central space. Leo made a clear distinction between esoteric and exoteric astrology, emphasizing synthesis and integrity in esoteric astrology, values that are key to astrological psychology:

> We may define Esoteric Astrology as that side of the subject which views all stellar phenomena from the standpoint of unity; whilst Exoteric Astrology begins its study from the side of diversity and separateness.[279]

Taking an increasingly psychological perspective, Leo's successors would recognize that the suffering caused by divided consciousness at the exoteric level generates the self-awareness that motivates the individual to close the gap between observer and observed, undergo initiatory challenges, and build a bridge from the separative personality to the unified soul at the esoteric level.[280] The raising of consciousness to higher levels of awareness, compassion, and potential to make regenerative changes for the benefit of humanity and the Earth is intrinsic to the Huber education programme.

Leo died in 1917. Charles Carter, his successor at the Astrological Lodge, was a Theosophist concerned with astrology of the soul, founder of the *Astrological Quarterly*, and first President of the Faculty of Astrological Studies, who took forward Leo's mainstream work on character and destiny and developed astrological education, but he was uninterested in his esoteric astrology and took a sceptical approach to New Age ideology.[281]

---

279. Leo, *Esoteric*, p. xiv.

280. Nigel Wellings, 'Naked Presence', in *Transpersonal Psychotherapy*, pp. 177-205 (p. 195).

281. Farnell, 'Leo', p. 8; Campion, Astrology and Popular Religion, p. 47; Mari Garcia and Joy Usher, 'An Introduction to Charles Carter', <www.skyscript.co.uk/carter_intro.html> [accessed 23 December 2014].

Bailey, on the other hand, adopted and transformed many of his ideas, and the Hubers assimilated selective insights directly from Leo. Besides the blank circle in the centre of the chart, they are indebted to Leo for his depiction of Jupiter as 'the great synthesizer', the 'seed planet on the physical plane', and 'the magnetic aura' ruling the four elements, which anticipates Bruno's portrayal of Jupiter as orchestrator of sensory perception, keeping the visionary intelligence grounded in earthly reality.[282] When the Hubers reworked Bailey's seven rays, they appointed Jupiter, not Uranus, as 'Lord of the Seventh Ray of Ceremonial Magic, Ritual and Order'. This makes perfect sense because, although Uranus is the modern exoteric ruler of Aquarius, Jupiter, as the esoteric ruler of Aquarius, brings grounding and humanity to the Uranian higher mind that can be cold in its adherence to ideology. The changes made to Bailey's connections between planets and rays nevertheless raise complex questions regarding the relationship between hers and the Hubers' esoteric astrology. Bruno's dissatisfaction with the Geneva Arcane School's over-emphasis on spiritual progress, and neglect of psychological preparation is referred to earlier. In the final section of this chapter, I outline some transformational exercises used by astrological psychologists that derive directly from Bailey and some inspired by other sources, and I question whether the most significant evidence of esotericism in Huber astrology lies in their adaptation of Bailey's rays. A number of these questions were addressed at an APA seminar, 'The Golden Seam', held at Buckland Hall in the Brecon Beacons, in 2006.[283] I quote from a subsequent article by Joyce Hopewell:

> The term 'esoteric astrology' conjures up all manner of mysterious unknowns... The books of Alice Bailey are often recommended as a source of understanding more about esotericism, but they can be pretty daunting to read and are laced with archaic language. Louise Huber has a deep understanding of esoteric astrology and in seminars she would often base her presentations around significant elements of the

282. Leo, *Esoteric*, p. 23; Leo, *Synthesis*, p. 80.
283. *Astrology and the Seven Rays*, p. 47.

> esotericism of Alice Bailey. The Huber Method is underpinned with the psychosynthesis of Roberto Assagioli, who was himself a follower of Alice Bailey's teachings. It could be said that the Huber Method is one corner of a triangle, with psychosynthesis and esotericism at the other two corners.[284]

Bailey emphasizes the transformative journey from the exoteric to the esoteric ruler of the Ascendant, or rising sign on the horizon at the time of birth:

> This sign and its qualities are often described as the mask or persona we assume and project when we meet the external world... Esoterically the ascendant sign indicates the qualities we should strive to move towards, acquire and express when on the spiritual path.[285]

Louise has developed similar transformative exercises across the axes for elevating the Moon signs' fluctuating desire nature to an expression of unconditional love able to heal emotional wounds.[286] Leo wrote: 'Full Moon, the opposition of the two luminaries, represents the personality illuminated by the Sun, or spirit, and throwing its borrowed light upon the earth, physical consciousness', Bailey allotted a special place to full Moon meditations in the new world religion, and Louise assembled monthly meditations into *Reflexions and Meditations on the Signs of the Zodiac*, taking the disciple or aspiring group on transformational journeys at full Moon across the axis from the Sun sign motivated by the traditional ruler into the opposing Moon sign, and then back to the Sun sign operating at the higher level of the esoteric ruler in consonance with the seed thought.[287] Oppositions between planets generate tension, involving a tug of war relating, perhaps, to a former life, and there is a need to learn from experience and redress the balance. Huber astrology suggests working with axial tensions through the

284. Joyce Hopewell, 'Esoteric Rulers and Seed Thoughts for the Signs', 1, *Conjunction*, 59 (2013), p. 16.

285. Hopewell, *Living Birth Chart*, p. 175.

286. *Planets*, pp. 239-84.

287. Leo, *Esoteric*, p. 3; see esoteric rulers, seed thoughts, axes, pp. 7, 10.

third pole, the other axis in the same motivational cross.[288] Besides planetary energies, special attention is paid to the directional line between the South Node or dragon's tail and the North Node or dragon's head. These points indicate the familiar space we have come from and the direction in which we are encouraged to move when meeting this life's challenges. The North Node is always included in the aspect structure in Huber charts, to show the way into uncharted territory.[289] This heightened awareness of opposites and their potential to bring about a change of perception can be likened to Klee's approach to the *Thinking Eye*, where 'Chaos as an antithesis is not complete and utter chaos, but a locally determined concept relating to the concept of the cosmos', introducing 'an idea of procedure in which no actor is in an absolutely fixed position'.[290] This comparison of the motion and shifting vision of artist, actor, and astrological initiate vis-à-vis earth and cosmos can be extended to include the wave sequences of the intensity curve, outlined below, as well as the cycle of age progression touched upon in the next chapter.

Although Bruno related the esotericism of astrological psychology to ancient practice, he always paid attention to contemporary research, in particular the work of Michel Gauquelin, whose statistical tests indicated that people with Saturn stressed behind the angles of especially the Ascendant or Midheaven were motivated towards science, while those with stressed Mars in a similar position often became leading athletes.[291] Huber chart interpretation incorporates a double wave sequence, or intensity curve. Dynamic quadrants peak immediately behind the four cardinal angles of the chart and dip at low points in the fixed houses, reflecting the Gauquelin effect. Each of the twelve houses is divided into a cardinal section from the cusp to the balance point, a fixed section from the balance point to the low

288. *Transformation*, pp. 7-9; *Astrological Houses*, pp. 71-85.

289. Hopewell, *Living Birth Chart*, pp. 159-74.

290. Rosenthal, pp. 33-38, citing *Paul Klee Notebook, I: The Thinking Eye*, trans. by Ralph Manheim and ed. by Jürg Spiller.

291. *Transformation*, pp. 46-47.

point, and a mutable section from the low point to the next cusp, with the divisions based on the pentagram and the golden mean.[292] The mutable section is divided into three parts, and any planet in the zone immediately behind the next cusp is stressed because it is both pulled back to the issues of the house it is leaving and forward to those of the house it is approaching. In addition to seeking transcendence through vertical ascent and equilibrium by balancing polarities, the esotericist using the Huber method examines the location of planets according to their house positions to see whether they resonate to the crest or the undercurrent of a wave.

In my chart, considered in the next chapter, Jupiter is on the crest of a wave, stressed behind the cusp of a 2nd house preoccupied with self-worth, opposing the Sun across the encounter axis between houses one and seven, and making a quincunx to a low point, introspective Mars in the 6th house. Jupiter, Sun, and Mars combine in a cardinal-mutable irritation triangle, full of longings and insecurities, and Jupiter dominates most of the Eastern hemisphere of the natal chart. The astrologer Marc Edmund Jones coined the term 'bucket handle', while the Hubers call such a controlling planet the 'tension ruler', and they have developed a three-stage process for managing stressed planets through compensation requiring a change of attitude, sublimation or refinement, and transformation of consciousness so that 'we realize the deeper meaning of the whole developmental event and can identify ourselves with it'.[293] My prominent Jupiter—traditionally, the greater benefic, although all planets have beneficial and contrary characteristics—endows me with good health and what my mother described as 'a facility for falling on my feet'. Nevertheless, as Rudhyar explained, Jupiter can only be a 'beneficent power of expansion... if balanced by the steady restraint of the Law of Saturn', and its inflated vision can

292. *Transformation*, pp. 13-15, 43-78; *Astrological Houses*, pp. 88-89; see intensity curve, p. 12.

293. *Transformation*, pp. 43-78 (p. 51); see my chart, p. 129.

harbour enormous stresses.[294] In my case, they relate primarily to overemphasis on scholarly achievement as a measure of self-worth, a sense of inadequacy arising from inevitable infiltration of subjective material into intellectual endeavour at a crucial period, the necessity for full-scale separative analysis prior to reassembly, and the struggle to regain self-confidence and integrity. Boundaries between psychological and spiritual journeys of transformation are blurred, as individuals seek to understand their 'calling', in the sense of being 'on this earth for a reason', and motivational drives behind the writing of this book include needs for clarity, synthesis, and sharing.[295]

Astrological psychology adopts three initiations from Bailey that refine and elevate the physical, emotional and mental ego of the personality represented by Saturn, Moon, and Sun to the level of the transpersonal planets, Uranus, Neptune and Pluto, whose forces connect with the higher self. The first, from Saturn to Uranus, involves physical rebirth, letting go of material dependency and fear of the unknown prior to leading a healthier life, becoming responsible, discerning, and adept with skilful will. The second, from Moon to Neptune, is an emotional purification leading to baptism that takes the initiate into a dark tunnel to confront the astral world of illusions, learn acceptance, forgiveness, and goodwill, and open the heart centre to find the eternal soul. The third, from Sun to Pluto, has been likened to the Way of the Cross, in which doubts and temptations hinder the creative power of thought and strength of will, as they strive to integrate the threefold personality and build a bridge to the soul:[296]

---

294. Dane Rudhyar, *New Mansions for New Men*, 3rd edn (Alameda, CA: Hunter House, 1978), pp. 133-34.

295. Hanegraaff, *Guide*, p. 137; Thomas Moore, *A Life at Work: The Joy of Discovering what you were Born to Do* (London: Piatkus, 2008), p. 17.

296. Alice. A. Bailey, *The Soul: The Quality of Life*, ed. by a student (New York and London: Lucis, 1974), pp. 256-62; *Planets*, pp. 82-117.

> The symbol of this initiation is the goat of Capricorn, the human personality with its mental focus, climbing the mountain of achievement. On reaching the top the goat is transfigured into the unicorn, the symbol of the soul.[297]

A complex blend of Christian, Buddhist, and Hermetic symbolism underpins these initiations:

> The Tibetan Adept DK refers to the third initiation as that of the 'transfiguration'. This draws an immediate parallel with the experience of the initiate Jesus on the Mount of Olives (before his final arrival in Jerusalem), where his three senior disciples (like the three Masonic apprentices) see him surrounded by an aura of spiritual light within which they can also discern two other figures—supposedly Elijah and John the Baptist—these being perhaps symbolic of the two spiritual (atmic and buddhic) states of being. A further proof of the third initiation having been passed and of the individual's now achieved capacity for the beginnings of spiritual sight was shown symbolically by the ancient Egyptians in their picture of the head of the neophyte emerging above the open lotus flower.[298]

One of Dr Douglas Baker's many volumes based on Bailey's seven rays devotes a section to the opening of the lotus petals.[299] By completion of the third initiation, the disciple is starting to experience the seven rays in daily life.[300] So how should we interpret them and their interface with the signs and planets, and ourselves?

According to Bailey, 'the theory of the seven rays lays the foundation for the psychology of the New Age' and, in the half-century since her death in 1949, much of the daunting amount that has been written about them by Michael D. Robbins and others has aimed at drawing down their emanations from supercelestial heights to enable the esoteric psychologist 'to help human beings

297. Errol Weiner, *Transpersonal Astrology: Finding the Soul's Purpose* (Shaftesbury: Element, 1991), p. 39.

298. Gordon, pp. 332-33.

299. Dr Douglas Baker, *The Jewel in the Lotus*, 2nd edn (Essendon: Claregate, 1985), pp. 107-76.

300. *Astrology and the Seven Rays*, pp. 78, 82.

learn to bring the soul or psyche into full expression in their lives'.[301] This requires knowledge of the human constitution comprising soul, personality, mind, emotions, and etheric-physical body and—in order to understand 'the next step ahead'—

> a very clear idea of one's spiritual and personal energy patterns (i.e., the ray and astrological energies which continuously condition the spiritual Self, as well as those which condition the personal self during any one incarnation).[302]

When Rudhyar united astrology with depth psychology in his pioneering work, *The Astrology of Personality* (1936), he described astrology as

> the most significant index to man's practical philosophy of living. Philosophy per se speculates about life and man. But astrology, in every age, characterizes, directly or indirectly, the deepest quality of man's actual response to life.

This perceptive comment, with which I wholeheartedly agree, leads into a more controversial statement regarding the relative significance of exoteric and esoteric astrology:

> As various types of philosophy have always existed simultaneously in man's effort to interpret reality at various levels of thought and intuitive perception, so in every period... astrology has been divided into more exoteric and more esoteric systems. This division must not, however, blind us to the fact that 'esoteric' and exoteric' represent merely two ways of expressing, at any time, the basic keynote of an epoch. It is more important to know what the keynote is than to find out whether it is expressed exoterically or esoterically.[303]

---

301. Astrology and the Seven Rays, p. 4; Michael D. Robbins, Tapestry of the Gods, 1, The Seven Rays: An Esoteric Key to Understanding Human Nature; 3rd edn (Mariposa, CA: University of the Seven Rays, 1996), repr. <http://www.makara.us/04mdr/mdr_home.htm> tapestry1.pdf, p. 21; Astrology and the Seven Rays, p. 82.

302. Robbins, 1, p. 21.

303. Rudhyar, *Personality*, pp. vii, 3-4.

Being in poor physical health, Rudhyar—an aspiring musician—was exempt military service in his native France during the First World War, travelled to the States at the end of 1916, and embraced Theosophy, which was in vogue among young intellectuals, shortly after his arrival in North America. By the mid-1930s, his enthusiasm for Theosophy was waning, in the 1940s he published fresh insights into the soli-lunar cycle, and by 1970, he was promoting a 'philosophical-cosmic and humanistic approach' to astrology, a 'person centred' perspective aimed at helping people to achieve their greatest potential in preparation for the 'transpersonal path', which he equated to 'what esoteric traditions have spoken of as the Path of Initiation'.[304] His multilevel approach, incorporating a re-evaluation of the esoteric, is fundamental to the revival of transpersonal astrology in the twenty-first century considered in the final chapter.

Alan Oken is the astrologer who reinterpreted Bailey's esoteric astrology in the late twentieth century, keeping fairly closely to the attributions of the seven rays to signs and planets as recorded by Bailey, and appealing to the New Ager on the path of individuation, for whom

> This existence is one in which the orientation and the exigencies of the inner life of the Soul—the 'vertical' life rather than the 'horizontal' life of the personality—are becoming a predominating theme in your daily experience of the world around and within you.[305]

304. Ertan, pp. 30-31; Rudhyar, *Personality*, p. xii; Dane Rudhyar, *The Lunation Cycle: A Key to the Understanding of Personality* 2nd edn (Boulder, CO: Shambhala, 1971), p. vii; Rudhyar, *Person Centred*, pp. 8-10; Rudhyar, *Multilevel*, p. xv.

305. Alan Oken, *Soul-Centred Astrology: A Key to Expanding Self* (Freedom, CA: Crossing Press, 1996), p. 4.

Oken outlines the fundamental relationship between personality and soul, and the linking force, known in Sanskrit as the Antahkarana and often referred to as the rainbow bridge. As Louise explains, 'the seven cosmic rays are seven types or manifestations of light' of which 'the colours of the spectrum are an example':

> When a ray of light is reflected in smooth glass or in a drop of water, the whole of the spectrum is visible. This is a good way to represent the effect of the seven cosmic rays. They are all pervasive; they bring to life everything and are the source of our existence. This is why they transcend normal astrology. They are primal energies that condition our lives, they are forms of energy that generate and sustain creativity.[306]

An unformed personality tends to be oblivious of the etheric energy he or she is projecting, and only becomes aware of his or her rays through the reactions of others.[307] An integrated personality or lower self is prerequisite to union with the soul:

> The personality consists of the physical body, the emotional (also known as the 'astral' or 'desire') body, and the lower mental body (the rational mind). In a fully developed personality, these three vehicles are synthesized into a harmoniously working unit. This means that there is an alignment of the mind and the feelings so that our outer actions are expressed in a balanced manner... (The transcending force—the use of the will to 'weave' the pattern of the horoscope into a cohesive whole—is a primary factor leading to the free use of that will and the co-creation of our character and destiny.)
>
> This type of personality is usually quite creative or, at the very least, quite able to function under all social pressures and circumstances. It is the goal of every spiritually active and aspiring person to create such an integrated lower self, for it is only with the correct alignment of forces that consistent Soul contact can occur.[308]

---

306. *Astrology and the Seven Rays*, p. 5.
307. *Astrology and the Seven Rays*, p. 82.
308. Oken, pp. 16-17.

A coordinated personality, synthesized with the help of skilful will, and intermittently in touch with the soul, represents the level of attainment expected of the APA Diploma student nearing the end of the course, although the seven rays are not included in the training, and the student may or may not have read *Astrology and the Seven Rays* by the Hubers and consulted the MegaStar computer programme that calculates physical, emotional, mental, and personality rays. Although there is a suggested formula for finding the soul ray, the onus is on the individual to develop the self-will and spiritual consciousness to bring about synergy between personality and soul.[309]

The workshop on the seven rays that forms the basis of their book took place in 1998, one year before Bruno's death, by which time many graduates in astrological psychology had adopted the correspondences between rays, signs, and planets presented by Bailey, Oken, and other interpreters. The Hubers, fully aware of disparities between the astrological method they carefully crafted over forty years and Bailey's cosmos with its sacred and non-sacred planets, emphasized the need for analogical thinking.[310] Their alignment of the rays with Assagioli's psychological types corresponds to their own planetary hierarchy in a way that makes perfect sense to the Huber scholar who has not previously adopted another system:[311]

309. *Astrology and the Seven Rays*, pp. 68-78.

310. *Astrology and the Seven Rays*, pp. 47, 114; Alice A. Bailey, *Esoteric Astrology*, A Treatise on the Seven Rays, 3, 3rd edn (New York and London: Lucis, 1997), pp. 506-07, 648-49. Bailey lists the seven sacred planets as Vulcan, Mercury, Venus, Jupiter, Saturn, Neptune, and Uranus, and the five non-sacred planets as Mars, Earth, Pluto, Moon veiling a planet, and Sun veiling a planet.

311. *Astrology and the Seven Rays*, pp. 16, 35, 80, 124-25.

Major Rays	**Types**	**Words of Power**	**Crosses**	**Pla-nets**
Will and Power; Atma	Will	I assert the fact	Cardinal	♇ ☉
Love and Wisdom; Buddhi	Love	I see the greatest light	Mutable	♆ ☽
Active Intelligence; Manas	Active-Practical	Purpose itself am I	Fixed	♅ ♄
Minor Rays			**Elements**	
Harmony through Conflict	Creative-Artistic	Two merge into one	Water	♀
Concrete Knowledge	Scientific	Three minds unite	Air	☿
Devotion and Idealism	Devotional-Idealistic	The highest light controls	Fire	♂
Ceremonial Magic, Ritual and Order	Organiza-tional	The highest and the lowest meet	Earth	♃

This rearrangement of celestial energy patterns is not so surprising, given that at least two psychotherapists with Theosophical connections—Assagioli, and Gordon-Brown, who was a director and trustee of the Lucis Trust as well as the CTP—made seamless transitions to transpersonal psychology during the 1960s-70s. Assagioli's conception of psychosynthesis has been aligned with the integral psychology of transpersonal philosopher Wilber, and a most useful rendering of the 'will to wholeness and the seven main archetypal energies', corresponding to the seven rays, can be found in the printed edition of transpersonal workshops led by Gordon-Brown and Somers.

The transpersonal aspires to wholeness not perfection, and the four components of will are: 'the will to power, the will to love, the will to knowledge, and the will to truth'.[312] Avoiding controversy, the descriptions in *The Raincloud of Knowable Things*, from which I have taken excerpts,[313] do not include astrological correlatives, but by connecting them with Huber initiation and designation of planets,[314] it becomes clear how well they interrelate.

Quotations from Gordon-Brown and Somers	**Paraphrased summaries from Huber**
1. Ruler. *The will to power* is about direction and purpose, force, energy and action... As forces of justice, they are bent upon human rights and freedoms, valuing the power to accomplish—and using it well... The *drawbacks* of natural rulers include isolation... In its *shadow* are violence, destructiveness and brute force... They *need* to link with other people—become inclusive, heart-based, decentralized...	Ray 1 is connected with the third initiation on the cardinal cross, from Sun to Pluto, and the renunciation of personal power to work for the divine plan.
2. Priest-healer. *The will to love...* doctors, healers... motivated by the need for expansion, initiation and fulfilment, longing for awareness and wisdom... inspiring others with their compassion... The *drawbacks* cluster mainly around invasion... Inflation is in the *shadow* of their longing for inner subjective truth... They *need* protection, to be pulled back from people with tremendous neurotic or psychotic needs...	Ray 2 is connected with the second initiation on the mutable cross, from Moon to Neptune, and the replacement of separateness by compassion for all creation.

312. Gordon-Brown and Somers, *Raincloud*, pp. 285-95 (p. 285).

313. *Raincloud*, pp. 285-95.

314. *Astrology and the Seven Rays*, pp. 118-22.

3. Thinker, philosopher (higher mind). *The will to knowledge* characterizes a different kind of teacher, one who values consciousness, the light of the mind and pure understanding... the thrust is towards ideas and intelligence... The *drawbacks...* lie in the very activity of their thought processes, the constant mental manipulation... In the *shadow* of the Thinker lies a dogmatic manipulator who may try to brainwash other people... They *need* to select and discriminate, to be still... reflecting on the problem or issue or need.	Ray 3 is connected with the first initiation on the fixed cross, from Saturn to Uranus, with 'stillness, restraining the urge to act, cultivating peace, learning to be silent; developing the love of truth... showing integrity, honesty, magnanimity, developing goodwill'.
4. Mediator, conciliator. Moved by the *will to harmony*, they seek peace *through* conflict and its resolution... explorers... artists seeking to capture vision harmoniously through music, acting, painting... The *drawback...* involves falling into chaos and despair... Subject to bi-polar swings, they lurch from over-enthusiasm and recklessness into a *shadow* of depression and self-flagellation. Their *need* is to make decisions and to act, to develop steadfastness.	Ray 4, connected with Venus and water, suffers decision-making crises and pathological sensitivity, while longing for harmony and unity. Transformation results from the awakening of intuition, generosity, quick understanding and perception.
5. Scientist, alchemist—knowledge through research. *The will to truth*, the objective practical fact... searching, analyzing, experimenting, measuring... The *drawbacks* include possible lack of ethics...Wedded to research, some seekers after truth may be less detached that they believe... Detachment is needed. Science is changing. There are new paradigms. Scientists themselves, taking a new position, have begun to speak of consciousness.	Ray 5, connected with Mercury and air needs to recognize the transience of matter, develop a 'delusion-free sense of reality and a sense of reverence for life', and study 'the science of the soul'.

6. Devotee, idealist. The energy of *the will to perfection* has given rise to the idealists and adorers of the Christian era. The last two thousand warlike years have elevated this ideal above the archetype of wholeness (which would have led us to integrate, not fight). When a minor archetype is lifted over a major, problems ensue... The *drawbacks* are many. Devotees love... particularly and selectively... Their *shadow* includes bigotry and exclusivity... their devotion to causes and ideals, their fanatical energy, are both splendid and terrifying.	Ray 6, connected with Mars and fire, requires the idealist to replace fanatical one-sidedness with serenity, inner balance, respect for the opinions of others, and constructive goals.
7. Magician—making manifest. Those under this archetype can anchor and earth, bringing components together coherently, understanding people... Their *drawbacks* include inflexibility... The *shadow* of the magician includes inflation, manipulation and deception... all magicians *need* humane purpose—to develop true magic, true ritual.	Ray 7, connected with Jupiter and earth, has organizational ability and loves rhythm, 'the cyclical, ritual process of things'. He is 'able to wait until paths open up for him to reach his goal', and transformation involves collaboration with others, sharing spiritual development and helping to implement a collective or cosmic plan.

Increasing awareness of 'the ray energies which we are told emanate from the Great Bear in seven great out-raying streams of force' generates greater harmony with the cosmos, so that integrity of soul and self radiate into daily life and, in the course of the last half-century, what we understand by the rays and how we can become better aligned with them so as to support humanity, the earth, and the cosmos more effectively has been drawn down from the stars into psychosynthesis, inclusiveness, and unity.[315]

315. Bailey, *Esoteric Astrology*, p. 421; *Astrology and the Seven Rays*, p. 114.

In her response to the question, 'What is esotericism?' Louise moves on from defining the seven rays, the spectrum, and light as 'the centralizing life principle' to the Akashic records

> ...in which everything that has ever lived is preserved. In old esoteric books, the ethereal dimension was also compared to a desert in which the traces of all the ages remain, including those of every human life. The moon node horoscope includes these traces in the sand.[316]

Her introduction of the moon node chart at this point is no accident and, although I have largely concentrated here on astrological psychology and the seven rays, arguably the Hubers' greatest gift to esotericism is the moon node chart, considered with reference to the three charts of individuals in chapter 4 and the ongoing relevance of astrological psychology in chapter 5.

---

316. *Astrology and the Seven Rays*, pp. 5-6.

4. Moon Node Astrology, Karma, and the Three Charts

Astrologers will eventually find it necessary to cast three horoscopes.[317]

The necessity for three charts to capture the complexity of modern life was recorded by Alice Bailey in *A Treatise of White Magic*, and astrological psychology works with a moon node chart as the key to karma, the unconscious, and past lives, and a house chart as an extended guide to our interface with the environment and its demands, as well as the natal chart—which is an imprint of the living personality with its underlying motivations, and an essential expression of who we are. This chapter begins by explaining the mechanics of the moon node chart and how it connects us with the past. The second section outlines the meaning of the house chart and how it reflects our engagement with this world and our contribution to it. The third part examines the chart of Professor Alan Deyermond, who encouraged me to explore astrological symbolism in medieval Spanish poetry and was kind enough to share his birth data with me. His three charts each portray a different motivation, and provide an example of how an individual can draw on diverse resources to make the most of a fulfilling life and leave a lasting legacy. I then consider my three charts—also motivationally different in aspect structure—to demonstrate working with karma. I pay special attention to Saturn, often referred to as the Lord of Karma, and to the Uranus cycle. There are some concluding remarks to round off this chapter.

317. Bailey, *Treatise of White Magic*, p. 439.

4.1 The Moon Node Chart: A Mirror of the Past

In his *History of Astrology*, Kocku von Stuckrad singled out the moon node chart—always shown to the left of the natal chart—as an example of how innovative twentieth-century astrology in the esoteric and Theosophical traditions could be.[318] It is like a mirror image of the natal chart in which the North Node and Ascendant switch places, and the signs rotate in the opposite direction, clockwise instead of anticlockwise:

> By comparing the Moon Node horoscope with the natal chart, we can discover the deeper meaning of "blows of fate" and find out what learning process awaits us.[319]

Alternatively, the nodal chart can enable us to make sense of things that happened imperceptibly in the early part of our lives, and help us find our way through the labyrinth. It offers invaluable assistance to a therapist, by uncovering material that

> can exhibit spiritual connections, reveal deeper roots, and examine questions raised in connection with the laws of evolution, human karma, reincarnation, the meaning of life, and further growth.[320]

Feedback recorded by the Hubers indicates that some students discover the roots of their problems in former lives, whereas others are able to make sense of circumstances in their present lives, get them into perspective, and see them as part of a greater whole.[321] In this map there may be skeletons lurking in cupboards, a treasure trove of hidden resources, or a blend of darkness and light. Here we find Jung's shadow landscape.

A full understanding of how the natal chart interfaces with the nodal chart requires a brief introduction to the Hubers' system of age progression. The circle of the natal chart is divided into twelve houses using Walter Koch's birthplace house system, which calculates houses of unequal size relating to the latitude and

---

318. Stuckrad, *Astrología*, p. 414.

319. *Moon-Node*, p. xv.

320. *Moon-Node*, p. xv.

321. *Moon-Node*, p. xvi.

longitude of the place of birth, the date, hour, and season of year, and the angle of the earth. Some houses focus on one sign, whereas others may cover three, and the energy contained in the intercepted middle sign lacks easy access to the outer world. The significance of this arrangement is captured by Louise:

> The house system is structured around the human being and constitutes a field of sensitivity with respect to the environment. You could say that a human being always carries his house system with him and that it forms part of his aura and vital space.[322]

Each of the twelve houses represents six years of life in a 72-year cycle. This does not imply that life closes down after seventy-two years. A notable example to the contrary is that of Nelson Mandela, who was released from prison in his seventy-second year to lead South Africa into a new era. The 'cyclic phenomenon has much to do with the law of cause and effect', known as karma.[323] Every house has a rhythmic wave sequence, starting at its most extrovert point on the crest or house cusp, gently receding with measured energy flow towards the balance point before ebbing to its lowest point of introspection and rising again to meet the crest of the next wave. The natal chart life clock measures out the passage on earth from cradle to grave. By contrast, the nodal chart timepiece flows through equal houses disconnected from time and space, recording what the philosopher, Henri Bergson called *la durée*, or duration. As explained by Rudhyar:

> The Bergsonian concept of duration is quite similar to that of time experienced by an existential whole as 'the passing', that is, before the concept of separate moments—or we might say, of time units—dominates the intellectualized consciousness of the human being.[324]

---

322. Louise Huber, cited in Solé, p. 63, and translated by me from Spanish into English.

323. *Transformation*, p. 6; for more information on age progression and how it works, see Joyce Hopewell, *Using Age Progression: Understanding Life's Journey* (Knutsford: HopeWell, 2013).

324. Rudhyar, *Planetarization*, p. 41; see intensity curve, p. 12.

A flashback releasing a flood of ancestral memories, unfinished business from a previous incarnation, or records of childhood trauma consigned to oblivion is more likely to appear in moon node progression than in natal house age progression but will, in all probability, be backed up by transits of slow-moving planets in aspect to the natal chart. Every thirty-six years the natal and nodal progression points coincide, and their crossing point represents not so much an immediate crisis as the gradual approach of a crossroads, where cumulative experience will fundamentally alter life direction. The indications of a crossing point can either appear in external events or reflect a subtle psychological transformation, and often one crossing point will manifest at one level and the second at another. If—despite switching Ascendant and North Node and rotating the signs in reverse—any planet falls in the same house in both charts, themes associated with that planet signpost ongoing work to be done.

4.2 The House Chart: Our Interface with the Environment

Whereas natal chart houses vary in size, signs representing archetypal inheritance are of equal size, and aspect patterns depict a 'person's profoundly-felt life motivation', the house chart has equal houses, and the extending and squeezing of signs can dramatically change the aspect patterns, revealing how inherent motivation might fall under environmental pressure to perform certain tasks. In psychotherapy, this tension might be expressed in terms of nature and nurture. Where the two charts are similar, the individual experiences fewer discrepancies between inner will and outer duty or expectation than where the radix and house charts are radically different. This third chart, developed by Bruno and Louise's son Michael Alexander, and tested by groups in 1975, offers an explanation as to why some children are misunderstood by their parents:[325]

325. *Transformation*, pp. 80-84.

> The house horoscope shows the influence of nurture... It may take the form of the environmental stimulus that spurs us on to further development, or of restrictions and constraints from which we want to free ourselves.[326]

Whereas, in Michael's view, it primarily 'shows the effects and influences of the environment in which we grew up', it can also help to identify the modification of attitudes required to live in harmony with the mores of a country to which someone has migrated. Huber astrology is non-predictive, and the house chart is not necessarily a vision of the future. It offers a picture of what the world asks us to handle and, by juxtapositioning natal and house charts, we can draw from both and learn how to synthesise the two.

4.3 The Three Charts of Professor Alan Deyermond FBA

The three charts of Alan Deyermond are strikingly dissimilar, each with a different motivational structure. The nodal chart (bottom left) has a monumental solidity, the natal chart has the linearity of a pioneer, while in the house chart (bottom right) relational triangles are cemented by a dynamic learning figure. Alan's natal chart depicts an enthusiastic and impetuous individual, ever eager to research new territory, while the Ascendant in Cancer, Sun in Pisces, and Moon in the 4th house are hallmarks of an affectionate family man, and these two sides of his life were, according to his daughter, 'wholly interdependent'.[327] Yet, with only the natal chart for guidance, the astrologer might wonder how this much loved Hispanist managed to complete so many major projects, and give such great attention to reference detail, especially if the session took place in the disorderly office, where:

326. *Transformation*, p. 92.

327. Ruth Deyermond, 'Forward', *Medieval Hispanic Studies in Memory of Alan Deyermond*, ed. by Andrew M. Beresford, Louise M. Haywood, and Julian Weiss, *Serie A, Monografías*, 315 (Woodbridge and Rochester, NY: Támesis, 2013), p. xiii.

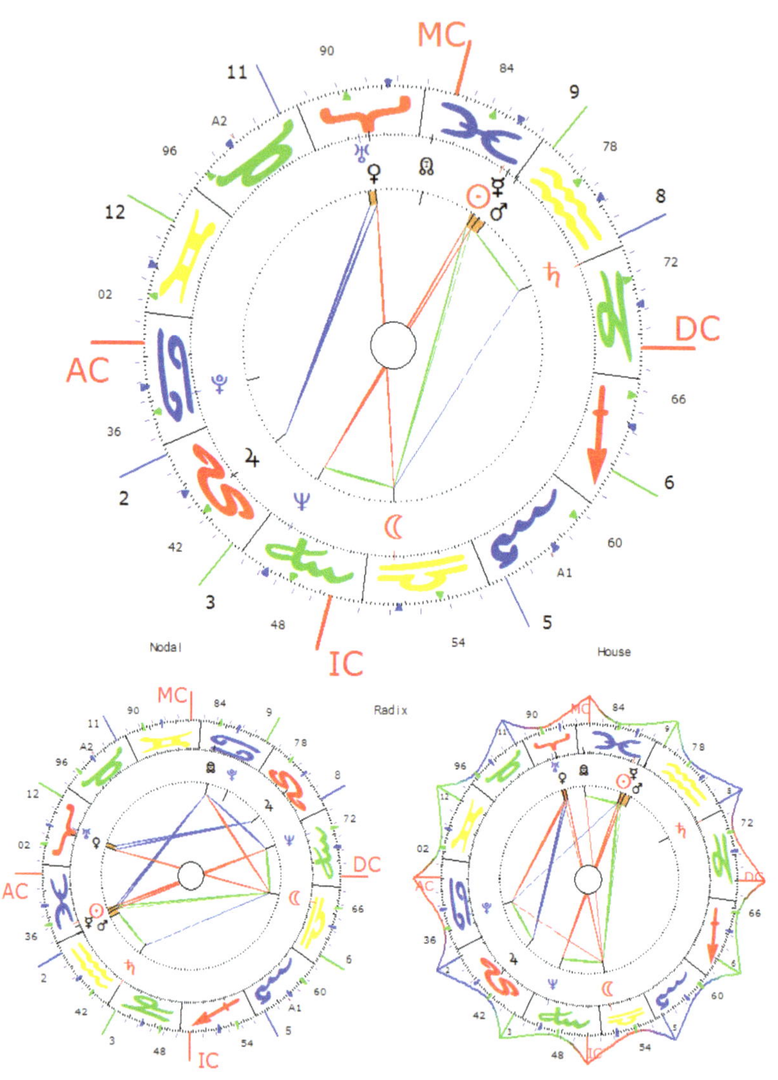

Alan Deyermond

b. 24 February 1932, 13:15, Cairo, Egypt (RR: A)

> The family included a succession of poodles, whose presence among the heaped papers in Alan's office could disconcert visitors as he located with implausible speed the offprint or typescript they needed to discuss.[328]

Invariably, he found the necessary paper with military precision, whether it crouched beneath a teetering pile on a desk or lurked behind three rows on a bookshelf. The pioneering energy and directness of his compass-like natal chart is supported by the solid structure of the nodal chart, where a fixed pattern, known to Huber astrologers as a streamer, processes volumes of information and generates powerful currents. Resembling the Great Pyramid of Giza, it shows how this sensitive intellectual, born in Cairo's Army hospital, harnessed the military strategy and tactics of his ancestors to locating books and scripts, meticulous research and editing, dedication to duty, and completion of the tasks he had undertaken.[329] The union of past and present manifested in his life at more than one level. In his *Guardian* obituary, Nicholas Round likened him to a modern-day Franciscan—Christian, family-oriented, vegetarian, and a lover of animals.

However much Alan appreciated history, choosing medieval Spanish literature as his subject, he was not entrenched in the past, and he did everything to make his subject relevant to the present and to prepare for the future. He established a Medieval Hispanic Research Seminar that continues to be vibrant. Not only did he extend the scope of standard texts of medieval Christian Spain taught in an undergraduate course, he actively encouraged research into Kabbalah, astrology, alchemy, the evil eye, the dance of death, the frontier ballad, and the Catalan inheritance put on hold during Franco's regime. His successful students, recollected:

> Alan Deyermond combined formidable knowledge with comic idiosyncracy, and the combination, though at times unsettling,

---

328. Nicholas Round, 'Alan Deyermond obituary', <http://www.guardian.co.uk/education/2009/oct/14/alan-deyermond-obituary/print> [accessed 16 October 2009].

329. *Aspect Pattern*, pp. 235-36.

> inspired our eventual university careers. It was not just the obviously quixotic moments of his lectures—battling with class furniture to illustrate scenes from the *Poem of the Cid*, engaging in dialogue with Tom, his poodle—that brought the subject to life. Nor was it just the clarity with which he expounded the complex and unfamiliar. It was also the ability to make students feel that they, too, could participate in the academic debate.[330]

The mutable house chart shows two people debating. Alan was not only enthusiastic about his subject, he actively encouraged students worldwide to believe in themselves, treating them as equals, and was genuinely interested in whatever their knowledge and experience might bring to his expanding field of research. In a Festschrift, his daughter describes a favourite photograph from his later life, taken at a conference in León:

> He is sitting by a wall in the sunshine, writing down a bibliographic reference for a graduate student. He looks delighted and completely absorbed, doing what he most enjoyed: sharing knowledge...[331]

The key to his immense success as a teacher lies in Pluto. Unaspected in the natal chart, it became his larger than life teaching persona and, in the house chart it linked up with Venus-conjunct-Uranus and Jupiter in a medium learning triangle, to become one side of a stimulating debate. Increasingly, he grew into this personality, which became a manifest expression of his soul. This ensured the transmission of his legacy through his students, though there was a downside, reflected in the disconnection of Saturn in Aquarius in the house chart. Inevitably those around him, and his own quixotic nature, would make impossible demands and—as Alan's health deteriorated—fewer of the schematic typescripts of his investigative and entertaining lectures became finished articles.[332] So the latest monograph in his memory, lovingly assembled by colleagues and former students, adds little to his scholarly portfolio but is a most fitting tribute to a master of transmission who showed others how to follow their dream.

---

330. Round, 2009.

331. Ruth Deyermond, p. xiv.

332. Intro. by David Hook to Alan Deyermond, '"Esta tan triste partida" (*Conde Dirlos*, v. 28a): maridos y padres ausentes', *Deyermond*, pp. 293-95.

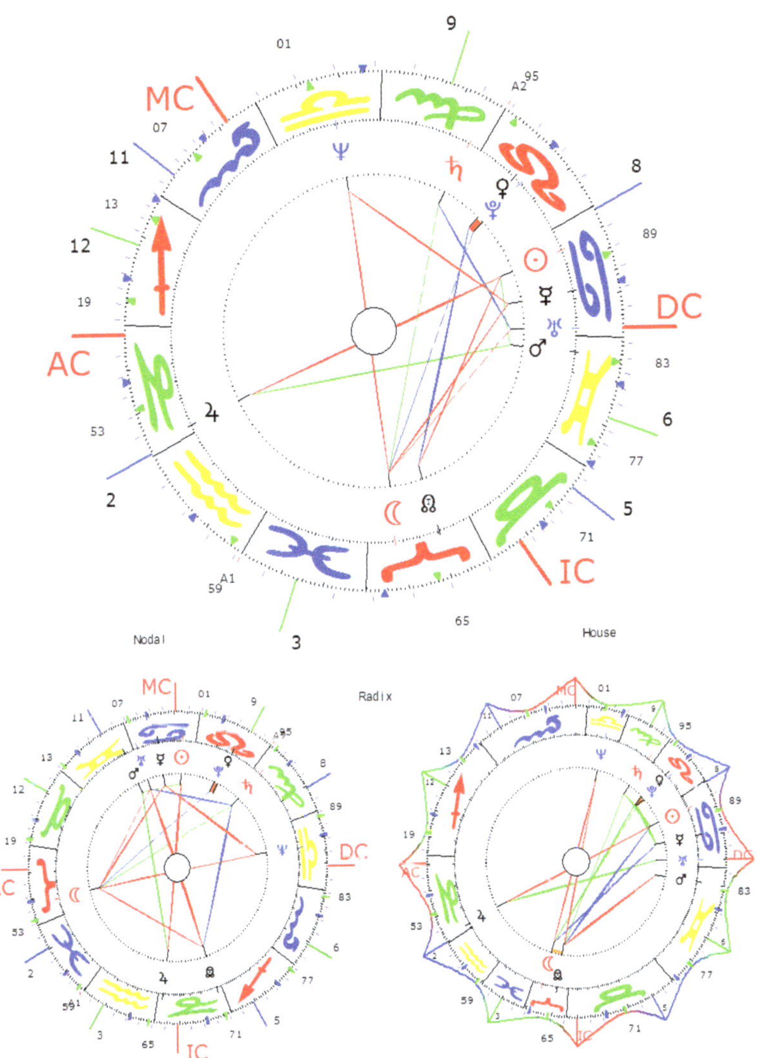

Sue Lewis

b. 16 July 1949, 19:45 BST, London, UK (RR: A)

4.4 Saturn and Uranus in the Three Charts of the Author

On Saturday 16 July 1949, at 19:45 British Summer Time, I was born in a nursing home in Wanstead, to the East of London on the edge of Epping Forest, during a heavy thunderstorm on a hot summer evening. My birth was later than expected, and I had grown too large for my mother's small frame by the time I made my reluctant entrance into the world. She had an out-of-body experience just prior to my birth, but returned to her body to help my head safely out into the world before being sedated. The drama surrounding my birth is aptly portrayed by Uranus on the Descendant. A practical outcome of my mother's frailty was that she was unable to breastfeed me because she couldn't produce any milk. Nor could she carry me upstairs, which meant that from an early age I was often handled by the men of the family. My mother had married a widower eighteen years older than she, who had wooed her with poetry and impressed her with his intellect. He had a son by his first marriage, almost nineteen at the time of my birth, who lived with us until I was three years old. Reflecting with hindsight on the period of time between my brother's departure and starting school at age five, I can see how my father loomed large in my emotional life, with lots of hugs, a head full of romantic poetry, and the Christian message.

The first image I have for my natal chart is of a flowerpot with a tender sapling blown over in the storm. Some of my students picture a bow and arrow, and on occasion I shoot myself in the foot! I can also imagine an umbrella, which I hold onto tightly as I walk straight into the driving wind of Uranus. This mostly mutable chart of a shy personality, who values relationships and shared activities as well as independent research, is complicated by three separate manifestations of the crab archetype in the 7th house of partnerships: an over-responsive and people-pleasing Sun at the end of the sign and house, linked to a prominent Jupiter in Capricorn stressed behind the 2nd house cusp and an introspective Mars in Gemini close to a low point; a generally balanced and thoughtful

Mercury in the middle acting as a mouthpiece for emotional Moon and imaginative Neptune whose ease of communication is thwarted by the interception of their signs; and an independent, reactive, resourceful, and transpersonal Uranus, over-exposed on the angle at the beginning of the sign and house, and linked to Moon and Saturn in a large learning triangle. If the mutable natal chart depicts a battered sapling, then the fixed nodal chart is a glass conservatory into which the bruised plant retreats for respite care. The more fluid and cardinal house chart resembles a barrow with a guy on top, wheeling purposefully forward, seeking reparation and renewal however painful the process may be. Drawing on Grof's findings that conditions surrounding our birth have a symbolic significance on the pattern of our lives, Louise links Uranus on the horizontal axis with 'the cracking and transcending of boundaries' and the ability to 'hit on unusual solutions'.[333] Uranus in Cancer is not only prominent in my horoscope; it is also uniquely representative of the different motivations of each of my three charts. Uranus, Saturn, Moon, and North Node participate in an irregular, four-sided, fixed ambivalence figure in the nodal chart that nurtures cherished memories like tender plants, guarding their roots. Moon reaches out to Saturn and Uranus in a mutable, retrograde learning triangle in the natal chart, which often has to go through several cycles to find a solution. While Uranus escapes from more conservative partners in the house chart to join forces with Jupiter in a freewheeling green quincunx that raises doubts and dilemmas, and seeks solutions to demoralizing circumstances. Because it is on the 'you' side of the chart, Uranus is not as self-initiatory or innovative as Uranus on the 'I' side might be, and it can be subsumed by stronger influences, but it has an uncanny ability to scent the way forward and find a half-concealed path through life's confusing maze. In my experience, Uranus transits hit hard, while opening up new gateways to self-becoming.

---

333. Louise Huber, 'Birth Time Imprinting and the Transpersonal Planets', *Conjunction*, 30 (2001), p. 4.

Saturn is both the exoteric and esoteric ruler of my Capricorn Ascendant. Situated in the earth sign of Virgo, making a sextile to Uranus and receiving a one-way quincunx from Moon, it occupies the angle of doubt and resolution in a large learning triangle. In the family chart of Huber astrology, Saturn represents mother, Sun father, and Moon the child, so Saturn's high location in the chart towards the end of the 8th house of inheritance gives an indication of the dominant role my mother would assume. At another level, Saturn is associated with storing of memory and preference for structure, and in Virgo there is a liking for precise detail.[334] Despite the reversal of planetary positions in natal and nodal charts outlined above, Saturn appears in the same house in both, emphasizing the karmic nature of themes relating to Saturn in the 8th house that need addressing as part of the process of self-becoming. Rosa Solé's vivid description of the issues facing people with planets in the eighth house of fixed water is translated below:

> People with planets in the 8th house need to experience some kind of character corrective, transforming or purifying their motives before they feel and become useful members of any society, group, or team. The spiritual task of this house can be condensed into the single word detachment, given that a constant search for self-honesty accompanies such a person through crises and disappointments along the road to transformation. Everything that at one moment represents security, success, social value, etc. is but a role or mask that can suddenly disappear, casting the individual into a state of suffering until with phoenix-like ability s/he attains a new state of consciousness, just as rusty metal needs an acid bath before it can once again sparkle like gold.[335]

By translating *desapego* as 'detachment' I aim to convey several concepts: the observer subpersonality, keeping watch; stoic control of unruly emotions by careful direction, not denial, suppression or sublimation; disidentification with the immediate concerns of the human ego; and adoption of a cosmic perspective.

---

334. *Astrological Psychosynthesis*, p. 42.
335. Solé, p. 97.

Designated tasks come to a head at appointed times in a person's life, and Huber astrology identifies these firstly through its specific method of age progression, and secondly through the transit cycles of slow-moving planets observed and interpreted by most astrologers. My first crossing point, when the natal and nodal age points converged, was on 8 September 1959 on the cusp of Aquarius and Pisces in the 2nd house, in opposition to Saturn in the 8th and trine Uranus in the 7th. Looking back over the previous year, on 8 November 1958 my father died, after Christmas my mother returned to full-time teaching, in May 1959, my maternal grandmother died, and that September, my half-brother married and went to live permanently in Canada. Looking forward to the next year, in April 1960, we moved from a largish semi-detached house with a private garden in East London to a new two-bedroom, fourth-floor flat with shared grounds in South London, where I would attend a local school for one term before going to boarding school for several years. Aged ten, I grew up fast, rapidly becoming my mother's partner in a world where widows were treated with so little respect that I questioned many social values. Later I would realize I had been out of touch with my emotions since January 1955 when my father's heart condition had deteriorated and he retreated into himself. With Moon, Venus, Neptune, and Pluto intercepted in my chart, it would take me time to learn how to read my own feelings. This first crossing point, in 1959, involved many circumstantial changes and was outwardly a real turning point in my life, overriding and concealing subtle changes that had taken place before, whereas the second crossing point in autumn 1995 precipitated my inner journey.

Although my mother and I always trusted each other, we did not start out as the ideal companions we became, and the one-way quincunx from Moon, representing the emotional child, to Saturn as protective mother provides evidence that ours was a relationship worked on by both. Much was expected of the daughter of a highly qualified, well-read, and distinguished father of mature years, and my mother often complained that I was not operating to my full potential. She was critical of indifferent teaching, but towards the end of 1966 an Italian graphologist suggested I might be living under some kind of defence mechanism. The natal age point was making a small talent triangle with natal Saturn and Uranus, while the nodal age point was in opposition to the Sun, and transiting Saturn and Uranus were in opposition to each other, both in harmonious aspect to the Sun. New horizons were opening and much more seemed possible. In the opinion of the graphologist, my intelligent ego would soon break out of this constraint. Huber astrology relates Uranian transformation to breaking eggshells, and I became aware of the need to progress beyond restrictive but protective boundaries. I was eager to learn and discover.

My mother must have been one of very few people who subscribed simultaneously to *The Humanist* published by the Rationalist Press and *Prediction Magazine*. She soon dropped former while maintaining a lifelong, but surface interest in the latter. In March 1969, she suggested I see a palmist-clairvoyant and, with trepidation, I went for a consultation. Uranus was squaring itself in the early degrees of Libra, with transiting Jupiter in conjunction. Although Jupiter and Uranus are in different aspect patterns in my natal and nodal charts, they form a linear quincunx in my house chart illustrating a scary experience taking me well outside my comfort zone. I struggled to relate to a reconstruction of my early history based on the map of my palm and clairvoyant perception, but I did not. The palmist said I had experienced a tragic loss around the age of five. I told him my father died when I was nine. He objected to the time frame and tried to describe an emotional loss in my early childhood of which I had no recollection.

Two years later, this accurate timing of unacknowledged trauma in my early life enabled me to catalogue the emotional volcano that erupted from my unconscious in 1971, stimulated by a combination of essential reading for a dissertation on theatre of cruelty and a one-to-one encounter with a man who pressed all the right buttons. My first meeting with a hitherto forgotten emotional past morphed into an alchemical trial by water and days of unstoppable weeping.[336] I went home that weekend and my mother corroborated my withdrawal into a shell around the age of five-and-a-half with the unaccountable deterioration of my father's heart condition while she was visiting her mother. She knew her husband had changed in character as well as health, although he never spoke about what had upset him, and a wall of silence between father and daughter was camouflaged by intelligent family games and shared programmes on television.

There was, therefore, tangible evidence of something more than primal phantasy, in the form of honest recognition by my mother that the apparently charming relationship between her charismatic husband and highly responsive daughter, which she had initially encouraged, had transgressed safe boundaries, and she had not known how to broach such a delicate subject with her husband. Events took over. Thereafter she focused her efforts on nursing him back to health and finding suitable diversions and creative outlets for her daughter. Two years later, she had an operation for breast cancer followed by radiotherapy, and made a miraculous recovery, becoming the parent who would teach me how to survive.

Freud's theory of trauma, as explained by the psychoanalyst Jean Laplanche, is of relevance to my experiences in the spring and early summer of 1971, as I approached my twenty-second birthday:

> Trauma consists of two moments: the trauma, in order to be psychic trauma, doesn't occur just in one moment. First there is the implantation of something coming from outside. And this experience, or the memory of it, must be reinvested in a second moment, and then it becomes traumatic. It is not the first act which is traumatic, it is the internal reviviscence of this memory that becomes traumatic.[337]

---

336. Somers, *Fires of Alchemy*, pp. 75-76.

337. Cathy Caruth, 'An interview with Jean Laplanche' (2001) <pmc.iath.virginia.edu/text-only/issue.101/11.2caruth.txt> [accessed 25 November 2014], p. 1, searched following a lecture by John Fletcher, 'The Unconscious, the Id and the Other: Laplanchean Developments of Freud', at a conference, 'Histories and Theories of the Unconscious', Queen Mary University of London, 22 November 2014.

In my case, retrieved memories slotted into place in a series of tempestuous flashbacks during an emotional voyage lasting several weeks, as I was tossed by the swell towards an imagined harbour. I took comfort in the belief that the future envisioned by the clairvoyant two years previously would be as accurate as his reconstruction of my past, but it was not. Evidently my fanciful Neptune square Mercury had sprung into action in response to anticipated need for the person who pressed the start button to be there for me at the end of the journey. I must have conjured an involuntary thought form that took control of the clairvoyant session, supplying a happy ending not destined to become a reality. Mercury, the most balanced planet in my chart in terms of sign strength and energy output had, with lightning speed aided by Neptunian imagination, supplied the creative solution that would enable me to complete a difficult journey to recover lost memories without totally breaking down, though it was one that would embarrass me for many years to come.

By spring 1971, transiting Uranus had moved deeper into Libra, making a conjunction to natal Neptune, so transpersonal intuition and imagination joined forces beyond the field of consciousness. The nodal age point, in opposition to natal Uranus, was on the Ascendant representing the persona in the natal chart and on the North Node in the nodal chart, in the 4th house of family and roots deep in the collective consciousness. This is the fourth corner of the ambivalence figure in the moon node chart that I have likened to a fragile glass conservatory shattering under the impact of material washing up from the unconscious. My natal age point and transiting Saturn squared Venus conjunct Pluto in the 8th house, exacerbating emotional anguish, while forcing me to detach from the immediate desire for human love and warmth to complete a journey to self-discovery on which I had embarked.[338] This crisis devastated treasured memories, revisiting a childhood full of mental, emotional, and spiritual stimuli that suddenly appeared in a tainted light. Emotional distress was compounded by the

338. See Joyce Hopewell, *Using Age Progression*, pp. 68-69.

discovery that my inner drive to self-knowledge had manipulated my choice of academic subjects, though I should not have been so surprised at a time when I had to write French philosophical essays on Blaise Pascal, whose most memorable thought is: 'Le coeur a ses raisons que la raison ne connaît pas'. Notwithstanding my knowledge that heart supersedes reason, my enthusiasm and self-belief melted away. In the words of Linda Schierse Leonard:

> My ego identity, my notions about who I was, crumbled. There was in me a power stronger than my consciously acknowledged self. This power rolled over my attempts to control my life and events around me, as an avalanche changes the face of a mountain.[339]

I was unmasked, I had no credibility, and my thoughts and feelings were irrelevant. How could anyone take me seriously? Most people did not. While acknowledging that I was and am no more than an average linguist, I had over-identified with an ability to interpret some literary texts with flair, a predisposition I associate with stressed Jupiter, discussed in the previous chapter. The boundaries between scholar and seeker had been breached so comprehensively that I felt a complete fraud. The rational world, in which I had believed, disintegrated before my eyes.

Recovery would come in stages, as I established a practical career. For my mother's sake, I would do my best. With Saturn as my exoteric and esoteric ruling planet, I have an inbuilt stoic and pragmatist, capable of navigating 'a narrow ridge between two chasms'.[340] Knowing I could only solve a few problems at a time, I postponed whatever I could not immediately handle. There was so much sorrow and self-recrimination. The quest for freedom had brought tragic knowledge and labyrinthine complications. Access to the source of my problems in 1971 only through use of a fiction generated in the unconscious and mouthed by a clairvoyant utterly depleted my self-confidence. The well-developed critic, epitomized by Saturn, objected strongly to the engagement of such

339. Linda Schierse Leonard, *The Wounded Woman: Healing the Father-Daughter Relationship* (Boston and London: Shambhala, 1985), p. 155.

340. Klibansky, p. 254.

nebulous tactics in an honest search for truth, and my Saturnian and Mercurial-Neptunian subpersonalities have taken years to accommodate each other and declare a truce.

I have been extremely fortunate in having an insightful and dedicated mother, good physical health, and an ability to manage the practical side of life at times of emotional and mental upheaval. Saturn and Uranus have mostly worked well together, balancing common sense and method with resourceful intuition. In autumn 1977, around the time of my first Saturn return, I had a brief relationship with a man who introduced me to serious astrology and showed me how to draw and interpret a horoscope. At last I started to make sense of my destiny and begin the slow reparation. Between 1977 and 1988 I learnt a great deal of astrology and psychology, but not enough to prevent another emotional crisis in mid-life, as transiting Saturn and Uranus opposed Mars prior to Uranus opposition Uranus. There had been too many compromises and too few risks. Arroyo gives some profound insights into the nature of 8th house karma:

> One must give oneself to involvement with others and must learn to take risks now and then in order to allow the energy to flow freely and the deepest feelings and drives to come to the surface. The eighth house can be... related to the assimilation of many lifetimes' experiences with sexuality, the values attached to intimate human relationships, and the responsibilities involved in using any kind of power that has an impact on others.[341]

During my second crossing point, I booked a week of psychodrama, facilitated by Marcia Karp in Southern Spain. This second crossing point on the cusp of Leo and Virgo made a green quincunx to natal Jupiter as well as a sextile to Uranus, and there was a lot of goodwill in my environment. One November morning in 1995, as gales battered the Alpujarras, an amazing group of people I had only just met facilitated re-enactment of the crisis I had suffered twenty-four years earlier, bringing to a close the

---

341. Stephen Arroyo, *Astrology, Karma, and Transformation: The Inner Dimensions of the Birth Chart* (Davis, CA: CRCS, 1978), pp. 16-17.

multiple projections that had dogged the intervening period. This transformational experience was supported by transiting planets. Uranus and Neptune at the end of Capricorn brought transpersonal insight and unconditional love to my natal opposition between Jupiter and Sun, while my natal conjunction of Venus and Pluto in Leo, in the 8th house, received a square from Sun in Scorpio, trines from Mars and Jupiter in Sagittarius, and a quincunx from Saturn in Pisces. The effects would take time to filter through, but they would be lasting.

By the end of 1998, as my age point was nearing the end of Virgo, making a trine to Jupiter and a square to Mars, creating a new aspect structure—a dominant learning triangle—I was close to completing a paper on astrological symbolism in a fifteenth-century Spanish poem, starting the APA diploma in astrology, and embarking a CTP course in transpersonal perspectives, supplemented by transpersonal psychotherapy. Then I met the man of my life. Our physical alchemy was and is transmutative, but our minds operate differently, and he has had to be tolerant with my intellectual and soul-searching endeavours. Whereas he has transformed my emotional wellbeing, the encouragement of two skilful mentors, Alan Deyermond and Nicholas Goodrick-Clarke, has played a crucial role in the recovery of my intellectual mind, as well as the support of many friends.

Astrological interpretation has helped me trace this journey, enabling much negativity in my past to be transformed into love and enjoyment, and this synthesis of self enables me to make a more positive contribution to humanity and our world. The three charts of Huber astrology are particularly insightful in this kind of reconstruction, because the nodal chart can reach back into early or ancestral history, while the house chart can reach out into the environment, and the structure of the natal chart illustrates the individual psyche with all its sensitivities, conflicts, and ambitions.

4.5 Family Inheritance

In astrological psychology, the position of the Sun and its aspects describe the subject's perception of the person playing the role of the father in an individual's chart, while Saturn and its aspects reveal insights about mother, and the Moon represents the child. The Hubers, who associate reincarnation archetypes with the houses, their elements, and predominant planetary axes, highlight a karmic problem on the 'I-you' encounter axis across houses one and seven, regarding the self-preservation and self-assertion drives of the infant, especially during the first four years.[342] This is the axis of my Sun/Jupiter opposition. Although critical issues did not constellate until the age of five-and-a-half, when the age point came into conjunction with Jupiter, they were incipient before the age of four. While I was enveloped by my father, giving rapt attention to his reading or recital of romantic poetry or Christian prayer, my mother—concerned by my passivity and apparent lack of initiative—made strategic efforts to thrust me out into the world. My father loved me as a little girl, but unwittingly discouraged the development of my separate identity.[343] Confusion around this area can be astrologically related to the 7th house Sun's square to the nodal axis as well as its opposition to Jupiter. In Huber charts, the North Node forms part of the aspect structure, acting as a signpost towards growth, and drives associated with a planet that makes a square to the South and North Nodes are notoriously difficult to develop. My timid Cancerian Sun, squaring both Nodes, is inclined to take the line of least resistance by being compliant rather than assertive, whereas my Aries Moon square Uranus in Cancer bristles in annoyance when someone tries to take advantage. Working with these two sub-personalities is an ongoing process that requires strong and skilful will to achieve balance, harmony, and synthesis. My courageous mother tuned into these issues early on and assumed the compensatory role indicated by the high position of Saturn in

---

342. *Moon Node*, pp. 159-69; *Transformation*, pp. 6-9; see axis cross, p. 10.

343. Barbara Somers and Ian Gordon-Brown, *Symptom as Symbol: A Transpersonal Language*, ed. by Hazel Marshall (Dorset: Archive Publishing, 2010), pp. 156-57.

the upper hemisphere of my chart. At times, her criticism could be demoralizing but I always trusted her implicitly and, as I grow older, I realize what a wise and dedicated mother she was. Her character is reflected in my large retrograde learning triangle of Moon, Saturn and Uranus, a more uncertain and more probing structure than my mother's creative small talent triangle with Sun—three degrees deeper into Aries than my Moon—at the apex, making a sextile to Saturn in Gemini and Uranus conjunct Jupiter in Aquarius, all of them strong in sign, resourceful and determined. On occasions, she would comment on her own superficiality, knowing full well that her buoyant approach to life depended on her resistance to plumbing its depths.

Whereas, with the Sun in Cancer in the 7th house, brought up in the leafy suburbs of London in an educated family, I might have anticipated a conventional marriage, cementing a secure social position with that sense of containment and belonging every Cancerian craves, Uranus on the descendant signposts my appointment with destiny along an independent route. Uranus in the house chart tugs the strings of Jupiter, whose opposition to the Sun replicates an aspect in my father's chart. His Sun, at 4 degrees of Aquarius was in exact opposition to Jupiter in Leo. Strong aspects between Sun and Jupiter have been linked with complicated relationships between father and daughter, involving intellectual and spiritual as well as emotional issues, by Greg Bogart and Liz Greene. Greene considers that such an aspect 'says a great deal about Jupiterian qualities which the individual shares with his or her father', and she associates these characteristics with the *puer aeternus*, the eternal youth, who 'is usually promiscuous, intellectually and spiritually as well as physically and emotionally'.[344] Her interpretation is very relevant to my story so far, although I do not go along with her further comments about lack of commitment. Members of my family were by nature committed, ethical, and

344. Liz Greene, 'Jupiter as a Parental Significator in the Birth Horoscope', in *Orpheus*, pp. 33-47 (pp. 34-35); Bogart's interpretation of Sonia, in *Astrology and Spiritual Awakening* is referred to in the next chapter.

thoughtful, not least my father, and this tragedy occurred as a result of joyful self-indulgence in late middle-age, while the incisive mind switched off. Sadly, we never really knew each other, and I have had to construct an artefact of memory from photographs, hearsay, twisted recollections, and distorting myths. I supposedly inherited his feeling for literature. Yet I was his 'little cover girl', and we never had an intellectual conversation. His mother died shortly after his birth, so he spent his early years reading the Bible with his grandmother until his father remarried and took him back. At my father's funeral, his half-sister told my mother how their father had beaten him mercilessly as a boy. That was something he never spoke of. He was a lifelong pacifist who was horrified at the prospect of hurting anyone. Whereas his Christian faith sustained him after the unexpected death of his first wife, and he became an occasional lay preacher, his later jottings called Christianity into question and found no adequate answers.

I am abundantly aware of this Jupiter/Sun inheritance, with its propensity to spill over boundaries and, while I have had misgivings about including this personal narrative in an ambitious project covering a broad canvas, I also need to share it as part of a healing process that will resonate more widely. There is doubtless a transgenerational story that I was destined to excavate, expose, and transcend.[345]

4.6 Concluding Remarks

My narrative focuses on this life of relationships and their evolving patterns, as might be expected of someone in whose natal chart eight out of ten planets are in the Western, 'you' hemisphere, and seven in the thinking quadrant comprising houses seven, eight, and nine—the equivalent of Wilber's exterior individual

345. Anne Ancelin Schützenberger, *The Ancestor Syndrome: Transgenerational Psychotherapy and the Hidden Links in the Family Tree*, trans. by Anne Trager (London and New York: Routledge, 1998), pp. 90-92.

quadrant.[346] This deeply personal drama also resonates in the collective. Transpersonal psychology, as presented by CTP, makes an important change to Assagioli's egg diagram:

> The higher unconscious is the seedbed from which come inspiration, intuitive flashes, future knowledge. This upper, or deeper, supra-conscious level, overlying and underlying all, doesn't just lie on the top but permeates through. This is where we could put samadhi.[347] It is the inner area from which come flashes of intuition. It holds our future potential, that which lies just beyond reach, the evolution of consciousness. Here we meet Patanjali's 'raincloud of knowable things' being processed in the present and moving back into the past.[348] But we remember that this map too is not the country.
>
> Assagioli placed a symbol for the Self above even this. Here at the top of the egg, with the sun indicating the mystery of the Other, nirvana could be mapped.
>
> However, transpersonal psychology adds to Assagioli's map. Unlike some other psychologies, it holds that in each of us the Self—that which chooses the life—both knows and intervenes. So we map the transpersonal Self not only at the top, but also down below the bottom of the egg. Thus we map the link both up from down and down to the Self—from 'me', the little everyday ego. The Self is about the deep; it goes into the depths. We need to be clear about the difference between the two centres: the small personal 'I' in the middle, and the higher Self, here mapped at the top and bottom.[349]

In 1971, when I experienced a breakthrough in understanding, I encountered my Self in the depths. By choosing to write a dissertation on twentieth-century French theatre, I was tasked with comparing the verse drama of the *Cenci* by Percy Bysshe Shelley

---

346. Ken Wilber, *Integral Psychology: Consciousness, Spirit, Psychology, Therapy* (Boston and London: Shambhala, 2000), p. 62; see quadrants, p. 11.

347. Samadhi: a Vedic/Indian/Sanskrit term: a non-dualistic, one-pointed state where the consciousness of the experiencing subject becomes one with the object experienced; repr. in Gordon-Brown and Somers, *Raincloud*, p. 13 n. 8.

348. Bailey 1927, *The Light of the Soul: The Yoga Sutras of Patanjali*, 4, 29, p. 425, cited *Raincloud*, p. 13, n. 9.

349. Gordon-Brown and Somers, *Raincloud*, pp. 12-14; see egg, p. 13.

(1819) with Antonin Artaud's 1935 adaptation into condensed and jerky French, emphasizing fragmentation and naked pain. My father had introduced me to Shelley's *Skylark*, rising 'higher still and higher', not to his sadistic tragedy of incest and parricide, based on a manuscript from the archives of the Cenci Palace in Rome recording events that took place in 1599, and a painting by Guido Reni supposedly of Beatrice Cenci.[350] The appalling nature of the father-daughter relationship depicted in the play jarred hidden memories of our relationship through antithesis, not similarity. Insofar as Artaud's intention was to create a theatre 'that would be like a shock treatment, galvanize, shock people into feeling', you could say that I was a posthumous success story though, of course, it was not the only activating factor at that crucial time.[351]

1971 spawned a dismal British film, *Family Life*, in which hypocritical parents and self-righteous doctors accentuate the problems a pregnant young woman called Janice, who is struggling to coordinate body, mind and heart. Her father made the chance remark that he and Janice had had fun when she was little, and it stuck in my mind as if it were the underlying mantra. Again, there is no direct parallel, but memory is selective as it tries to fit together the pieces of an emerging story. I was in touch with a universal archetype but the connecting images I encountered did not resonate with my own experience, so I would need a far more subtle symbolic system to unfold its essence. According to the principles of Jung's method, as explained by Ira Progoff:

> When we practice the method of amplification in order to enlarge our inner symbolic experiences, we can maintain the integrity of the process only when we work with images and symbols that are actually our own in the sense that they have happened within our own inner experience. Otherwise there is an unnecessary dishonesty that breaks the authenticity of the individuation process.[352]

350. *The Poetical Works of Percy Bysshe Shelley*, intro. by Richard Garnett (London and Melbourne: Ward, Lock, 1931), pp. 205-50, 374-76.

351. McGilchrist quotes Artaud in conversation with Anaïs Nin, p. 396.

352. Ira Progoff, *Jung, Synchronicity, and Human Destiny: Noncausal Dimensions of Human Experience* (New York: Delta, 1973), p. 33.

Transpersonal astrology, in particular the Huber method, has enabled me to own and transcend my experiences, though Rudhyar is cautious regarding what we might expect:

> Transpersonal astrology should not be approached with the expectation that it may solve any or all personal problems. It can only help an individual... transcend these problems by clearly, objectively, and unemotionally understanding where they fit into the larger, transformative pattern of a step-by-step unfoldment of innate, but mostly latent potentiality.[353]

Increasing numbers of accusations are being aired on the media in the twenty-first century, as cases of historical trauma come into the light, their revelations corresponding astrologically to the transiting squares between Uranus in Aries and Pluto in Capricorn. In some instances, there is evidence of evil and abusive behaviour with cover-ups linked to financial gain, misplaced loyalty, or changing social mores. Other situations are more nebulous, reflecting perhaps a slippage of boundaries with varying repercussions for the individuals concerned. What is the meaning of each situation, and how can it be brought to a close so that those involved can breathe new life? Each episode has its own story, while also being part of a greater upheaval in our society as we re-examine codes of behaviour.

Several astrologers have written insightful books on karma in the birth chart without necessarily adopting the Huber method. Arroyo emphasizes the imprint of karmic patterns on the water houses four, eight, and twelve, making a useful distinction between the latter two:

> The primary difference between the eighth and the twelfth houses is that, whereas eighth house planets have to be confronted immediately and worked through, twelfth house planets can often be transcended. In the first case, one brings to the surface the old tendencies in order to transform them through immediate and intensive involvement, whereas in the latter case, one rises above the problems entirely.[354]

353. Rudhyar, *Multilevel*, p. 122.
354. Arroyo, *Karma*, p. 17.

Judy Hall makes clear: 'Belief in karma and reincarnation does not exclude a belief in fate or chance, nor does it imply a fatalistic viewpoint'. Rather,

> The pattern of cause and effect laid down in previous incarnations is reflected in the heavens at the moment of birth and the incarnating soul chooses a time of entry which will offer the conditions most conducive to growth and development... it has freewill built into it.[355]

Our task is to work with our script to bring about synthesis of self and spiritual progress.

Behind the three charts of astrological psychology, more deeply embedded complexes can be accessed with the guidance of a karma click chart, used by the German depth psychologist Wolfhard König.[356] At these levels of intricate analysis and synthesis, Huber astrology can help both the individual and the therapist reach into the depths and shore up the fragmented personality as it strives towards synthesis and builds a bridge to the soul. As Faivre wrote:

> It must be realized that on the most elevated plane, the esoteric, astrology is less a science of divination than a body of knowledge—a gnosis—of invisible relationships between stars and men.[357]

---

355. Judy Hall, *Patterns of the Past: The Birthchart, Karma and Reincarnation*, 2nd edn, rev. (Bournemouth: Wessex Astrologer, 2000), pp. 4 and 45.

356. Wolfhard König, *The Karma Click Horoscope: The Astrologer's Secret Weapon*, trans. by Heather Ross, and ed. by Barry Hopewell (Knutsford: Astrological Psychology Association, 2009).

357. Faivre, *Access*, p. 34.

5. Chaosmic, Transpersonal, and Huber Astrology in the 21st Century

5.1 The Competing Worldviews of Astrology and Science

Over many centuries, from the earliest recorded star paths in ancient Mesopotamia through to the Elizabethan age when the astrologer Dr John Dee was the foremost mathematician and navigational expert in England and Wales, astrology was aligned with science. Although the heliocentric theory of Copernicus was published in 1543, the confrontation of the old worldview with the new came to a head in 1619 when Johannes Kepler published his *Harmonices mundi* with a lengthy appendix attacking the superbly illustrated *Histories* of the macrocosm and microcosm by Robert Fludd—physician, alchemist, Hermetic philosopher, and Rosicrucian—for presenting outdated 'Neoplatonic harmonies of the universe'. The polemic between these two outstanding interpreters of the cosmos continued for four years.[358] The years 1614-16 saw the publication of the Rosicrucian manifestos *Fama* and *Confessio*, and the *Chemical Wedding*, heralding a secret brotherhood and presenting 'an allegory that can open us to the mystery of inner transformation, if we but meditate upon and immerse ourselves deeply in its symbolic substance'.[359] On the other hand:

---

358. *Robert Fludd*, ed. by William Huffman, Western Esoteric Masters Series (Berkeley, CA: North Atlantic Books, 2001), pp. 41-42; Christopher McIntosh, *The Rosicrucians: The History, Mythology, and Rituals of an Esoteric Order*, 3rd edn rev. (San Francisco, CA: Weiser, 1997), pp. 33, 41.

359. *The Chemical Wedding of Christian Rosenkreutz*, trans. by Joscelyn Godwin, and ed. by Adam McLean, Magnum Opus Hermetic Sourceworks, 18, (Grand Rapids, MI: Phanes, 1991), p. 8.

> Kepler's views on cosmic harmony, essentially based on quantitative, mathematically demonstrable premises, were incompatible with... an archaistic-magical description of nature culminating in a mystery of transmutation.[360]

This dispute saw a parting of the ways of esotericist and scientific materialist.

Kepler was an astrologer as well as an astronomer, but he wanted to reform astrology and could not be described as an esotericist.[361] When I became a student in the late 1970s, astrologers set great store by the engagement of significant figures in the evolution of science, like Kepler, with our much maligned method of interpreting the interface between macrocosm and microcosm. A lot of serious astrological research was being done by John Addey, Charles Harvey, and others, and it was fully expected that, sooner or later, a return to the first principles of number and extensive statistical research would validate astrology and bring to an end to the ongoing war being waged by dogmatic scientists and media sceptics. Esotericists like the Hubers followed this research with great interest, and incorporated the findings of that most scrupulous of statisticians, Michel Gauquelin, into the wave sequences of quadrants and houses in their intensity curve, followed through by age progression, and the diagnosis and interpretation of stressed planets behind house cusps, discussed in earlier chapters. Notwithstanding the rigorous methodology used for compiling and testing statistics, narrow-minded scientific materialists, determined to invalidate astrology, managed to find fault with something somewhere. All three of these valiant astrological researchers have passed away, two from natural causes and one from an overdose. It has been said that the soul of astrology might be lost if it conformed to science, and this is a thought to bear in mind.[362]

---

360. Wolfgang Pauli, 'The Influence of Archetypal Ideas on the Scientific Theories of Kepler', pub. with Carl Jung, 'Synchronicity: An Acausal Connecting Principle', in *The Interpretation of Nature and the Psyche*, Bollingen Series, 51 (New York, NY: Pantheon, 1955), repr. Huffman, pp. 121-45 (p. 121).

361. Campion, *Medieval and Modern*, p. 139.

362. Brady, *Chaosmos*, quoting Curry, p. 121.

Science, too, has changed and, in a posthumous publication, Gauquelin, referring to James Gleick's *Chaos: Making a New Science* (1987), suggested that chaos theory might come to the aid to his neo-astrology:

> Chaos represents the world in a completely different way. Whereas science has until now searched for order in the disorder of things, Gleick tells the story of researchers who, on the contrary, have seen in disorder the key to many phenomena previously inexplicable. Purely mathematical in origin, chaos is a doctrine that leads to something concrete...
>
> Here is a definition evocative of the chaotic diversity of astrology, where, searching hard I have nevertheless observed some sort of order.[363]

Chaos and chaosmos are considered in a later section.

5.2 The Postmodern Paradigm of Science

Introducing the third edition of his book on Rosicrucianism, Christopher McIntosh wrote:

> There is a synchronicity in the fact that, as this book goes into its third edition, we stand at the threshold of a new millennium. Millenarian ideas helped to launch Rosicrucianism, and it is tempting to see parallels between the present age and that of the Rosicrucian manifestos. The two eras have much in common: momentous changes, bitter divisions and conflicts, a sense of this world having gone wrong and a yearning for a better one.[364]

This ideal has been taken up by Richard Tarnas in his call for 'heroic communities', aware of their 'crucial role in the postmodern world' as builders of 'a framework of values or a vision of the true and the good'.[365] For Tarnas, who is a historian, Uranus equals Prometheus, the stealer of fire for humanity, the 'catalyst of the new'—attributes

363. Gauquelin, pp. 176-78.

364. McIntosh, *Rosicrucians*, p. xxiii.

365. Tarnas, 'Carter, 2013', p. 31.

presented with great conviction in *Cosmos and Psyche*—but do these attractive ideas hold up to the scrutiny of forward-thinking scientists and twenty-first century astrologers?[366] The high profile given to Uranus is in line with New Age excitement about the forthcoming Age of Aquarius, and with the worldwide web that has changed the way we communicate. So alignment of the planet with Prometheus, the mythical competitor of Zeus (Jupiter)—traditional ruler of Pisces—adds an alternative dimension, though this is not the way that Tarnas presents the story. In fact, as Armand Diaz points out, he largely discounts signs which, to the Huber astrologer at least, represent the archetypal level of a chart that has five distinct levels from the inner core to the outer environment:

> One of the key points of archetypal cosmology is that astrological symbols are multivalent and multidimensional, and thus can manifest at any level of existence, internally within an individual, externally in their lives, in our collective life, and so on. Astrological symbols describe archetypal patterns, not specific manifestations, according to archetypal cosmologists, and the proper focus is not exactly what will happen (or has happened), but on the deeper meaning of archetypal interactions. Archetypal cosmologists frequently use the images of myth as a means of transcending the limitations of verbal astrological interpretations. In that sense, they point to the archetypal dimension that informs our spatiotemporal experience.[367]

Phoebe Wyss does include signs in *Inside the Cosmic Mind: Archetypal Astrology and the New Cosmology* (2014), which she relates to the twelve faces of the dodecahedron, one of the five platonic solids, in a beautifully written book, but the 'top-down' only approach and excessively wide aspects leave many questions unanswered. By bending over backwards to persuade the academic establishment and the scientific community to view the cosmos through the eyes of an astrologer, archetypal astrologers are taking to extremes the trend identified by Hyde in the 1990s, whereby

366. Tarnas, *Cosmos and Psyche*, p. 94.

367. Armand Diaz, *Integral Astrology: Understanding the Ancient Discipline in the Contemporary World* (USA and UK: Integral Transformation, 2012), p. 122; see five levels, p. 6.

'the borrowing of archetypes from Jung' encourages 'a loose and undisciplined approach' to astrology.[368] Whereas it is fascinating to explore the archaeoastronomy of ancient sites and much can be learnt from drawing parallels between the holistic worldview of ancient civilizations and the 'deeper supersensible order, permeated by patterns of interconnection' uncovered by leading physicists, this should not preclude recognition that while astrology has been 'an organizing system, a scheme for identifying order in chaos, and meaning in otherwise random events' since time immemorial, it has also evolved over the centuries, adding new techniques to analyze an increasingly complex scenario.[369] Oversimplification leads to generalization, stereotyping, and caricature, ignoring the subtleties that can be discerned in a carefully constructed horoscope.

One word that arises with frequency is 'synchronicity', coined by Jung and presented as 'a means of filling a gap in the world view of science, specifically as a balance to the principle of causality'.[370] Whereas this concept was rejected at the time, in recent years physicists have begun to speak and write about 'the connection between physical and meaningful events' and 'their common origin in the fields below the world of subatomic particles', but they have preferred to sideline Jung's experiments with astrology.[371] These were inconclusive regarding the astrological synastry between married couples they were set up to prove, but they did draw attention to Heisenberg's uncertainty principle, demonstrating that 'it is impossible for a human being to act as an impartial, objective observer':[372]

> The emotionality and psychic state of the participating observer goes beyond his or her own personal sphere... it keys in with the apparently objective factors so that it matches the astronomical data and the married couples. Thus the participating observer, the married

368. Hyde, p. 91.
369. Wyss; Le Grice, *Archetypal*, p. 102; Campion, *Medieval and Modern*, p. 139.
370. Progoff, p. 4.
371. Diaz, *Integral*, p. 11.
372. Hyde, pp. 130-33; Le Grice, *Archetypal*, p. 139.

> couples and the physical fact of the astronomy are all underpinned by an archetype in the collective unconscious which is acting autonomously.[373]

The 'synchronicity trickster' is primarily associated with Mercury, while the discipline of astrology involves 'learning to think in new categories':[374]

> It embodies a system of categories that are as different from the ones to which we are habituated, as the warp is from the weft. In this system objects and events that at first sight appear to have nothing whatever to do with each other are shown to be intimately connected.[375]

Whether or not synchronicity provides evidence of astrology, astrology enables those of us who can read its language to make sense of synchronistic events, and our awareness that every human being is a participating agent in the wellbeing of the earth and the cosmos accentuates our sense of responsibility. That is why we need an astrology that operates in both directions, concerning itself with humanity as well as the cosmos.[376]

The system theorist and philosopher of science, Ervin László, has chosen the Sanskrit word Akasha, meaning 'cosmic sky' and 'higher spheres of life and existence', as the umbrella term under which to assemble first-hand accounts of expanded consciousness, making a more explicit link between science and spirit:

> In the spiritual context we could call it the consciousness or intelligence of the world, and in the scientific context we can best view it as the logic or 'program' of the world. It is what makes the world intelligible, makes the stars and planets and the atoms and organisms behave in a way we can comprehend. The Akasha paradigm conveys insights that were traditionally the domain of spirituality and religion.[377]

---

373. Hyde, p. 133.

374. Hyde, pp. 134-37; Dennis Elwell, *Cosmic Loom* (London: Urania Trust, 1999), p. 245.

375. Elwell, p. 42.

376. Llewellyn, 'Carter, 2001', p. 13.

377. Ervin Laszlo, *The Akasha Experience: Science and the Cosmic Memory Field* (Rochester, VT: Inner Traditions, 2009), pp. 1-3; Ervin Laszlo, *The Self-Actualizing Cosmos: The Akasha Revolution in Science and Human Consciousness* (Rochester, VT: Inner Traditions, 2014), p. 93.

László's accounts cover varied experiences, among them observations of a professor of religious studies on the growing awareness of his students and their capacity for absorbing the subject:

> Students were becoming more porous not only to me but to each other. They sometimes showed up in each other's dreams in significant ways. Synchronicities between them were increasing, and life-expanding coincidences were becoming increasingly common in my courses... Sometimes insights surfaced in the room that seemed to come not from me nor from any individual student but from the strength of our combined collective consciousness... Slowly I began to recognize that there was a meta-learning taking place behind the scenes, a pattern of learning that ran deeper than the learning of individual students. I began to recognize that there were learning fields growing around my courses, fields of consciousness that registered the learning taking place semester after semester, fields of influence that were making it easier for subsequent generations of students to learn the same material.[378]

This evidence of how much we—and younger people in particular—interact with the environment, picking up information through unseen antennae, is both exciting and scary. If our descendants can learn more quickly, so much the better; but, with such heightened sensitivity to the environment, how do they resist its call if whatever is beckoning out there challenges their beliefs, or seems too good to be true? We cannot ignore the shadow archetype in its many manifestations, and a system of interpreting unseen influences has never been more essential. Bailey asserted the necessity for three horoscopes, and astrological psychology compares the radix chart imprinting the cosmos at the time of inception, with the moon node chart as a mirror of the past, and the house chart depicting the attractions, threats and expectations of the environment. This method of astrological interpretation, used primarily on the charts of individuals, can equally well be applied to significant events.

378. Christopher Bache, 'The Living Classroom', in Laszlo, *Akasha Experience*, pp. 82-93 (pp. 90-92).

Akasha, the most fundamental of five elements in Hindu philosophy, embraces the properties of air, fire, water, and earth, expressing 'the enduring memory of the cosmos'. In Huber astrology, these memory traces are found in the moon node chart, situated in indeterminate time and space.[379] Although it is not the only system that accesses ancestral records, astrological psychology can immediately relate to a paradigm that appears to invite astrologers into the fold.[380] Akasha was referred to both by Bailey and Louise:

> Akasha, in manifestation, expresses itself as Fohat, or divine energy... It is the sum total of that which is active, animated, or vitalized, and all that concerns itself with the adaption of the forms to the needs of the inner flame of life.[381]

Expanded consciousness and collective memory in Akasha and the moon node chart share common ground with morphic resonance, introduced by Rupert Sheldrake, in 1981:

> The formation of habits depends on a process called morphic resonance. Similar patterns of activity resonate across time and space with subsequent patterns. This hypothesis applies to all self-organizing systems, including atoms, molecules, crystals, cells plants, animals and animal societies. All draw upon the collective memory and in turn contribute to it.[382]

---

379. Laszlo, *Akasha Experience*, pp. 3-4; *Moon Node*, p. 132.

380. Many astrologers work with regression and karma. Patricia Walsh has combined evolutionary astrology, pioneered by Jeffrey Wolf Green, making extensive use of the Nodal Axis and outer reaches of Pluto, with deep memory process developed by Roger Woolger in *Understanding Karmic Complexes: Evolutionary Astrology and Regression Theory* (Bournemouth: Wessex Astrologer, 2009).

381. Alice A. Bailey, *A Treatise of Cosmic Fire* (New York, NY: Lucis, 1951), pp. 43-44, cited *Moon Node*, p. 132.

382. Rupert Sheldrake, *The Science Delusion: Freeing the Spirit of Enquiry* (London: Coronet, 2012), p. 99.

Astrology has advanced enormously over the years and evolved a language of its own. The interpretive skills of the astrologer could envisage connections and provide insights for the scientist to work with, but such interpretations involve the use of symbolism and imagination that perform badly when subjected to the control group testing required to validate scientific data. Instead of prostrating itself before science, Brady argues that cultural cosmology would do better to formulate a method based on Stoic sympathy and place its 'astrological soul... in the hands of chaosmos'. I am inclined to agree with her and discuss these ideas in later sections.[383]

5.3 Sensitive-Intuitive Seeing

In earlier chapters, I drew attention to the importance of gazing inwards to the soul centre, with reference to Theosophical art, Kabbalistic dreaming, and the way we look into the chart in astrological psychology, initially focusing on and visualizing the aspect structure to find a motivational picture in the inner circle. Whereas the Hubers referred to Goethe's approach to colours and the spectrum, Henri Bortoft has demonstrated the efficacy of this intense way of looking through the surface to the underlying pattern in Goethe's work on the metamorphosis of plants, which has subsequently been ratified by modern biology:[384]

> What Goethe said about metamorphosis is confirmed today by developmental genetics. The puzzling thing is, as one professor of genetics put it to me, how Goethe could have got it right over two hundred years ago without the resources of modern genetics. The answer is that he did it by learning 'to think like a plant lives' through practice of active seeing and exact sensorial imagination.[385]

---

383. Brady, *Chaosmos*, p. 121.

384. *Transformation*, pp. 154-59.

385. Henri Bortoft, *Taking Appearance Seriously: The Dynamic Way of Seeing in Goethe and European Thought* (Edinburgh: Floris, 2012), p. 62, quoting Craig Holdrege.

The presence of nature experienced through the senses correlates with the characteristic of esoteric thought defined as living nature or *Naturphilosophie.*

Not only is the sensorial imagination brought into focus in the initial formation of an image and overview of the chart, it is also factored into our understanding of the thinking planets, Mercury and Jupiter. Mercury represents the 'verbal-intellectual mode of apprehension... developed through education in modern western culture':

> The verbal-intellectual mind functions in terms of abstract generalities that take us away from the richness and diversity of sensory experience—this is both its strength and its weakness. It is focused on what is the same in things, their commonality, so that even without our realizing it we become immersed in uniformity and cease to notice differences... This is a consequence of what psychologists call the process of automatization or habituation.[386]

The contrasting function of Jupiter involves 'redeployment of attention into sensuous perception by active looking' and development of 'exact sensorial imagination', by

> creating a 'space' for the phenomenon by means of our attention so that we can receive it instead of trying to grasp it—so that we become participant in the phenomenon itself instead of an onlooker who is separate from it... we become aware of the more subtle qualities of the phenomenon... Whereas the intellectual mind can only bring us into contact with what is finished already, the senses—enhanced by exact sensorial imagination—bring us into contact with what is living, so that we begin to experience the phenomenon dynamically in its coming into being.[387]

386. Bortoft, p. 53.
387. Bortoft, pp. 54-55.

Bortoft relates Goethe's dynamic way of seeing to Iain McGilchrist's divided brain—'the left hemisphere tends to deal more with pieces of information in isolation, and the right hemisphere with the entity as a whole, the so-called *Gestalt*'—and concludes:[388]

> We can see that Goethe's way of working, by returning to the senses through active seeing and exact sensorial imagination, brings about a shift from left hemisphere dominance of the verbal-intellectual mind to right hemisphere wholeness of what is livingly present... What we can now add to this is the discovery is the neuropsychological correlation between Goethe's way of science and the difference between the modes of functioning of the two hemispheres of the brain. Perhaps such a contemporary approach could provide a doorway through which Goethe's sensuous-intuitive way of science can be introduced into the world today.[389]

This was what Bruno brought into astrology, that most cerebral of esoteric crafts:

> Viewed in its entirety the aspect structure is a symbolic representation of our consciousness, formed by the life energies available to us. That's why it is possible to see the inner motivation inherent in a chart only by using our senses, by means of a meditative approach... We'll have to cultivate our ability to think and feel ourselves into the picture... learn to work with our powers of empathy and perception, not using the analytical Mercurial mind but relying on the Jupiterian function of sensing and visualizing and opening our inner awareness. In this way we may just be able to intuit the quintessence of the person concerned in visual form... the aspect structure is a symbol, a mandala, which has an energy of its own, with the faculty to speak to our intuition. We can think of it as an energy field in which life energies radiate and interweave, and whose basic pattern conveys to our inner eyes the plan, purpose and potential of our whole existence.[390]

---

388. McGilchrist, p. 4.
389. Bortoft, p. 61.
390. *Astrological Psychosynthesis*, p. 32.

5.4 The Stoic Revival

What we understand by Stoicism has undergone a makeover in the last half century. The severe countenance of a passionless individual, who bows before his or her inevitable fate has been replaced by that of a sage with the 'ability to endure painful feelings and rise above them, with magnanimity, while continuing to maintain his relationships and interaction with the world'.[391] Stoicism, which started to flourish in the 1970s partly owing to the success of cognitive behavioural therapy (CBT), is becoming a popular philosophy of life in a secular age where we are assaulted by so much material and so many expectations that we need to learn to tell the difference between good and bad, and what we can and cannot control, self-management concerns that we might relate to Saturn in the astrological chart.[392]

At a recent conference, a connection was made between the Stoic view that we are 'integral parts of nature' and our 'need to think more about the impact of human actions on the natural environment'.[393] An article by Jessica Murray, in a collection of 'explorations at the frontier' of transpersonal astrology voices similar concerns:

> It would seem that the urgent realities of our epoch impel a running leap into outer-planet thinking. The human race is at a point in its growth arc where our infatuation with material and technological knowledge has outstripped our connection with deep wisdom, throwing us out of whack. From a lack of transpersonal understanding, our stewardship of the earth has gone derelict.[394]

---

391. Donald Robertson, 'Stoics are not Unemotional!' in *Stoicism Today: Selected Writings*, 1, ed. by Patrick Ussher (2014), p. 36.

392. Jules Evans, *Philosophy For Life And Other Dangerous Situations* (London: Rider, 2013), pp. 25-38.

393. Christopher Gill, 'Stoicism, Nature and the Environment', Stoicism Today, Queen Mary University of London, 29 November 2014.

394. Jessica Murray, 'The World Moment', in *Transpersonal Astrology: Explorations at the Frontier*, ed. by Armand Diaz, Eric Meyers, and Andrew Smith (USA and UK: Integral Transformation, 2013), pp. 25-41 (p. 27).

Despite the urgency of the situation, Murray reiterates the need to integrate the energy drives of inner planets with outer planets, deal with 'unresolved hurts' and 'take responsibility':

> It is hazardous to take on the outer planets without factoring in Saturnine responsibilities. This point is often missed by adherents of the transpersonal realm, which can lure us with the glamour of the exotic.[395]

Faivre, too, draws attention to the 'necessity of knowing the concrete universe by combining wisdom and technique', while also underlining the importance of intermediaries creating a passage between opposing forces to bring about harmony, the doctrine of cosmic sympathy binding all things, common to Mesopotamian magic, Pythagoreanism, Platonism and Stoicism.[396] This concept is fundamental to Brady's view of astrology as

> neither a pseudo-science nor a spiritual subject but is instead a product of the desire to domesticate chaos, a blending of the chaosmic nature of *sumpatheia* with the cosmic surety of heavenly numbers.[397]

5.5 Chaos, Chaosmos, and Astrological Research

Brady's investigations comprehensively demonstrate astrology's greater affinity with chaos theory and complexity than with the cosmic perfection delineated by Ptolemy, and application of this approach does not require the use of any specific techniques, rather a change of attitude on the part of the astrologer:[398]

> Complexity research has found that... new order emerges when the system is ruffled by increasing its networks, by moving it a little away from its established orderly systems, by pushing it gently towards 'the edge of chaos'. As we move the system towards turbulence or a time of potency where it can be tripped by what is known in complexity as the tipping point, so the system enters a fertile zone, a tiny phase of

395. Murray, pp. 29-36.
396. Faivre, 'Ancient and Medieval', in *MES*, p. 3; Campion, *Dawn*, p. 186.
397. Brady, *Chaosmos*, p. 2.
398. Brady, *Chaos*, pp. 29, 82, 109, 132.

> transition between a place of no change and a place of total change, and it is in this place that new patterns, new opportunities and new ideas emerge. The 'edge of chaos' is not... a place of upheaval but rather, in complexity, it is the phase or zone where even the smallest of changes at the right time can produce a cascade of new order.[399]

Her quest is to develop a research methodology that is acceptable to the astrological community as a whole, potentially capable of giving its qualitative research projects greater credence, and of steering it into the future. In general, astrologers

> believe that complex systems will evolve into established patterns, whether in the life of an individual, the history of a nation or the behaviour of non-living systems like weather. Indeed the astrological community is in its strongest position when talking about cycles, for at the heart of their culture are the measurable and predictable cycles of the celestial sphere and the planets.[400]

By combining the word 'chaos', meaning infinite space, chasm, and gulf, with 'cosmos', meaning order, ornament, and universe, we get the word 'chaosmos', coined by James Joyce in *Finnigans Wake* (1939).[401] When expounding this method of interpreting literature, science and theory—which Brady suggests extending to astrology—Philip Kuberski, addresses 'the paradoxical coincidence of order and disorder' and presents

> a chiasmic concept of the world as a field of mutual and simultaneous interference and convergence, an interanimation of the subjective and objective, an endless realm of chance that nevertheless displays a persistent tendency toward pattern and order. Everything in the world can be seen as chaosmic.[402]

---

399. Brady, *Chaos*, p. 70.

400. Bernadette Brady, 'Astrology and Research', <https://www.academia.edu/ 8823841/Astrology_and_Research_Astrologers_attitudes_to_research_methodologies_and_the_implications_of_these_attitudes_for_the_contemporary_communities_of_astrologers?auto=download&campaign=upload_email> [accessed 18 October 2014], p. 21.

401. Philip Kuberski, *Chaosmos: Literature, Science, and Theory* (Albany, NY: State University of New York, 1994), p. 37.

402. Kuberski, p. 3.

Chaosmos reconnects with the non-dualistic worldview of the ancient philosophers, characteristic of the esoteric way of thinking, while developing a postmodern 'nonlinear, nonidealized, ragged enactment of holism', deepening reality, enabling it to 'play up and down various scales of size and perspective simultaneously', making it 'less easily satisfied with closure'.[403]

> The chaosmic self, as an aspect of a self-organizing, organic process, is expressed at different levels or reference within different temporalities by corresponding contexts.[404]

It would therefore seem to be eminently applicable to the cosmology of our expanding universe, the astrology of humanity in relationship with nature and cosmos, the birth of new nations and the cycles of civilization, to name but a few corresponding readings of the stars.

Conceived as 'the in-between-between two milieus, rhythm-chaos or chaosmos' it has, unsurprisingly, been applied to the German-Swiss artist, Paul Klee, whose approach to chaos as a prelude to creative reordering is discussed with reference to the intensity curve on pages 108-09. His depiction of the trajectory of the artist's brush at the start of a new composition as 'an active line on a walk, moving freely, without goal' can be likened to a person starting life's pilgrimage before meaning and structure crystallize through age progression.[405] The Huber life clock not only expresses the passage of life on earth, as the individual progresses anticlockwise through the mundane houses interacting with people and situations, it also represents the ebb and flow of cardinal, fixed, and mutable energy through quadrants and houses in the course of a lifetime. Planets at the cardinal angles are most assertively engaged with the world around them, while those at the balance point have a measured flow of energy, and low-point planets are

403. Kuberski, p. 192.

404. Kuberski, p. 139.

405. John David Dewsbury and Nigel Thrift, 'Genesis Eternal: After Paul Klee', in Ian Buchanan and Gregg Lambert, eds, *Deleuze and Space* (Edinburgh: Edinburgh University Press, 2005), pp. 102-03, 105; Gale, p. 18.

most inward-looking. When the age point is conjunct a low point, this may herald a period of introspection during which the world can be hard to deal with, so the astrological psychologist can appreciate how the individual's perception changes, just as Klee's artist 'moves and finds himself indeed in motion in relation to the motion of the rest of the earth—most often, most productively in opposition to it'. Huber transformation exercises often involve working with polarities across the axes. In *Dream City* (1921) Klee selected ethereal colour tones—white, pink, green, and black—to ground imagination, and geometrical forms with unusual angles to 'shift one's view of things', making visible recesses of dream and memory previously shrouded in secrecy.[406]

The artist is often at the forefront in presenting alternative experiences of the cosmos. The contemporary German artist, Anselm Kiefer, inspired by Fludd's vision of cosmic man standing in the path of the Sun, expresses a sombre vision of the cosmos through blackened heads of sunflowers.[407] The pop artist Sigmar Polke pictured himself as an astronaut suspended in space. The transpersonal astrologer Eric Meyers is experimenting with heliocentric astrology 'as a portrayal of our awakened selves, how we might approach the world as realized beings'.[408]

Chaosmos, with its kaleidoscopic vision, can encompass astrology, whether it is pseudo-scientific, psycho-spiritual, pragmatic, mundane, tropological, or transpersonal.

---

406. Rosenthal, pp. 33-38; Will Grohmann, *Klee*, trans by Norbert Guterman, abr. (London: Thames and Hudson, 1987), pp. 60-61; see axes, quadrants, intensity curve, pp. 10-12.

407. Matthew Biro, *Anselm Kiefer* (London: Phaidon Focus, 2013), p. 88.

408. Eric Meyers, 'A Transpersonal Vision for Astrology', in *Transpersonal Astrology*, pp. 6-24 (p. 18).

5.6 Transpersonal and Astrological Psychology

Huber astrology, founded in the 1960s around the same time as transpersonal psychology, was greatly influenced by the psychosynthesis of Assagioli and the esoteric astrology of Bailey, and responded to needs within the society of that time. Rudhyar was not only quick to support the transpersonal movement, he also revealed he had been using the word transpersonal since 1930, but with a slightly different emphasis:

> I defined as transpersonal a process of descent of transcendent spiritual power and illumination through the normal consciousness, and eventually through the whole personality of a human being. The source of that power and light exists in a realm beyond the personal consciousness and the ego, but I saw in the transpersonal action a descent of power rather than an ascent of a person's consciousness and emotions. In traditional religious terms, as a man prays to God his soul reaches up to the Divine; and God answers by an outpouring of 'grace'—a descent of the Holy Spirit. The transpersonal approach I have been presenting does not follow any strictly religious system of thought; neither is it mystical in the usual sense of the term. It is essentially metaphysical and cosmological—or one may say cosmontological, as it refers to cosmic being (ontos).[409]

CTP adds a second transpersonal energy centre to the base of Assagioli's egg, allowing room for its expression in the depths as well as the heights, and sometimes the breakthrough that opens up the path to wholeness begins in a very dark space.[410] Often the individual, whether working with a therapist or responding to some intuitive intelligence or inner voice, has only the faintest idea of where a critical journey into the unknown might be heading. It may seem as if s/he is climbing towards the pinnacle of a mountain hidden in the clouds until a chasm appears, as the sacred space opens into a deep gorge and the individual goes spiralling into the abyss. König cites the inscription above the Asklepion, the temple of healing on the island of Kos—'We ask the gods to help us better

---

409. Rudhyar, *Multilevel*, pp. ix-x.

410. Gordon-Brown and Somers, *Raincloud*, pp. 12-14; see egg, p. 13.

understand what is happening within us'—in an article that takes the reader into a therapy space, created in a spirit of integrity and allowing in an element of risk:

> The therapist may expect sexual images but religious ones come instead. A religious therapist may expect religious images but may be confronted by sexual ones.[411]

The whole human being matters—body, heart, mind, and spirit. Seminal esoteric movements of the late nineteenth century working with expanded consciousness were sometimes pioneered by celibate couples whose abstinence might seem unnecessarily monastic and unhelpful to the growth of the whole person. Theories about humanity's provenance and destiny couched in pompous language might appear prejudiced, and directives from Himalayan Masters questionable, out of sync with postmodern paradigms of science and spirituality. Nevertheless, these movements exerted an enormous influence on postmodern thinking by opening up new fields of study and alternative methods of perception. Ugly shadows have emerged in the lives of twentieth-century New Age gurus, including sex scandals and financial mismanagement, emphasizing human frailty and the labyrinthine paths we travel in an effort to achieve balance and synthesis in our lives. In his profile of Sonia, Bogart acknowledges that the practice of spiritual disciplines does not treat issues around self-esteem, sexuality, and career pressure:

> Sonia was confused about her downwardly spiralling situation. She was distressed to discover that the spiritual disciplines of yoga, pranayama, chanting and meditation she'd practised for many years didn't shed any light on what she was going through. They didn't touch the pain she was feeling or calm the energies agitating inside her, yearning for an as yet indefinable state of freedom.[412]

---

411. Wolfhard König, 'Talk Therapy for Astrologers 3: Non-Directive Counselling', trans. by Heather Ross, *Conjunction*, 58 (July 2013), pp. 20-23 (p. 23).

412. Bogart, p. 138.

The astrological birth chart, which is unique to each one of us while also being an imprint of the cosmos, can help us to centre ourselves. To guide clients like Sonia, Bogart proposes the transformation process of the six shaktis, a model derived from the teachings of Kashmir Shaivism and described by Rudhyar, accessing 'the instinctual evolutionary drives signified by the outer planets' to awaken the spiritual force through the serpent power of kundalini, 'a principle of coordination between the individual and the universe'.[413] The use of such methods outside the intimacy of a partnership evidently requires expertise in advanced yoga and psychotherapy as well as astrology. Bogart concludes that:

> Whereas astrology at the humanistic level is to aid our fulfilment as individuals, the goal of transpersonal astrology is to transform personal problems by referring them to a new purpose: the opening to an infusion and descent of supramental forces.[414]

In the late 1950s, Bruno became aware that many participants in the spiritual programme run by the Arcane School in Geneva were in need of grounding psychotherapy to prepare for their vocation, motivating the Hubers to move to Florence, work with Assagioli, and incorporate psychosynthesis into their astrological psychology. The differences between so-called humanistic and transpersonal astrology are perhaps not as clear cut as Bogart has suggested, and we might think of esoteric astrology, like psychotherapy, 'as a bridge between psychology and spirituality'.[415] By choosing to call their method a psychology rather than a transpersonal astrology, the emphasis is on psychological preparation, although it incorporates some spiritual exercises, facilitating imagination and mediation on the ladder of the esotericist poised between the natural world and the cosmos. Michael Huber has developed further techniques for finding the soul and interpreting the inner spaces of the chart, and he has worked closely with the Spanish school, which

413. Bogart, pp. 165-77 (p. 175).

414. Bogart, p. 177.

415. John Rowan, *The Transpersonal: Psychotherapy and Counselling* (London/New York: Routledge, 1993), p. 2.

has introduced lucid dreaming inspired by Kabbalah. There are several small schools and groups in German-speaking Europe and Scandinavia, one of which emphasizes depth psychology. König has presented alternative holistic models of the psyche, suggesting that 'elements of free association can be incorporated into a horoscope consultation'. He describes free association and depth psychology as 'spiritual processes' that require 'the relinquishing of power' to access deep memories in the collective unconscious, and the way he uses astrological psychology is a testament of how well it combines with psychotherapy.[416] To work with the depth and freedom he recommends the astrologer needs to be a fully trained and experienced psychotherapist. However, a consultation with a Huber astrologer is not generally directed by the astrologer who, having undertaken preparatory work on the charts beforehand, will begin by encouraging the client to open up and share his or her preoccupations, and the level of the two-way exchange that develops will depend largely on what the client brings to a session that focuses on drawing out and synthesizing helpful insights, and is never predictive.

As Richard Llewellyn stated at his Carter Memorial Lecture, delivered at the Astrological Association Conference, in 2001, Huber incorporates both 'top down' and 'bottom up' approaches:

> In the same way as we can see Assagioli's Egg as symbolizing the individual, so we can also see it as symbolizing humanity as a whole. For me this begins to define a purpose for astrology because it gives a sense of the larger plan. Not only a reason for us being here but also for doing something with our lives. Something which helps with the manifestation of these transpersonal qualities in matter and therefore with the evolution of humanity. These transpersonal qualities which originate from the source of everything are looking for a Form in which to manifest. And you and I are that form. What are these transpersonal

416. Wolfhard König, 'Talk Therapy for Astrologers 4: Non-Directive Counselling in Astrological Consultation', trans. by Heather Ross, *Conjunction*, 59 (November 2013), pp. 13-15 (p. 15), and 3, p. 23.

> qualities? In case the concept is unfamiliar, they include such things as joy, beauty, peace, will, freedom, wisdom, power, and so on.[417]

To be able to express these qualities and direct them to the service of humanity, we first need to develop our inner will and bring the transpersonal soul into everyday life. Meditation practice is helpful, and deeper work might be desirable to uncover past history, shift blocked energy, challenge fear, dissociate from controlling people, so as to regain the power and integrity to speak from the heart and choose the good things that can make a difference.[418]

This final section takes a further look at what is understood by the transpersonal, why this approach to life has gained ground the twenty-first century, how it relates to Huber astrology, and why astrological psychology continues to have an important role to play.

Although I considered transpersonal psychology with astrological psychology under the umbrella of New Age in chapter 3, since both are indebted to Bailey, who popularized the term, some practitioners object to what has become a degenerate term for a subculture with a 'holistic and syncretistic orientation' that has spawned a vast array of books and paraphernalia, 'all suitable for vulnerable people'.[419] To describe what we mean by transpersonal psychology, we could say that it is 'concerned with experiences and aspirations that lead people to seek transcendence, as well as with healing potentials of self-transcendence', or with 'experiences involving an expansion or extension of consciousness beyond the usual ego boundaries and beyond the limitations of time and/or space'.[420] By extending this line of thought we can differentiate 'the Self as the centre of the psyche' from 'the ego as the centre of the

---

417. Llewellyn, p. 13; see egg and combined model, pp. 13-14.

418. Piero Ferrucci, *Your Inner Will: Finding Personal Strength in Critical Times*, trans. by Vivien Reid Ferrucci (New York, NY: Tarcher/Penguin, 2014)

419. Hanegraaff, *New Age*, p. 75; Rowan, *Transpersonal*, p. 12.

420. Frances Vaughan, *The Inward Arc: Healing in Psychotherapy and Spirituality*, 2nd edn (Nevada City, CA: Blue Dolphin, 1995), p. 39; Stanislav Grof, *Realms of the Human Consciousness* (London: Souvenir Press, 1979), p. 155, cited by John, Rowan, pp. 6-7.

conscious personality', both of which may be accommodated in the central core of the Huber chart:

> This definition of the Self as an organizing principle is useful in mapping advanced stages of psychological growth and spiritual development. Awakening self-awareness at this level may be marked by a shift from personal, egocentric motivation to more altruistic, socially conscious values, or it may focus for a time on inner development. When attention turns to spiritual development, it may at first appear to be narcissistic and self-absorbed. But the shift in values inherent in genuine spiritual aspiration is reflected in behaviour that is characteristically ethical, well-intentioned, and concerned with the effects of one's actions on others. Healthy spiritual development is not bent solely on personal gain.
>
> The transpersonal Self is discovered by turning inward, sometimes in the practice of meditation or contemplation. Self-knowledge cannot be attained by searching outside of oneself. The value of inner searching is affirmed both in depth psychology and in every major spiritual tradition.[421]

The process being described here corresponds to the process of learning on the APA diploma course, where the student takes a multilevel approach his or her own astrological charts, the tutor's and those of a friend, building a bridge to the next stage. I have not defined spiritual, because it is not circumscribable and does not mean the same for everyone. According to Wilber, 'there are at least five very different definitions, two of which seem to involve stages, and three of which do not'.[422]

In *New Age Religion* (1998), Hanegraaff describes Grof as 'the leading empirical researcher', and Wilber as 'the foremost theoretician in the transpersonal movement', and highlights Wilber's rejection of the holographic paradigm characteristic of New Age for reasons of incompatibility with his updated perennial philosophy describing reality as 'a hierarchy of different

---

421. Vaughan, pp. 39-40.

422. Wilber, *Integral Psychology*, p. 129.

levels'.[423] A Western esotericist would not necessarily agree that a hierarchical perception of spiritual progress was equivalent to a belief in Perennialism. Yet, later texts by Wilber and Grof that underline their mutual respect and the stimulating nature of their dialectic, also confirm their allegiance to Perennialism. The Hubers incorporated Grof's research on birth-time imprinting into their method. Parallels have been drawn between the quadrants of Huber and Wilber, and between Assagioli's 'pluridimensional conception of the human personality' and Wilber's 'Great Nest of Being':[424]

> Reality according to Wilber is composed of a hierarchy of levels, which he prefers to call holarchies, because the basic levels are holons (wholes within wholes) of consciousness. When the self moves through these basic levels of consciousness, as part of its evolutionary journey and development it experiences them as direct experiential realities, reaching from sensory experience to mental experience to spiritual experience. The development of the self is a vertical climb, using a height metaphor, through the different inner levels of reality and increasing complexity.
>
> The levels are not rigid patterns of consciousness but according to Wilber are more like the colours of the rainbow that interpenetrate and grade into each other or like waves in the great river of life, through which its many streams run.[425]

Wilber has inspired Diaz's book setting out 'a more inclusive astrology', whose evolutionary scheme and approaches to consciousness and karma are pretty similar to those of Huber introduced half a century earlier.[426]

These interconnections are unremarkable. More difficult to explain is how Assagioli, intent on helping humanity out of the basement and onto the sunlit terrace, and Huber, motivated to raise awareness and banish fateful predictions, have somehow become

423. Hanegraaff, pp. 57-58, 75.

424. Collier; Assagioli, *Psychosynthesis*, p. 16; Wilber, *Integral Psychology*, pp. 5-27 (p. 6), 61-64.

425. Sørensen, p. 6.

426. Diaz, *Integral Astrology*.

entangled with Perennialism that disdains our fallen world 'as a product of the Kali Yuga'. In fact, this is not the worldview Wilber adopts, and it becomes clear why Faivre sketched out a third strand of contemporary esotericism, isolated by Sheldon R. Isenberg and Gene R. Thursby, and described as an 'evolutionary' current within *philosophia perennis*, as opposed to the 'devolutionary' Traditionalism of Guénon and other purists.[427] Faivre's preferred label of 'humanist' is not only ambiguous for reasons I outlined in chapter 2, but also fails to take account of the iconic status accorded by early experimenters and founders of the transpersonal movement to Aldous Huxley, author of *The Brave New World* (1932) and *The Doors of Perception* (1954). Huxley introduced *The Perennial Philosophy* (1945) as:

> The metaphysics that recognizes a divine Reality substantial to the world of things and lives and minds; the psychology that finds in the soul something similar to, or even identical with, divine Reality; the ethic that places man's final end in the knowledge of the immanent and transcendent Ground of all being.[428]

Jorge Ferrer does take on board the influence of Huxley in *Revisioning Transpersonal Theory* (2002), which effectively deconstructs the perennial philosophy, piece by piece, and rebuilds a participatory worldview in its place. He begins by tackling the dangers of spiritual narcissism and failure to integrate spiritual experiences into everyday life: the 'goal of the spiritual quest... is not to have spiritual experiences, but to stabilize spiritual consciousness, live a spiritual life, and transform the world accordingly'.[429] Next, he tackles what he calls 'the empiricist colonization of spirituality', which he relates to 'Maslow's self-validating peak-experiences' that 'were not merely emotional and ecstatic states, but frequently possessed a cognitive or noetic element':[430]

---

427. Faivre, *Access*, p. 40.

428. Ferrer, p. 74, cites Huxley, p. vii.

429. Ferrer, pp. 15, 37.

430. Ferrer, p. 46.

> the similarities between spirituality and science are more apparent than real, and... efforts to legitimate spiritual knowledge by appealing to its scientific status may be both misleading and counterproductive.[431]

We might draw the same conclusions regarding the relationship between science and the psycho-spiritual discipline that astrology has become. Notwithstanding the revival of traditional astrological methods in the late 1980s, in *Astrology, Science and Culture* (2004), Patrick Curry found it necessary to include a subheading for 'psychological astrology'—despite its evident descent from 'Neoplatonic/Hermetic astrology'—precisely because it had become 'the dominant kind of astrology among contemporary practitioners'.[432]

According to Ferrer, Maslow's approach to 'mystical or peak-experiences' as the same in essence in all religions is a factor behind the almost unquestioned acceptance of 'the universalist account of spirituality espoused by the perennial philosophy', as well as the strong influence of Wilber, and a tendency for transpersonal scholars to work in isolation, overlooking dialogues in cross-cultural philosophy and religion that might have encouraged earlier exploration of 'alternative visions for understanding interreligious relations and the nature of spiritual phenomena.[433] Behind the influence of specific individuals and circumstances, Ferrer digs deep to reveal a scenario in which experiential vision seeking to validate itself came to rely on perennial philosophy in a late twentieth-century environment that marginalized 'spirituality as subjective and epistemically sterile' and viewed 'valid knowledge as essentially objective and public'.[434] With the new millennium, it was time to move on:

---

431. Ferrer, p. 41.

432. Campion, 'Traditional Revival'; Willis and Curry, p. 73.

433. Ferrer, pp. 105-07, citing from Maslow, *Religions, Values, and Peak Experiences* (1970)

434. Ferrer, pp. 108-09.

> Spiritual knowing is a participatory event: It can involve the creative participation of not only our minds, but also our hearts, bodies, souls, and most vital essence. Furthermore, spiritual energies are not confined to our inner world, but can also flow out of relationships, communities, and even places.[435]

This participatory vision, 'more consistent with the view of spiritual knowing embraced by most contemplative traditions', is achieved through a 'participatory turn', meaning 'a radical shift of emphasis from intrasubjective experiences to participatory events in our understanding of transpersonal and spiritual phenomena'. Just as William James said that 'mystical states seem to those who experience them to be also states of knowledge' so, instead of having experiences, the transpersonal participant realizes 'special states of discernment... insight into depths of truth unplumbed by the discursive intellect'.[436] The participatory approach embraces 'a diversity of spiritual truths and cosmologies', among which 'there is no final, privileged, or more encompassing spiritual viewpoint'.[437]

Ferrer has set out a radically different transpersonal viewpoint but, although many astrologers embrace this participatory vision, according to Cornelius, only a few have introduced it into their practice. At the end of chapter 2, there is a brief mention of how the Huber astrologer is encouraged to develop the sensory-intuitive side represented by Jupiter to complement the verbal-intellectual mode personified by Mercury and operate at the tropological level. This method of intense visualization to reveal the essential self, directional energy, and evolving form has been elaborated earlier in this chapter in the context of Goethe's study of plants. König's non-directive counselling in a psychotherapeutic healing chamber creates an environment that invites a 'participatory turn'. My narrative in chapter 4 uses astrological symbolism as an analogical connecting principle on the healing journey.

435. Ferrer, p. 115.

436. Ferrer, pp. 126-27.

437. Ferrer, pp. 166-67.

Transpersonal astrologers have been aware of changing dimensions in what we understand by reality for over forty years. In 1975, Rudhyar wrote in his 'Introduction to the Galactic Level of Consciousness':

> What we are witnessing today is the gradual emergence of a picture of the universe which... demands the acceptance of a new dimension of reality. This 'fourth dimension' can be defined by the elusive, yet revealing word: INTERPENETRATION... The era of isolated, irreducible, and quasi-absolute individualities, as well as of totally distinct and unrelated physical-material objects, is passing away. Everything not only connects to everything else; all there is interpenetrates everything...[438]

As I hope I have demonstrated in the course of this text, many of the techniques introduced into astrology by Bruno and Louise in the 1960s were attuned to the need to redress the balance between cognitive and sensory perception. What has significantly changed over the last half century is the widespread awareness of extended consciousness. The impact of communication via the Internet cannot be underestimated, not to mention that of films and television. Esotericism as the third pillar of Western culture is no longer shrouded in secret societies, because everything is out there if you are sufficiently motivated to find it. A specialized centre of research, the Institute of Noetic Sciences, became a household name when Dan Brown chose to base his heroine on its former CEO in a thriller that took a canter round Freemasonic Washington.[439] The term 'chaosmos', buried for decades in the linguistic complexity of *Finnigans Wake*, has been appropriated for an Internet game challenging players to outwit imminent global catastrophe. Most of us can access the vocabulary of esotericism, astrology, and the transpersonal however we choose to use it.

---

438. Dane Rudhyar, *The Galactic Dimension of Astrology: The Sun Is Also A Star* (Santa Fe, NM: Aurora, 1982), p. 7.

439. Dan Brown, *The Lost Symbol* (London: Bantam, 2009).

John Rowan put out a recent reminder that, notwithstanding political correctness, we do not all live 'on a level playing field', and often we fail to communicate satisfactorily with one another because we are operating on different levels of perception and using words in a nuanced way.[440] One person may be using the logic of formal education, another the dialectical logic of psychotherapy, while a third may be talking about angels, daemons, and other spiritual beings of the imaginal world. Whereas medieval astrologers and astronomers once spoke the same language, today's astronomers codify planets as entities in space, while astrologers explain them in terms of human, national, or collective qualities, possibly amplified by a mythological connotation. Such diversities mostly relate to the vertical axis of individuation without being discriminatory. Wilber's answer to the question—'does psychological development have to be completed before spiritual development can begin?'—highlights the complicated nature of our society:

> Because the developmental lines themselves can unfold independently, an individual can be at a very high spiritual stage (transpersonal or post-post-con) in one line and still be at a very low personal or psychological stage (con or precon) in others. For example, a person might be at a transpersonal level of cognition (perhaps attained by meditative development), and yet still be at a personal or psychological (con or precon) stage of moral development.[441]

Uneven levels of self-development can lead to spiritual narcissism—which Ferrer discusses at some length—or open up vulnerability to shadow archetypes in the collective. There is general consensus that it is preferable to ground oneself first and work towards psychosynthesis in preparation for spiritual gnosis.

440. John Rowan, 'Levels of Flattery', *Network Review*, 116 (Winter 2015), Journal of the Scientific and Medical Network, pp. 18-19.

441. Wilber, *Integral Psychology*, p. 135.

We no longer operate in a rigid class structure, and most of us are not contained within societies bound to one religious faith. Sometimes we encounter situations that transform our perception of the world and how we understand our mission in life so radically that we have to find a new way of expressing ourselves. Our openness to many more influences, requests, vibrations, pressures, and sensitivities of all kinds makes it ever more necessary to develop discernment and cultivate strong will, skilful will, and good will, as Assagioli recommended. That is, if we wish to make a difference for the better, instead of being scooped up like pawns or steered into becoming catalysts or scapegoats in collective issues to which we are only partially committed. Not that we can control everything in our interconnected world, and we can benefit from recognizing when we perform best and knowing when to let go. Psychosynthesis helps us to choose our commitments wisely and we cannot, I think, wholly abandon the image of a stairway to climb. Nor can we with health, heart and conscience dissociate ourselves from those things we would prefer to bury that return with insistence, because we do not live in isolation and whatever we neglect to do resonates out there in the ether. The horizontal line of consciousness, between 'I' and 'you', subject and object, is—initially at least—more challenged by the postmodern paradigms. Issues around intrasubjective reductionism arise in a variety of contexts, as do questions concerning the objectivity of the observer in our interconnected chaosmos.

Not everyone is attracted to the same organizing system for making sense of ourselves and our kaleidoscopic world. This book sets out the credentials of the astrological psychology of Bruno and Louise Huber, which is no ephemeral New Age wonder. The roots of its method lie in the esoteric wisdom of ancient civilizations, to which modern methods of restoring equilibrium between cognitive and sensory learning have been applied. The astrologer's gaze extends over three principal charts for interpretation, one facilitating insight into the Akashic records of the past, and another mapping the collective environment of the present, as well as the central imprint of birth, the beginning of the journey, showing the way to psychosynthesis and transpersonal development, and using that most appropriate of symbolic systems, the language of the cosmos.

Bibliography

A. Works by Bruno and Louise Huber

Huber, Bruno, *Astrological Psychosynthesis: The Integration of Personality, Love, and Intelligence in the Horoscope*, 2nd English edn (York Beach, ME: Weiser, 1996)

—*The History of Astrology*, three articles trans. from *Astrolog* by Heather Ross (Knutsford: API [UK], 2007)

—'Sol Sagitario y signos en el AC', ed. by Rita Keller for Astrolog 124, 125, and 126 (2001-02), and trans. by Joan Solé <www.escuelahuber.org/Private/Sol_Sagitario_signos_Ascendente_BH.pdf> [accessed 2 December 2014]

Huber, Bruno and Louise, *The Astrological Houses: A Psychological View of Ourselves and Our World*, trans. by Haloli Richter, 3rd edn, rev. by Barry Hopewell (Knutsford: HopeWell, 2011)

—*Astrology and the Seven Rays: Interpreting the Rays through the Natal Chart*, 2nd edn revd, transcribed from workshop at Beacon Centre, Exeter (1998), with additions, trans. by Heather Ross, and ed. by Barry Hopewell (Knutsford: HopeWell, 2006)

—*Astrology and the Spiritual Path: The Spiritual Significance of Age Progression* (York Beach, ME: Weiser, 1990)

—*The Development of Astrological Psychology*, trans. by Agnes Shellens and Heather Ross (Knutsford: API [UK], 2006)

—*LifeClock: The Huber Method of Timing in the Horoscope*, trans. by Haloli Q. Richter, Transcript, and Agnes Shellens, vols 1 and 2, 2nd edn revd (York Beach, ME: 1994)

—*Moon-Node Astrology*, trans. by Transcript, (York Beach, ME: Weiser, 1995; repr. Knutsford: HopeWell, 2005)

—*The Planets and their Psychological Meaning: Capabilities and Tools of the Personality*, trans. by Heather Ross, and ed. by Barry Hopewell (Knutsford: HopeWell, 2002)

—*Transformation: Astrology as a Spiritual Path*, trans. by Heather Ross, and ed. by Barry Hopewell (Knutsford: HopeWell, 2008)

Huber, Bruno and Louise, et al, *Astrolog 1: Life and Meaning*, trans. by Heather Ross, and ed. Barry Hopewell (Knutsford: HopeWell, 2008)

Huber, Bruno, Louise and Michael Alexander, *Aspect Pattern Astrology: A New Holistic Horoscope Interpretation Method*, trans. by Heather Ross, and ed. by Barry Hopewell (Knutsford: HopeWell, 2005)

Huber, Louise, *Reflections and Meditations on the Signs of the Zodiac*, trans. by Moray Patterson (Tempe, AZ: American Federation of Astrologers, 1984)

—'Birth Time Imprinting—Planets at the AC and DC', 1st pub. in *Astrolog*, 118, 119, and 120, trans. by Agnes Shellens, and repr. in *Conjunction*, 30, 31, and 32 (2001-2002)

B. Other Sourcebooks

Agrippa of Nettesheim, Henry Cornelius, *Three Books of Occult Philosophy*, trans. by James Freake, and ed. by Donald Tyson (Woodbury, MN: Llewellyn, 2007)

Allen, Don Cameron, *The Star-Crossed Renaissance: The Quarrel about Astrology and Its Influence in England* (London: Frank Cass, 1966)

Arroyo, Stephen, *Astrology, Karma, and Transformation: The Inner Dimensions of the Birth Chart* (Davis, CA: CRCS, 1978)

—*Exploring Jupiter: The Astrological Key to Progress, Prosperity and Potential*, ed. by Barbara McEnerney (Sebastopol, CA: CRCS, 1996)

Assagioli, Roberto, *The Act of Will: A Guide to Self-Actualization and Self-Realization*, 2nd edn (Woking: Platts, 1999)

—*Psychosynthesis: A Manual of Principles and Techniques*, 2nd edn (Wellingborough: Turnstone, 1975)

—*Los siete tipos humanos y la psicosíntesis*, trans. by Lluïsa Sallés, and ed. by the API Escuela Española Huber de Astrología (Barcelona, 1994)

—*Transpersonal Development: The Dimension beyond Psychosynthesis*, ed. by Maria Luisa Girelli, 2nd edn (London: Thorsons, 1993)

Atwood, Mary Anne *A Suggestive Inquiry into the Hermetic Mystery and Alchemy* (London: Trelawney Saunders, 1850), repr. <www.archive.org/details/suggestiveinquir00atwo> [accessed 10 February 2014]

Bagley, Demetrius, and Nan Geary, eds, *Astrology, The New Generation: Essays from 14 Rising Stars of Astrology* (London: Flare and London School of Astrology, 2012)

Bailey, Alice A., *A Treatise on White Magic or The Way of the Disciple* (New York and London: Lucis, 1951)

—*Esoteric Astrology, A Treatise on the Seven Rays, 3*, 3rd edn (New York and London: Lucis, 1997)

—*The Soul: The Quality of Life*, ed. by a student (New York and London: Lucis, 1974)

Baker, Dr Douglas, *The Jewel in the Lotus*, 2nd edn (Essendon: Claregate, 1985)

Barbault, André, *The Value of Astrology from ancient knowledge to today's reality*, trans. by Kate Johnston, and ed. by Roy Gillett (London: Astrological Association, 2014)

Baring, Anne, *The Dream of the Cosmos: A Quest for the Soul* (Dorset: Archive Publishing, 2013)

Barton, Tamsyn, *Ancient Astrology* (London and New York: Routledge, 1994)

Beresford, Andrew M, Louise M. Haywood, and Julian Weiss, eds *Medieval Hispanic Studies in Memory of Alan Deyermond, Serie A, Monografías*, 315 (Woodbridge and Rochester, NY: Támesis, 2013)

Biro, Matthew, *Anselm Kiefer* (London: Phaidon Focus, 2013)

Blavatsky, Helena Petrovna, *Isis Unveiled: A Master-Key to the Mysteries of Ancient and Modern Science and Theology*, 1, Science, 2, Theology (Pasadena, CA: Theosophical University Press, 1976)

—*Isis Unveiled: Secrets of the Ancient Wisdom Tradition, Madam Blavatsky's First Work*, A New Abridgement for Today by Michael Gomes (Wheaton, IL: Quest, 1997)

—*The Key to Theosophy: A Clear Exposition based on the Wisdom Religion of All Ages*, repr. of 1st edn (1889), with glossary of 2nd edn and new index (Pasadena, CA: Theosophical University Press, 1987)

—*The Secret Doctrine: The Synthesis of Science, Religion, and Philosophy*, 1, Cosmic Evolution, 2, Anthropogenesis, 1st edn 1888, repr. 2008 <www.forgottenbooks.org>

Bogart, Greg, *Astrology and Spiritual Awakening*, 2nd edn (Tempe, AZ: American Federation of Astrologers, 2014)

Bortoft, Henri, *Taking Appearance Seriously: The Dynamic Way of Seeing in Goethe and European Thought* (Edinburgh: Floris, 2012)

Brady, Bernadette, *Astrology, A Place in Chaos* (Bournemouth: Wessex Astrologer, 2006)

—*Cosmos, Chaosmos and Astrology: Rethinking the Nature of Astrology*, Sophia Centre Master Monographs, 1 (Ceredigion: Sophia Centre Press, 2014)

Broek, Roelof van den, and Wouter J. Hanegraaff, eds., *Gnosis and Hermeticism from Antiquity to Modern Times* (Albany, NY: SUNY, 1998)

Buchanan, Ian, and Gregg Lambert, eds, *Deleuze and Space* (Edinburgh: Edinburgh University Press, 2005)

Campion, Nicholas, *Astrology and Cosmology in the World's Religions* (New York and London: New York UP, 2012)

—*Astrology and Popular Religion in the Modern West: Prophecy, Cosmology and the New Age Movement* (Farnham: Ashgate, 2012)

—*The Dawn of Astrology: A Cultural History of Western Astrology, 1: The Ancient World* (London and New York: Continuum, 2008)

—*The Medieval and Modern Worlds: History of Western Astrology, 2* (New York, NY: Continuum, 2009)

Campion, Nicholas, and Patrick Curry, eds, *Sky and Psyche: The Relationship Between Cosmos and Consciousness* (Edinburgh: Floris, 2006)

Campion, Nicholas, Patrick Curry, and Michael York, eds, *Astrology and the Academy: Papers from the Inaugural Conference of the Sophia Centre, Bath Spa University College, 13-14 June 2003* (Bristol: Cinnabar, 2004)

Campion, Nicholas, and Liz Greene, eds, *Astrologies: Plurality and Diversity: The proceedings of the eighth annual conference of the Sophia Centre for the Study of Cosmology and Culture, University of Wales, Trinity Saint David, 24-25 July 2010* (Ceredigion: Sophia Centre Press, 2011)

—*Sky and Symbol: The Proceedings of the Ninth Annual Conference of the Sophia Centre for the Study of Cosmology and Culture, University of Wales, Trinity St David, 4-5 June 2011* (Ceredigion: Sophia Centre Press, 2013)

Cavallo, Sandra, and Tessa Storey, *Healthy Living in Late Renaissance Italy* (Oxford: Oxford University Press, 2013)

Cohn, Norman, *Cosmos, Chaos and the World to Come: The Ancient Roots of Apocalyptic Faith* (New Haven and London: Yale University Press, 1993)

Collier, Catharine, *Celebrating the Quality of Four: The Human Condition as the Fourth Kingdom in Nature* (Knutsford: API [UK], 2004)

Copenhaver, Brian P., ed, Hermetica: *The Greek 'Corpus Hermeticum' and the Latin 'Asclepius' in a new English translations with notes and introduction*, (Cambridge: Cambridge UP, 1992; repr. 2000)

Cornelius, Geoffrey, *The Moment in Astrology: Origins in Divination*, 2nd edn revd (Bournemouth: Wessex Astrologer, 2003)

Curry, Patrick, and Angela Voss, eds, *Seeing with Different Eyes: Essays in Astrology and Divination* (Newcastle upon Tyne: Cambridge Scholars Publishing, 2007)

Dan, Joseph, ed., *The Early Kabbalah*, trans. by Ronald C. Kiener (Mahwah, NJ: Paulist, 1986)

Deyermond, Alan, *Points of View in the Ballad: 'The Prisoner, The Lady and the Shepherd', and Others*, The Kate Elder Lecture, 7 (1995), expanded (London: Department of Hispanic Studies, Queen Mary and Westfield College, 1996)

Diaz, Armand, *Integral Astrology: Understanding the Ancient Discipline in the Contemporary World* (USA and UK: Integral Transformation, 2012)

Diaz, Armand, Eric Meyers, and Andrew Smith, eds, *Transpersonal Astrology: Explorations at the Frontier* (USA and UK: Integral Transformation, 2013)

Ebertin, Reinhold, *The Combination of Stellar Influences*, trans. by Alfred G. Roosedale and Linda Kratzsch, 4th edn (Tempe, AZ: American Federation of Astrologers, 1972)

Ellwood, Robert, *The Politics of Myth: A Study of C. G. Jung, Mircea Eliade, and Joseph Campbell* (New York, NY: SUNY, 1999)

Elwell, Dennis, *Cosmic Loom* (London: Urania Trust, 1999)

Ertan, Deniz, *Dane Rudhyar: His Music, Thought, and Art* (Rochester, NY: Rochester UP, 2009)

Evans, Jules, *Philosophy for Life, And Other Dangerous Situations*, 2nd edn (London: Rider, 2013)

Faivre, Antoine, *Access to Western Esotericism* (Albany, NY: SUNY, 1994)

—*Theosophy, Imagination, Tradition: Studies in Western Esotericism*, trans. by Christine Rhone (Albany, NY: SUNY, 2000)

Faivre, Antoine, and Jacob Needleman, eds, *Modern Esoteric Spirituality* (London: SCM, 1993)

Faivre, Antoine, and Wouter J. Hanegraaff, eds, *Western Esotericism and the Science of Religion: Selected Papers presented at the 17th Congress of the International Association of the History of Religions, Mexico City 1995* (Leuven: Peeters, 1998)

Farnell, Kim, *The Astral Tramp: A Biography of Sepharial* (London: Ascella, 1998)

Ferrer, Jorge N., *Revisioning Transpersonal Theory: A Participatory Vision of Human Spirituality* (New York, NY: SUNY, 2002)

Ferrucci, Piero, *Your Inner Will: Finding Personal Strength in Critical Times*, trans. by Vivien Reid Ferrucci (New York, NY: Tarcher/Penguin, 2014)

Ficino, Marsilio, *The Book of Life* trans. by Charles Boer, 2nd edn (Woodstock, CT, Spring, 1996)

Firman, John, and Ann Gila, *Psychosynthesis: A Psychology of the Spirit* (Albany, NY: SUNY, 2002)

Gauquelin, Michel, *Neo-Astrology: A Copernican Revolution*, trans. by Stella Tomašević (London: Arkana, 1991)

Gilbert, R. A., *Gnosticism and Gnosis: An Introduction* (Bristol: Antioch Papers, 2012)

Godwin, Joscelyn, *The Golden Thread: The Ageless Wisdom of the Western Mystery Traditions* (Wheaton, IL: Quest, 2007)

—*The Theosophical Enlightenment* (Albany, NY: SUNY, 1994)

Goodrick-Clarke, Nicholas, ed., *Helena Blavatsky*, Western Esoteric Masters Series (Berkeley, CA: North Atlantic Books, 2004)

—*The Occult Roots of Nazism: Secret Aryan Cults and their Influence on Nazi Ideology*, 3rd edn (London: Tauris Parke Paperbacks, 2005)

—*The Western Esoteric Traditions: A Historical Perspective* (New York, NY: Oxford UP, 2008)

Gordon, J. S., *The Path of Initiation: Spiritual Evolution and the Restoration of the Western Mystery Tradition* (Rochester, VT: Inner Traditions, 2013)

Gordon-Brown, Ian, with Barbara Somers, *The Raincloud of Knowable Things: A Practical Guide to Transpersonal Psychology: workshops; history; method*, ed. by Hazel Marshall (Dorset: Archive Publishing, 2008)

Govinda, Lama Anagarika, *Foundations of Tibetan Mysticism: According to the Esoteric Teachings of the Great Mantra 'Om Mani Padme Hum'* (London: Rider, 1969)

Greene, Liz, *The Astrology of Fate*, 2nd edn (London: Unwin, 1985)

—*Barriers and Boundaries: The Horoscope and the Defences of the Personality* (London: CPA, 2002)

—*Magi and Maggidim: The Kabbalah in British Occultism, 1860-1940*, Studies in Cultural Astronomy and Astrology, 3 (Ceredigion: Sophia Centre Press, 2012)

—*Relating: An Astrological Guide to Living with Others on a Small Planet*, 2nd edn (New York: Weiser, 1978)

—*Star Signs for Lovers* (London: Arrow, 1980)

Greer, John Michael, and Christopher Warnock, trans. and ed., *The Picatrix: Liber Viridis*, Green Magic edn (Iowa City, IA: Renaissance Astrology Adocentyn Press, 2010-11)

Gregory, John, trans. and ed., *The Neoplatonists*, (London: Kyle Cathie, 1991)

Grof, Stanislav, *The Cosmic Game: Exploration of the Frontiers of Human Consciousness*, 2nd edn (Dublin: Newleaf, 1998)

Grohmann, Will, *Klee*, trans by Norbert Guterman, abr. (London: Thames and Hudson, 1987)

Hakl, Hans Thomas, *Eranos: An Alternative Intellectual History of the Twentieth Century*, trans. by Christopher McIntosh with Hereward Tilton (Montreal and Kingston: McGill UP, 2013)

Halevi, Z'ev ben Shimon, *Astrology and Kabbalah: a rewrite of The Anatomy of Fate* (London: Urania Trust, 2000)

—*Kabbalah and Psychology* (Bath: Gateway, 1986)

Hall, Judy, *Patterns of the Past: The Birthchart, Karma and Reincarnation*, 2nd edn, rev. (Bournemouth: Wessex Astrologer, 2000)

Hanegraaff, Wouter J., *Esotericism and the Academy: Rejected Knowledge in Western Culture* (Cambridge: Cambridge UP, 2012)

—*New Age Religion and Western Culture: Esotericism in the Mirror of Secular Thought* (Albany, NY: SUNY, 1998)

—*Western Esotericism: A Guide for the Perplexed* (London: Bloomsbury, 2013)

Hardy, Jean, *A Psychology with a Soul: Psychosynthesis in Evolutionary Context* (Arkana, 1987)

Harvey, Suzi, ed., *Orpheus: Voices in Contemporary Astrology* (Frome: Consider, 2000)

Hopewell, Joyce, *Aspect Patterns in Colour* (Knutsford: HopeWell, 2010)

—*The Living Birth Chart: Astrological Psychology: A Practical Workbook* (Knutsford: HopeWell, 2008)

—*Using Age Progression: Understanding Life's Journey* (Knutsford: HopeWell, 2013)

Hopewell, Joyce, and Richard Llewellyn, *The Cosmic Egg Timer: Astrological Psychology: An Introduction to the Huber Method*, ed. by Barry Hopewell and illustr. by Annabel Burton (Knutsford: HopeWell, 2004)

Hopper, Vincent Foster, *Medieval Number Symbolism: Its Sources, Meaning, and Influence on Thought and Expression*, Columbia University Studies in English and Comparative Literature, 132 (New York: Columbia University, 1938; repr. Mineola, NY: Dover, 2000)

Huffman, William, ed. *Robert Fludd*, Western Esoteric Masters Series (Berkeley, CA: North Atlantic Books, 2001)

Hyde, Maggie, *Jung and Astrology* (London: Aquarian, 1992)

James, William, *The Varieties of Religious Experience: A Study in Human Nature*, ed. by Jim Manis, <www2.hn.psu.edu/ faculty/jmanis/wjames/varieties-rel-exp.pdf> [accessed 26 July 2013]

Jung, Carl Gustav, *Four Archetypes: Mother, Rebirth, Spirit, Trickster*, trans. by R. F. C. Hull, 4th edn (London: Routledge Classics, 2003)

—*Memories, Dreams, Reflections*, ed. by Aniela Jaffé, and trans. by Richard and Clara Winston, 3rd edn (Glasgow: Collins Fount, 1977)

—*Psychology and Alchemy*, trans. by R. F. C. Hull, The Collected Works of C. G. Jung, 12, 2th edn (London: Routledge and Kegan Paul, 1980)

Kandinsky, Wassily, *Concerning the Spiritual in Art*, trans. by Michael Sadler, 1st edn, 1914 (Mineola, NY: Dover, 1977)

Klibansky, Raymond, Erwin Panofsky and Fritz Saxl, *Saturn and Melancholy: Studies in the History of Natural Philosophy, Religion and Art* (London: Nelson, 1964)

König, Wolfhard, *The Karma Click Horoscope: The Astrologer's Secret Weapon*, trans. by Heather Ross, and ed. by Barry Hopewell (Knutsford: Astrological Psychology Association, 2009)

Kuberski, Philip, *Chaosmos: Literature, Science, and Theory* (Albany, NY: State University of New York, 1994)

Lancaster, Brian L., *The Essence of Kabbalah*, 2nd edn (London: Arcturus, 2006)

Laszlo, Ervin, *The Akasha Experience: Science and the Cosmic Memory Field* (Rochester, VT: Inner Traditions, 2009)

—*The Self-Actualizing Cosmos: The Akasha Revolution in Science and Human Consciousness* (Rochester, VT: Inner Traditions, 2014)

Le Grice, Keiron, *The Archetypal Cosmos: Rediscovering the Gods in Myth, Science and Astrology* (Edinburgh: Floris, 2010)

Leo, Alan, *The Art of Synthesis*, 6th edn (New York: Astrologer's Library, 1978)

—*Esoteric Astrology* (Rochester VT: Destiny, 1983)

Leonard, Linda Schierse, *The Wounded Woman: Healing the Father-Daughter Relationship* (Boston and London: Shambhala, 1985)

McGilchrist, Iain, *The Master and his Emissary: The Divided Brain and the Making of the Western World* (Newhaven and London: Yale UP, 2010)

McIntosh, Christopher, *The Rosicrucians: The History, Mythology, and Rituals of an Esoteric Order*, 3rd edn rev. (San Francisco, CA: Weiser, 1997)

McLean, Adam, ed. *The Chemical Wedding of Christian Rosenkreutz*, trans. by Joscelyn Godwin, Magnum Opus Hermetic Sourceworks, 18, (Grand Rapids, MI: Phanes, 1991)

Maslow, Abraham H. *The Farther Reaches of Human Nature*, 3rd edn (New York: Penguin-Arkana, 1993)

Mayer, Michael, *The Mystery of Personal Identity*, 2nd edn, kindle (Orinda, CA: Bodymind Healing Publications, 2012)

Meader, William A., *Shine Forth: The Soul's Magical Destiny* (Mariposa, CA: Source, 2004)

Mebane, John S. *Renaissance Magic and the Return of the Golden Age: The Occult Tradition of Marlowe, Jonson, and Shakespeare* (Lincoln and London: University of Nebraska Press, 1992)

Moore, Thomas, *A Life at Work: The Joy of Discovering what you were Born to Do* (London: Piatkus, 2008)

—*The Planets Within: The Astrological Psychology of Marsilio Ficino*, 2nd edn (Hudson, NY: Lindisfarne, 1990)

Myss, Caroline, *Anatomy of the Spirit: The Seven Stages of Power and Healing* (London: Bantam, 1997)

Nasr, Seyyed Hossein, *An Introduction to Islamic Cosmological Doctrines*, 2nd edn rev. (London: Thames and Hudson, 1978)

Needleman, Jacob, *The Heart of Philosophy*, 2nd edn (New York, NY: Tarcher/Penguin, 2003)

Oken, Alan, *Soul-Centred Astrology: A Key to Expanding Self* (Freedom, CA: Crossing Press, 1996)

Ovid, *Metamorphoses*, trans. by A. D. Melville and ed. by E. J. Kenney (Oxford: Oxford UP, 1987)

Owen, Alex, *The Place of Enchantment: British Occultism and the Culture of the Modern* (Chicago and London: University of Chicago Press, 2004)

Papke, Werner, *Die Sterne von Babylon: Die geheime Botschaft des Gilgamesch—nach 4000 Jahren entschlüsseit* (Lübbe, 1989)

Parfitt, Will, *Psychosynthesis: The Elements and Beyond* (Glastonbury: PS Avalon, 2003)

Pasi, Marco, *Aleister Crowley and the Temptation of Politics* (Durham: Acumen, 2014)

Perry, Whitall N., *The Widening Breach: Evolutionism in the Mirror of Cosmology* (Cambridge: Quinta Essentia, 1995)

Plato, *The Collected Dialogues of Plato, including the Letters*, ed. by Edith Hamilton and Huntington Cairns, Bollingen 71, 2nd edn (Princeton, NJ: Princeton University Press, 1963)

Plotinus, *The Enneads*, trans. by Stephen MacKenna, abr. and ed. by John Dillon (London: Penguin, 1991)

Progoff, Ira, *Jung, Synchronicity, and Human Destiny: Noncausal Dimensions of Human Experience* (New York: Delta, 1973)

Ptolemy, Claudius, *Tetrabiblos*, trans. by F. E. Robbins, Loeb Classical Library, 435 (Cambridge, MA: Harvard UP, 1940, repr. 1994)

Regardie, Israel, *The Tree of Life: An Illustrated Study in Magic*, ed. by Chic and Sandra Tabatha Cicero, 3rd edn (Woodbury, MN: Llewellyn, 2010)

Reuchlin, Johann, *On the Art of the Kabbalah: De Arte Cabalistica*, trans. by Martin and Sarah Goodman, 2nd edn (Lincoln and London: University of Nebraska Press, 1993)

Robbins, Michael D., Tapestry of the Gods: 1, The Seven Rays: An Esoteric Key to Understanding Human Nature; 2, Psychospiritual Transformation and the Seven Rays, 3rd edn (Mariposa, CA: University of the Seven Rays, 1996), repr. <http://www.makara.us/ 04mdr/mdr_home.htm> tapestry1.pdf and tapestry2.pdf

Rowan, John, *The Transpersonal: Psychotherapy and Counselling* (London and New York: Routledge, 1993)

Rudbøg, Tim, *The Academic Study of Western Esotericism: Early Developments and Related Fields*, Introduction Series to Western Esotericism, 1 (Copenhagen: H-E-R-M-E-S Academic Press, 2013)

Rudhyar, Dane, *An Astrological Triptych: Gifts of the Spirit; The Way Through; The Illumined Road*, 3rd edn rev. (New York, NY: ASI, 1978)

—*Astrology and the Modern Psyche: An Astrologer Looks at Depth Psychology* (Davis, CA: CRCS, 1976)

—*The Astrology of Personality: A Re-formulation of Astrological Concepts and Ideals, in Terms of Contemporary Psychology and Philosophy*, 3rd edn (Garden City, NY: Doubleday, 1970)

—*The Astrology of Transformation: A Multilevel Approach* (Wheaton, IL: Quest, 1980)

—*The Galactic Dimension of Astrology: The Sun Is Also A Star* (Santa Fe, NM: Aurora, 1982)

—*The Lunation Cycle: A Key to the Understanding of Personality* 2nd edn (Boulder, CO: Shambhala, 1971)

—*New Mansions for New Men*, 3rd edn (Alameda, CA: Hunter House, 1978)

—*Person Centred Astrology*, 3rd edn (New York, NY: Aurora, 1980)

—*The Planetarization of Consciousness*, 3rd edn (New York, NY: ASI, 1977)

Ruperti, Alexander, *Cycles of Becoming: The Planetary Pattern of Growth* (Davis, CA: CRCS, 1978)

Sasportas, Howard, *The Gods of Change: Pain, Crisis and the Transits of Uranus, Neptune and Pluto*, 2nd edn (Bournemouth: Wessex Astrologer, 2007)

Schützenberger, Anne Ancelin, *The Ancestor Syndrome: Transgenerational Psychotherapy and the Hidden Links in the Family Tree*, trans. by Anne Trager (London and New York: Routledge, 1998)

Secret, François, *Les Kabbalistes Chrétiens de la Renaissance*, 3rd edn rev (Milan: Archè, 2006)

Sedgwick, Mark, *Against the Modern World: Traditionalism and the Secret Intellectual History of the Twentieth Century* (New York: Oxford UP, 2004)

Shainberg, Catherine, *Kabbalah and the Power of Dreaming: Awakening the Visionary Life* (Rochester, VT: Inner Traditions, 2005)

Sheldrake, Rupert, *The Science Delusion: Freeing the Spirit of Enquiry* (London: Coronet, 2012)

Shelley, Percy Bysshe, *The Poetical Works*, intro. by Richard Garnett (London and Melbourne: Ward, Lock, 1931)

Solé Gubianes, Rosa, *Psicología Astrológica: Bases prácticas del método Huber* (Barcelona: Sincronía, 2014)

Somers, Barbara, *The Fires of Alchemy: A Transpersonal Viewpoint*, ed. by Hazel Marshall (Morton: Archive Publishing, 2004)

Somers, Barbara, and Ian Gordon-Brown, *Symptom as Symbol: A Transpersonal Language*, ed. by Hazel Marshall (Dorset: Archive Publishing, 2010)

Stuckrad, Kocku von, *Astrología: Una historia desde los inicios hasta nuestros días*, trans. by Roberto H. Bernet (Barcelona: Herder, 2005)

— *Locations of Knowledge in Medieval and Early Modern Europe* (Leiden: Brill, 2010)

—*Western Esotericism: A Brief History of Secret Knowledge*, trans. by Nicholas Goodrick-Clarke (London: Equinox, 2005)

Szanto, Gregory, *The Marriage of Heaven and Earth: The Philosophy of Astrology* (London: Arkana, 1985)

Tarnas, Richard, *Cosmos and Psyche: Intimations of a New World View* (New York, NY: Viking, 2006)

—*The Passion of the Western Mind: Understanding the Ideas That Have Shaped Our World View* (New York: Ballantine, 1991)

Treitel, Corinna, *A Science for the Soul: Occultism and the Genesis of the German Modern* (Baltimore and London: Johns Hopkins UP, 2004)

Ussher, Patrick, ed., *Stoicism Today: Selected Writings*, I (Marston Gate: Amazon.co.uk, 2014)

Vaughan, Frances, *The Inward Arc: Healing in Psychotherapy and Spirituality*, 2nd edn (Nevada City, CA: Blue Dolphin, 1995)

Versluis, Arthur, *Theosophia: Hidden Dimensions of Christianity* (Hudson, NY: Lindisfarne, 1994)

Voss, Angela, ed., *Marsilio Ficino*, Western Esoteric Masters Series (Berkeley, CA: North Atlantic Books, 2006)

Waite, Arthur Edward, *The Holy Kabbalah: A Mystical Interpretation of the Scriptures* (New York, NY: Citadel, 1995)

Walsh, Patricia L., *Understanding Karmic Complexes: Evolutionary Astrology and Regression Theory* (Bournemouth: Wessex Astrologer, 2009)

Weiner, Errol, *Transpersonal Astrology: Finding the Soul's Purpose* (Shaftesbury: Element, 1991)

Wellings, Nigel, and Elizabeth Wilde McCormick, *Transpersonal Psychotherapy: Theory and Practice* (London and New York: Continuum, 2000)

Wilber, Ken, *The Atman Project: A Transpersonal View of Human Development*, 2nd edn (Wheaton, Il: Theosophical Publishing House, 1982)

—*A Brief History of Everything*, 2nd edn, (Dublin: Gateway, 2001)

—*Integral Psychology: Consciousness, Spirit, Psychology, Therapy* (Boston and London: Shambhala, 2000)

—*Sex, Ecology, Spirituality: The Spirit of Evolution*, 2nd edn rev.(Boston and London: Shambhala, 2000)

Willis, Roy, and Patrick Curry, *Astrology, Science, and Culture: Pulling Down the Moon* (Oxford and New York: Berg, 2004)

Wyss, Phoebe, *Inside the Cosmic Mind: Archetypal Astrology and the New Cosmology* (Edinburgh: Floris Books, 2014)

Yates, Frances, *Giordano Bruno and the Hermetic Tradition*, 3rd edn (London and New York: Routledge, 2009)

—*The Occult Philosophy in the Elizabethan Age*, 4th edn (London and New York: Routledge Classics, 2008)

Yeats, W. B., *Autobiographies* rev. edn (London and Basingstoke: Macmillan Papermac, 1980; repr. 1987)

Yiacoup, Şizen, *Frontier Memory: Cultural Conflict and Exchange in the 'Romancero fronterizo'*, MHRA Texts and Dissertations, 87 (London: Modern Humanities Research Association, 2013)

C. Articles and Lectures

Anonymous, 'Great Theosophists: Ammonius Saccas', *Theosophy*, 25 (1936), 53-59, repr. <www.wisdomworld.org/setting/ saccas.html> [accessed 1 March 2012]

Armistead, Samuel G., and Joseph H. Silverman, 'The Judeo-Spanish Tradition', *Oral Tradition* (1987), 633-44

Bachmann, Verena, 'Si tiene que ver con el ser humano, debe tener sentido', Interview with Bruno Huber (1930-1999), on 30 July 1999 in Adliswil, pub. in *Astrologie Heute*, 82 (December 1999/January 2000) and trans. into Spanish by Joan Solé i Girbau

Blavatsky, H. P., 'Letter 21 to Prof. Hiram Corson, dated 16 February 1875', in *H. P. Blavatsky Collected Writings: The Letters of H. P. Blavatsky*, 1, ed. by John Algeo (Wheaton, IL: Quest, 2003)

—'The Mystery and Sacredness of Number Seven', from *Collected Writings of H. P. Blavatsky*, 2, p. 408, repr. <www.theosophical-society.org.uk/html/ insight_articles/ spring2005_mystery_seven> [accessed 16 February 2012]

Brady, Bernadette, 'Astrology and Research', <https://www.academia.edu/8823841/Astrology_and_Research_Astrologers_attitudes_to_research_methodologies_and_the_implications_of_these_attitudes_for_the_contemporary_communities_of_astrologers?auto=download&campaign=upload_email> [accessed 18 October 2014]

Campion, Nicholas, 'The Traditional Revival in Modern Astrology: A Preliminary History', <astrologyfoundation.org.nz/2004/08/03/the-traditional-revival-in-modern-astrology> [accessed 10 November 2013]

Caruth, Cathy, 'An interview with Jean Laplanche' (2001) <pmc.iath.virginia.edu/text-only/issue.101/11.2caruth.txt> [accessed 25 November 2014]

Cornelius, Geoffrey, 'Astrology, Imagination, and the Imaginal', *The Astrological Journal* (January/February 2014), 12-16

Farnell, Kim, 'A Brief Biography of Alan Leo', <www.skyscript.co.uk/Alan_Leo.html> [accessed 22 April 2010]

Fletcher, John, 'The Unconscious, the Id and the Other: Laplanchean Developments of Freud', Queen Mary University of London conference on 'Histories and Theories of the Unconscious', 22 November 2014

Forshaw, Peter, 'Jewish Kabbalah', EXESESO module HISM 154 (University of Exeter, 2011)

Gale, Matthew, 'Carefully ordered confusion', in *The EY Exhibition—Paul Klee: Making Visible* (London: Tate, 2013), pp. 15-31

Garcia, Mari, and Joy Usher, 'An Introduction to Charles Carter', <www.skyscript.co.uk/carter_intro.html> [accessed 23 December 2014]

Gill, Christopher, 'Stoicism, Nature and the Environment', Stoicism Today, Queen Mary University of London, 29 November 2014

Goodrick-Clarke, Clare, 'The *Corpus Hermeticum*: A Founding Document of Western Esoteric Traditions', EXESESO Study Conference, 15 October 2011

Goodrick-Clarke, Nicholas, 'H. P. Blavatsky and the Ambiguities of Orientalism: Western Esotericism and Eastern Religion in Theosophy', EXESESO Study Conference, University of Exeter, 29 January 2012

—'The Hermetic Harvest of Goethe's Alchemical Retreat', EXESESO Study Conference, 18 October 2009

—'Rudolf Steiner and Anthroposophy', EXESESO module HISM 156 (University of Exeter, 2011)

—'Wheels of Fire: The Reception of Eastern Subtle Body Doctrines in the Western Esoteric Tradition', Scientific and Medical Network Conference, *The Body and Beyond: Cross-Cultural Understandings of Subtle Energy*, Bath Spa University, 22-24 August, 2008.

Hames, Harvey J., 'Exotericism and Esotericism in Thirteenth Century Kabbalah', *Esoterica*, 6 (2004), 102-112

Hopewell, Barry, 'Beauty, Truth and Goodness', *Conjunction*, 49 (2010), 18-20

Hopewell, Joyce 'Esoteric Rulers and Seed Thoughts for the Signs', 1, *Conjunction*, 59 (2013), 16-18

Introvigne, Massimo, 'Theosophy and the Visual Arts: The Nordic Connection', International Conference on Theosophical History, London, 20-21 September 2014

Kaulins, Andis, 'The "Text" and Interpretation of the MUL.APIN Tablets', <www.lexiline.com/lexiline/lexi179.htm> [accessed 17 November 2014]

Keen, Sam, 'The Golden Mean of Roberto Assagioli', *Psychology Today* (December 1974), repr. <samkeen.com/interviews-by-sam/ interviews-by-sam/the-golden-mean-of-roberto-assagioli/> [accessed 23 October 2013]

Klitsner, Yvonne Smith, 'The Astrology of Synchronicity in Healing Relationships', filmed for *Coniunctio* at the California Institute of Integral Studies, 10 September 2014, <www.youtube.com> [accessed 6 October 2014]

König, Wolfhard, 'In memory of Bruno Huber 1930-1999', trans. by Heather Ross, *Astrolog* (October/November 2014) repr.

<astrologicalpsychology.org/in-memory-of-bruno-huber-1930-1999/> [accessed 23 January 2015]

—'Talk Therapy for Astrologers 1: Psychological Models and Counselling', trans. by Heather Ross, *Conjunction*, 56 (November, 2012), 14-16; 'Talk Therapy for Astrologers 2: The Unconscious and Directive Counselling', trans. by Heather Ross, *Conjunction*, 57 (March, 2013), 16-19; 'Talk Therapy for Astrologers 3: Non-Directive Counselling', trans. by Heather Ross, *Conjunction*, 58 (July, 2012), 20-23; 'Talk Therapy for Astrologers 4: Non-Directive Counselling in Astrological Consultation', trans. by Heather Ross, *Conjunction*, 59 (November, 2013), 13-15

Lachter, Hartley, review of Kocku von Stuckrad, *Locations of Knowledge in Medieval and Early Modern Europe* (Leiden: Brill, 2010), <www.h-net.org/reviews/showrev.php?id=31482> [accessed 6 November 2013]

Llewellyn, Richard, 'The Carter Memorial Lecture, Astrological Association Conference 2001', *The Astrological Journal*, 43 (November/December 2001), 8-17

Meader, William, 'Practical Mysticism: The Way of the Future' (2007), <meader.org/articles/practical-mysticism-the-way-of-the-future> [accessed 4 April 2014]

Pasi, Marco, 'Oriental Kabbalah and the Parting of East and West in the Early Theosophical Society', in *Kabbalah and Modernity: Interpretations, Transformations, Adaptations*, ed. by Boaz Huss, Marco Pasi, and Kocku von Stuckrad (Leiden and Boston: Brill, 2010), pp. 151-66, repr. <www.academic.edu>

—'Western Esotericism and Artistic Creativity: Searching for a New Interpretive Method', *Visions of Enchantment—Occultism, Spirituality and Visual Culture*, an international conference at the University of Cambridge, 18 March 2014

Ringbom, Sixten, 'Art in "The Epoch of the Great Spiritual": Occult Elements in the Early Theory of Abstract Painting', *Journal of the Warburg and Courtauld Institutes*, 29 (1966), pp. 386-418.

Rosenthal, Deborah, 'A transparent world: the notebooks of Paul Klee', *The New Criterion* (1993), pp. 33-38

Round, Nicholas, 'Alan Deyermond obituary', <www.guardian.co.uk/education/2009/oct/14/alan-deyermond-obituary/print> [accessed 16 October 2009]

Rowan, John, 'Levels of Flattery', *Network Review*, 116 (Winter 2015), Journal of the Scientific and Medical Network, pp. 18-19

Schoener, Gustav-Adolf, 'Astrology: Between Religion and the Empirical', trans. by Shane Denson, *Esoterica*, 4 (2002), 29-60

Sørensen, Kenneth, 'Integral Psychosynthesis: Integral Perspectives on Psychosynthesis', MA thesis, Psychosynthesis and Education Trust (2008), rev. 2009, <www.psykosyntese.dk/a-198/> [accessed 17 June 2014]

Stuckrad, Kocku von, '*Astrologia Hermetica:* Astrology, Western Culture, and the Academy', in *Hermes in the Academy: Ten Years' Study of Western Esotericism at the University of Amsterdam*, ed. by Wouter J. Hanegraaff and Joyce Pijnenburg, eds (Amsterdam: Amsterdam UP, 2009), pp. 51-58

— 'Esoteric Discourse and the European History of Religion: In Search of a New Interpretational Framework', <ojs.abo.fi/index.php/ scripta/article/viewFile/398/1176> [accessed 8 October 2014]

Tarnas, Richard, 'The Carter Memorial Lecture, Astrological Association Conference 2013: Role of Astrology in a Civilization in Crisis', *The Astrological Journal*, 56 (January/February 2014), 27-34

Tilton, Hereward, 'Spiritual Alchemy and Transfiguration', EXESESO Study Conference, 27 March 2011

Versluis, Arthur, 'What is Esoteric? Methods in the Study of Western Esotericism', *Esoterica,* 4 (2002), 1-15

Voss, Angela, 'A Methodology of the Imagination', *Eye of the Heart: A Journal of Traditional Wisdom*, 3 (2009), 1-15

Weiss, Peg, 'Kandinsky and "Old Russia": An Ethnographic Exploration', *Syracuse Scholar*, 7 (1986), repr. <surface.syr.edu/suscholar/vol7/iss1/5> (2013)

D. Dictionaries

Cirlot, J. E., *A Dictionary of Symbols*, trans. by Jack Sage, 2nd edn (London and Henley: Routledge and Kegan Paul, 1983)

Fischer-Schreiber, Ingrid, ed. with Franz-Karl Ehrhard, and others, *The Rider Encyclopedia of Eastern Philosophy and Religion: Buddhism, Hinduism, Taoism, Zen*, trans. by Rider (London: Rider, 1989)

Grimal, Pierre, *A Dictionary of Classical Mythology*, trans. by A. R. Maxwell-Hyslop (Oxford: Blackwell, 1986)

Hanegraaff, Wouter J., ed., with Antoine Faivre, Roelof van den Broek, and Jean-Pierre Brach, *Dictionary of Gnosis and Western Esotericism*, (Leiden: Brill, 2006)

Pring, J. T., *The Pocket Oxford Greek Dictionary*, 3rd edn rev. (Oxford: Oxford University Press, 1995)

Zalta, Edward N., ed., *The Stanford Encyclopedia of Philosophy* (2014) <plato.stanford.edu/archives/sum2013/entries/>

E. Web Sites

Academia.edu Team, <www.academia.edu>

Astro-Databank, <www.astro.com/astro-databank>

Astrological Psychology Association, <astrologicalpsychology.org>

Cathar Software, <www.catharsoftware.com>

Escuela Huber de Psicología Astrológica, <www.escuelahuber.org> <www.psicologiaastrologica.es>

Skyscript by Deborah Houlding, <www.skyscript.co.uk>

Wikipedia, <en.wikipedia.org/wiki>

Index of Names and Dates

Subject Index